A Guide to

Small Boat Emergencies

D1260334

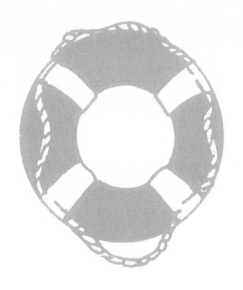

For Tom —
Safety at sea is a
state of mind!
Dad

A Guide to
Small Boat
Emergencies

John M. Waters, Jr.
Captain, U.S. Coast Guard (Ret.)

Naval Institute Press
Annapolis, Maryland

Library of Congress Cataloging-in-Publication Data
Waters, John M. 1930–1992
    A guide to small boat emergencies / John Waters.
       p.   cm.
    Includes index.
    ISBN 1-55750-913-1 (alk. paper)
    1. Boats and boating—Safety measures.   I. Title.
VK200.W38 1992
623.88'8—dc20   92-24103
                                                    CIP

Printed in the United States of America on acid-free paper ∞

9 8 7 6 5 4 3 2

First printing

Contents

Foreword

Safety at sea has always held a top priority among the many missions of the United States Coast Guard. Of the thousands of people we rescue or assist each year, by far the largest group consists of recreational boaters. Over the past three decades we have seen explosive growth in recreational boating, with 20 million Americans now owning boats and nearly 46 million participating in boating activities.

Despite the rate of growth, the fatality rate in boating accidents has dropped by two-thirds since 1971. Much of the credit must be given to the Federal Boat Safety Act of 1971, which established minimum safety and equipment standards as well as boating education programs and charged the Coast Guard with implementing the act in cooperation with the states.

Most accidents are the result of operator error rather than material or equipment failure. Further reductions in the accident rate will thus require emphasis on the role and responsibilities of the boat operator.

In this book the author clearly identifies the triad of prevention, self reliance, and search and rescue that all boaters need to know and understand to ensure safety on the water. He focuses on the problems of the coastal and weekend sailors, while emphasizing that many perils are common to all mariners, wherever they cruise.

Captain John M. Waters, USCG (Ret.), is well qualified to address the subject. An expert on emergency operations, Captain Waters has held both sea and aviation commands, has personally engaged in hundreds of rescues, and is an enthusiastic and experienced ocean-cruising yachtsman as well. His observations are those of a man who has been in the midst of the action. He was the principal author of the first National Search and Rescue Manual, which after nearly 30 years and several revisions is the world's definitive reference on the subject.

Drawing on his knowledge and experience, Captain Waters has offered this contribution to the safety of all who go down to the sea in small craft.

Paul A. Yost
Admiral, United States Coast Guard (Ret.)
Commandant, 1986–1990

Preface

Combat veterans nearly all declare, "If you aren't scared at times, you don't know what's going on." The principle applies to many small boat owners who venture into dangerous situations, confident that nothing will happen to them. Tens of millions of Americans go out in boats each year, but only one in twenty has had any formal training in boat maintenance and safe operation. Few states require qualification or licensing of boat operators as they do of vehicle drivers. This contributes to a toll on the water second only to that on the highways.

In a quarter century as a ship captain, search and rescue (SAR) pilot, and operational commander in the Coast Guard, I have witnessed a wide variety of small-boat mishaps and tragedies. At the time, many appeared to result from stupidity or gross negligence. But the view from a large ship or aircraft is far different than it is from a small boat with a small crew of limited experience. As the subsequent owner and skipper of three sailing sloops, I have seen the problem from "the other side of the hill" during frequent trips in coastal and offshore waters. Can an experienced professional sailor and airman, who has repeatedly seen the consequences of mistakes by others, encounter the same problems? You can bet on it.

A few of my near misses include a knockdown in 60-knot winds, a galley fire that nearly gutted the main cabin, a lost prop shaft that nearly flooded the boat, medical emergencies, several engine failures, a lightning strike that cremated the electronics suite, a man overboard, and many times aground in inland waters (those who say it has never happened to them will lie about other things too).

Trouble will seek out both professionals and amateurs; the difference is that professionals often handle the situation without outside help, as was done in all of the above mishaps. However, I have also been assisted twice and boarded once by the Coast Guard. I helped balance the record by rescuing five people from two boats offshore.

The surest way to avoid trouble is never to leave the dock, but even there lightning, fire, and severe weather can seek you out. Boats are built to sail the seas and rivers where mishaps do occur. This book helps to prepare you for that probability, using proven practices developed by seamen over the years. I have used actual cases, many from my own experience, to illustrate the principles of handling small-boat emergencies.

The wide differences in readers' experience and geographical environments are obstacles. What seems a fresh breeze to an experienced offshore sailor in a 40-foot ketch may appear scary to a family out in their new 22-foot runabout. Knowledge taken for granted by one may have to be laboriously spelled out for the other. Seeking a common ground, I have refrained from dealing with the issues of basic seamanship except where it is inseparable from the emergency being described. I have likewise avoided complex repairs and difficult maneuvers the average coastal boater will possess neither the materials nor the skills to execute.

Never assume that river and inland cruising is inherently easier and safer than ocean sailing and that preparations and vigilance can be relaxed. The reverse is often true. On an ocean passage, a boat is mostly clear of hazards; on inland waters and rivers, they are always nearby. Death and injuries are no less painful when they occur in familiar surroundings or in company. The dangers of inland and coastal cruising are mitigated, however, by the proximity of excellent navigational aids and the large and experienced U.S. Coast Guard Search and Rescue (SAR) system. Although North American waters are as safe as any in the world, the Coast Guard SAR statistics for 1989 disclose that some sixty thousand calls for assistance were answered by the Coast Guard, and 70 percent of them were from recreational boats in inshore or coastal waters. Nationwide, an American Red Cross survey that same year estimated that 291,000 boats were involved in significant accidents, with a toll of 1,000 deaths, 355,000 injuries, and $850 million in property damage.

Any prudent owner should complete a short safe-boating course (such as those taught by the Coast Guard Auxiliary or the U.S. Power Squadron) before taking out his boat as skipper. Inquire about these classes at local boating organizations or call BOATS/ US (toll free, 1-800-335-BOAT) for nationwide information.

Before venturing into unknown or unprotected waters, first do so as crew with an experienced skipper. Ask about or post a note on the bulletin board at a yacht club, marina, or boating association, where many skippers are frequently looking for crew members and most experienced sailors are more than willing to help a beginner.

A short course and hands-on experience should be augmented by studying a good broad coverage book such as *Chapman's Piloting, Seamanship, and Small Boat Handling.* For those seeking more detail, there are dozens of well-written specialty books ranging from first aid to sailing techniques, and from cooking to engine repair. These provide enjoyable reading on cold winter nights by the fire or in an anchorage. Unfortunately, some of the advice that sounds feasible when read in such surroundings is unrealistic or impossible for a sick and frightened crew in heavy weather or a severe emergency. A cardinal rule in distress situations is to *keep it simple.* I have attempted to do this.

If you have equipped and prepared the boat and navigation plans well, checked the weather, filed a float plan, and briefed the crew before casting off, it is unlikely that anything will occur that cannot be handled on the spot. There will be exceptions.

In serious cases in U.S. waters and the high seas contiguous to them, the Coast Guard will nearly always exercise SAR control. I therefore have covered in some detail the Coast Guard's SAR procedures. An early call to the Coast Guard is essential in a maritime emergency, but such an early call should not discourage self help, especially after the Coast Guard has been alerted and is en route. Most problems are resolved by those in trouble or with the help of other nearby boaters. But we must always remember that weekend sailors are neither as experienced nor as well equipped as offshore sailors who devote years to their vocation.

I am deeply indebted to hundreds of people for input and assistance in the preparation of this book. Much of the material obviously derives from my own experiences as a rescuer and occasionally as a small-boat sailor in trouble. The other primary source was the U.S. Coast Guard, the world's premier authority on small-boat operations. In visiting dozens of air stations, ships, shore units, and Headquarters divisions, I met with a cooperation and courtesy comparable to that normally shown a senior officer. Jack Schnabel, Chief of the National Oceanic and Atmospheric Administration and an enthusiastic boater, was most helpful in the development of the material on weather and hurricanes. John Hanninan, Esq., distinguished admiralty lawyer and experienced sailor, reviewed legal matters in the text and provided valuable insights.

I reviewed some ten years of boating and yachting articles written mostly by small-craft operators from firsthand experience. Some of the periodicals also featured industry and marine experts, as well as developments in the boating community.

I reviewed dozens of books and have recommended some of them in Appendix F. Revisions and new works make for constant change in any list, but some books have been considered authoritative for decades.

I regularly read the timely newsletters and reports from BOATS/US; this organization of some half million boat owners and operators is a highly effective voice, and I highly recommend membership. The small annual fee includes regular updates on anything from marine shopping centers to lobbying Congress for boaters' rights.

Some of my most enjoyable research involved hours of sea stories along the docks with sailors of varying experience. Many of the anecdotes illustrated once again that the boating public needs to be prepared to operate in a sometimes hostile environment.

Any small-boat sailor standing out past the sea buoy *should* be a little frightened. Those who seldom experience fear may substitute the term *heightened awareness*. This is part of the thrill of boating. At sea there is a sensible channel between excess complacency and undue anxiety. I have attempted to steer that course in this book.

A Guide to

Small Boat Emergencies

1
Pleasure Boats, Emergencies, and Search and Rescue (SAR)

How real are the perils of the sea and the dangers of recreational boating? The bad news is that in 1989 a third of all recreational boaters reported being in an accident or a threatening situation during the preceding year. The good news is that only 9 percent required help from others to reach shore, which speaks well for the self-reliance of the average pleasure boater. But these percentages must be applied to the huge number of boats and sailors (sail and power) to appreciate the magnitude of the problem.

The vast changes in pleasure boat construction and production since World War II, including the lower initial costs and maintenance for today's boats than for the older wooden boats, have enabled millions of Americans (1 in 13) to own a boat. More than forty-six million citizens, a fifth of the population of the United States, participate in boating activities on their own or friends' boats. The National Transportation Safety Board (NTSB) annually reports that boating accidents are second only to highway mishaps in lives lost and injuries incurred.

The extent of the problem has long been a matter of ambiguity. Under the provisions of the Federal Boat Safety Act of 1971 (FBSA71), the states are required to report certain boating accidents to the Coast Guard,* which then compiles an annual pub-

*Section 33, Code of Federal Regulations 173-4, requires that a report be filed on any boating accident involving deaths, injuries requiring more than first aid, damages exceeding $500, or total loss of the boat.

lication, *Boating Statistics*. Though fatal accidents are usually reported, the Coast Guard has long contended that the states submit only 5–10 percent of the accident reports required by the law. A landmark survey completed in 1991 by the American Red Cross indicates that compliance by the states is even worse than that—only 2.5 percent. The Red Cross study, funded by a Coast Guard grant of $400,000, is more comprehensive and inclusive than the accident summaries derived from the states' reports. Based on interviews with several thousand users, the Red Cross survey is extrapolated to the national population level to provide estimates of nationwide usage and experience. The Coast Guard's annual *Boating Statistics* is derived from some five thousand accident reports submitted annually by the states. Because these represent only the most serious accidents, conclusions that may be drawn from the data may be on the pessimistic side. On the other hand, the Red Cross study, which also reflects less serious accidents, discloses a far greater number of accidents than would be suspected from the Coast Guard report.

The Red Cross study bases fatality rates on deaths per million passenger hours; Coast Guard figures have been based on deaths per one hundred thousand boats. Although the Coast Guard's methodology seems to indicate a steady drop in the *death rate*, the new Red Cross study shows a slight increase in the last fifteen years. This is partially a result of owners' using their boats less, with a resultant drop in the number of hours of exposure.

Examining and reconciling the findings of both the Coast Guard and the Red Cross studies, we arrive at the following distribution of serious recreational boating accidents (see table 1.1): Although collisions are by far the leading category of accidents, the death rate is highest in falls overboard, capsizing, and swamping. Obviously, most such deaths are due to drowning. Lest we become lost in impersonal statistics, let us look at some individual accidents in widely differing environments.

PROFILE OF AN ACCIDENT

The popular concept of marine distress is a sailboat fighting for its life in a raging sea, but the actual event is far more likely to be

Table 1.1 Accidents with Damage and Injuries, 1990

Category	Percentage of Cases	Number of Fatalities
Collision	46.1	170
Fall overboard	9.2	239
Capsizing	7.5	289
Grounding	6.9	14
Waterskiing	5.7	—
Fall within boat	4.4	1
Swamping/Flooding	4.1	60
Fire or explosion	3.4	16
Hit by prop or boat	2.8	7
Sinking	2.3	11
Other/unknown	7.6	58

SOURCES: Derived from USCG *Boating Statistics,* 1990, and American Red Cross National Boating Survey, 1991

mundane and commonplace. Basing the characteristics on the Coast Guard's 1990 *Boating Statistics,* we arrive at a composite or typical accident as follows:

The thirty-seven-year-old operator, accompanied by his wife and a child, was cruising in his 20-foot fiberglass boat, periodically stopping to fish or swim. He was fairly experienced, with more than three hundred hours operating time, but he had never attended a formal boating education class. The 80-horsepower outboard was running smoothly, pushing the five-year-old boat along at 15 knots. Winds were light, waters smooth with a temperature of 75 degrees, and visibility clear. At 3:30 P.M. on a July weekend, there seemed to be little danger, and no one wore personal flotation devices (PFDs or life jackets), which were stowed below, nor was anyone specifically charged with maintaining a lookout.

At a bend in the river, another boat running at high speed suddenly loomed up ahead. Both operators turned in the same direction, neither sounded a warning signal, and neither reduced speed. The ensuing crash left three people injured and both boats heavily damaged (fig. 1.1). Fortunately both boats remained afloat after the impact because of their built-in flotation. The injured

Figure 1.1 Collisions are the largest category of serious water accidents. This fatal crash on Lake of the Ozarks shows the impact force of a speeding boat. *Courtesy USCG*

were picked up by passing boats and taken to a hospital by paramedics and the sheriff's department, which then conducted the accident investigation. The operator of the speeding boat was found to have a blood alcohol content of over .10 percent and was charged with operating a boat while under the influence of alcohol.

There are, of course, hundreds of cases bearing more resemblance to the popular stereotype of a storm-tossed boat on the high seas, but they are difficult to reduce to a composite because of the wide variations in circumstances. An actual case study can be more instructive.

The three-member crew of the 32-foot ketch *Dibya* did not lack experience as they sailed from Morehead City, North Carolina, on an October morning en route to the Bahamas. One of the crew, Edward M. "Emo" Osborne of East Hampton, New York, is an old friend and shipmate of mine and veteran of many Bermuda races and small-boat Atlantic crossings as well as command of a navy frigate. He is a thorough and conservative sailor. The departure had been delayed by misrouted airline baggage, and the three agreed to sail despite forecasts of 25 to 30 knot winds, since they would be running before them.

By the following morning, however, they were twenty miles southeast of Frying Pan Shoals Light and the northeast winds were up to 55 knots with 15- to 18-foot seas, which carried away their dinghy. Attempts to obtain the latest weather reports by VHF radio were futile because they were sixty miles offshore and well outside the range of the Coast Guard and National Weather Service (NWS) VHF radio net. Shortly afterward, the little ketch was hit by a rogue sea and rolled 360 degrees, wiping the deck clean of gear and leaving Ed Osborne paddling thirty yards astern. Acting quickly, Colin Fraser, the skipper, heaved him a line and hauled him to the boat. By this time the *Dibya* was without power or lights, dragging a maze of rigging and masts, and one crew member was injured. No distress call had been sent, nor was an EPIRB (emergency position indicating radio beacon) on board. For the next day and a half, the exhausted men worked to clear the wreckage and tried to get up a jury rig in order to close the coast but with little success. On Sunday night, however, they sighted the lights of a ship, signaled it by flashlight, and were soon picked up by the 80,000-ton tanker *Exxon San Francisco*. The boat was left to sink.

Even with the numerous radio stations along the coast, a sailor in distress must be within range, twenty to thirty miles, to alert them, and the *Dibya* was one hundred miles east of Charleston, South Carolina, when sighted by rescuers. The *Dibya* encountered seas in the coastal region as formidable as any that would accompany such winds in midocean, and they proved too much for the 32-foot ketch. Though the crew members were undoubtedly concerned about sea room, their distance offshore precluded VHF contact with shore stations, and they were most fortunate to be sighted by a passing vessel.

The near disaster of the *Dibya* was to have an eerie repeat seven years later on nearly the same date, when the 33-foot *Demon of Hamble* departed Beaufort for Fort Lauderdale on the same route taken previously by the ill-fated *Dibya*. The weather conditions were similar. The skipper, Angus Primrose, an English yacht designer, was an experienced sailor who had recently sailed the boat, one of his own design, from Plymouth, England, to Newport, Rhode Island, in a single handed transatlantic race. His crew on this latest leg was Dereka Dodson, a young English dentist.

The voyage was routine until the afternoon of 23 October 1980, when at the same position as the *Dibya* had capsized, the wind rose suddenly and the seas quickly built to "monstrous size." As seas began breaking over the small boat, Primrose told his companion that he thought the boat would capsize. Shortly afterwards it did but righted itself. The two launched a life raft and abandoned the boat. Dodson soon washed overboard but was hauled back to the raft by Primrose. Then Primrose was himself washed over by a wave and disappeared. Five days later, Dereka Dobson, who had survived on a diet of seaweed and rainwater, was sighted and picked up by the submarine tender USS *Canopus*, which reported that Dodson was in "amazingly good condition."

Other coincidences link the two emergencies at sea. Not only had the *Demon of Hamble* capsized under conditions nearly identical to those that had disabled the *Dibya*, but Primrose was a close friend of Ed Osborne of the *Dibya* and had designed a 40-foot sailboat for Ed, which had been built in France. It was named *Primevere*, the French word for "primrose," in honor of the designer. The loss of the two boats might incite speculation by believers in the myth of the Bermuda Triangle, but the reality is that both vessels lacked adequate stability and were unsuitable for the prevailing weather.

Despite such dramatic tales, less than 7 percent of Coast Guard SAR cases and 4 percent of fatalities involve sailboats. The lower percentage is probably the result of a combination of greater stability, slower speeds, the greater experience of sailing crews, the higher reliability of combined sail/engine propulsion, and the smaller number of sailboats compared with powerboats. Sailboats cruising offshore and along the coast also tend to be larger than the average powerboat. Coast Guard records show that over half of its pleasure boat assists involve boats 16–25 feet long, and another quarter are between 26 and 39 feet in length. Boats larger or smaller than this range are involved in serious accidents less than 20 percent of the time.

ACCIDENTS AND THE HUMAN FACTOR

The most common and costly accident by far is collision, which, like grounding, capsizing, and falls overboard or within the boat, is primarily caused by human error or inattention. The predominance of accidents traceable to human mistakes suggests that we have made more progress in improving boats and equipment than in training those who operate them.

Only a fourth of the people on the water have ever had a course in boat operation and safety, yet only a few states are making plans for operator licensing, which will be required if educational standards are to be enforced. This is a strange omission in a country that requires licensing for such varied activities as driving, flying, amateur radio, and barbering. This deficiency is even more glaring when we see the deaths and injuries, property losses, and SAR costs caused by incompetent boat operators. The boating public is well aware of the dangers of this situation, for the Red Cross study showed that 81 percent of all boaters were in favor of mandatory education while two-thirds favored licensing. Those on the water see the dangers from reckless and ignorant boat operators at much closer range than do politicians ashore.

LOCATIONS AND KINDS OF SEARCH AND RESCUE (SAR)

As the primary maritime SAR force of the United States, the U.S. Coast Guard conducts most of the significant rescue operations at sea and on the navigable waters where the United States has jurisdiction. The Coast Guard, the smallest of the armed services, has a strength of 39,000 officers and enlisted personnel, 250 cutters, 2,000 patrol and utility boats, and 200 aircraft. The regular forces are backed up by a ready reserve of 12,000 and a civilian Coast Guard Auxiliary of 35,000 people.

The Coast Guard has a unique multi-mission responsibility that includes aids to navigation, merchant marine inspection, small-boat safety, maritime law enforcement, fisheries and marine environmental protection, and polar operations, all in addition to its traditional national defense and SAR roles. In recent years an increased emphasis has centered on the war against drugs.

The Coast Guard is charged by law with developing and maintaining SAR facilities and for rendering aid to distressed persons and property, both civilian and military—on, over, and under the high seas and waters of the United States. It *may* render aid to persons or property at any time and any place at which Coast Guard facilities are available. It should be especially noted that the authorization to render aid is a *permissive* rather than a mandatory requirement. The Coast Guard is not *required* by law to help anyone, and the courts have repeatedly held that the Coast Guard is not liable for failure to act on learning of a distress incident. Once an attempt to assist is begun, however, it is obligated to see the matter through or to arrange for an equally competent source of help. In actual practice, operating personnel are indoctrinated to answer any call for help *in an emergency or when no other help is available.*

Under authority granted by the Congress, the Coast Guard may also render assistance anywhere in the world where it has forces available, without regard to the nationality of those in distress. This includes an area from the Arctic to the Antarctic, and from the Denmark Strait to the coast of Asia. Most of the far-flung cases involve large ships and aircraft in distress. But the major SAR load is in and adjacent to the United States, where of the 52,738 assistance cases handled by the Coast Guard in 1989, 35,341 were pleasure boats. Most such cases occurred within ten miles of the U.S. coast or on its rivers, bays, and lakes. The location of SAR cases is shown in table 1.2:

Table 1.2 Locations of Search and Rescue (SAR) Cases By U.S. Coast Guard, 1989

	INLAND		DISTANCE OFFSHORE (MILES)				
	Land	Water	0–3	3–10	10–20	20–50	50+
No. of Cases	2,022	25,956	25,475	5,646	1,854	1,662	1,365
Lives Lost	146	519	449	108	78	372	89
Lives saved	314	1,577	2,165	662	373	324	531

It should be noted, however, that the death rate farther offshore was much higher than that incurred within ten miles of the beach.

The kinds of SAR cases are shown in figure 1.2. The largest category by far consists of boats disabled or adrift, which by definition are not accidental events but the result of material failure, malfunction, or negligence. Even so, many of these boats may be in danger as time passes and must be assisted without regard to

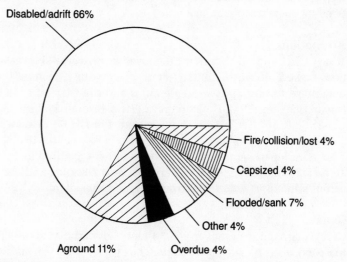

Figure 1.2 Kinds of search and rescue (SAR) cases by U.S. Coast Guard, 1989. *Courtesy USCG*

the cause of their predicament. It will be apparent comparing the numbers in figure 1.2 with the total number of boating accidents nationwide that the Coast Guard rescues only a relatively small portion of all boaters in difficulty. More incidents occur in inland regions where few Coast Guard facilities exist than in the coastal and offshore areas, but the latter cases are more difficult and often require sophisticated equipment and trained personnel.

COAST GUARD FACILITIES

Shore Stations and Boats

Numerous small Coast Guard shore stations are situated along the coastlines of the United States, the Great Lakes, and many major river systems. Equipped with various types of small boats designed to assist craft in distress, they conduct three-quarters of all Coast Guard SAR missions, including most of the pleasure boat cases (see figure 1.3). The boats range in size from 18 feet to 65 feet, and most are equipped with radar, radio direction finders, and adequate communications and are built to take heavy seas. These boats are the ones most likely to be encountered by the recreational boater.

Air Stations

Nearly two hundred aircraft are deployed from twenty-six air stations in the United States and overseas. Fixed-wing aircraft are the long-range turboprop HC-130 Hercules and the twin-jet HU-25 Falcon (see figure 1.4). Helicopters, all twin-turbine, include the HH-3F Pelican, the HH-65 Dolphin, and the HH-60 Seahawk. The Coast Guard's air arm is the same size as those of the British, French, or Japanese navies. Though aircraft are required in only 10 percent of SAR cases, these are the most complex and dangerous situations, where air coverage is indispensible.

Cutters

Coast Guard cutters range from 378-foot high-endurance vessels to 82-foot and 110-foot patrol boats. The big cutters as well as the medium-endurance 270-foot and 210-foot ones have flight decks

Figure 1.3   Coast Guard station near an inlet. The nearest (a 30-footer) and the middle (a 44-footer) are heavy-duty motor lifeboats. The larger boat (rear) is an 82-foot patrol boat used for coastal and off-shore work. *Courtesy USCG*

for helicopters and sophisticated armament, sensors, and communications. Most pleasure-boat rescues will be made by the patrol boats and boats from shore stations, though the larger cutters may be encountered offshore and in drug interdiction areas.

ANNUAL SAR OPERATIONS

In 1989, a typical year, the Coast Guard logged 64,030 responses to 52,738 calls for help and saved 3,961 people and $641 million in property. It also assisted 117,546 other persons in distress cases involving $2.1 billion of property; however, 1,106 lives were lost. This SAR load was double that of only twenty years ago. The cost to the Coast Guard (and taxpayers) for the protection of small-boat sailors is exceeded only by its budget for law enforcement and drug interdiction.

Figure 1.4   A long-range turboprop C-130 Hercules passes over the Coast Guard air station at Clearwater, Florida. *Courtesy USCG*

THE U.S. COAST GUARD AUXILIARY

A civilian volunteer organization, the Coast Guard Auxiliary was established by Congress to promote safety in recreational boating. Its thirty-five thousand members are experienced boat operators, amateur radio hams, or licensed aircraft pilots with nine thousand boats and aircraft owned by the individual members. Eligibility for the auxiliary extends to all U.S. citizens who are at least seventeen years old and who own at least 25 percent of a boat, aircraft, or a fixed or mobile radio station. The auxiliary carries out three basic programs: courtesy marine examinations (CME), public education, and operations.

Courtesy Marine Examinations (CME).   Specially trained members of the auxiliary conduct courtesy marine examinations of recreational boats upon request of the owners or operators. If a boat does not pass the examination, the owner is advised of the deficiencies but no report is made to any law enforcement official.

Public Education.   The auxiliary offers to the public a wide array of boating safety courses, each tailored to a specific need and taught by experienced boaters. The most comprehensive is the multilesson course "Boating Skills and Seamanship," which covers basic knowledge of aids to navigation, rules of the road, boat handling, legal requirements, piloting, marine engines, sailing, marlinspike seamanship, radio-telephone, weather, locks and dams, plus trailering and safe motorboat operation (see figure 1.5).

Operations.   To assist the Coast Guard, members of the auxiliary perform SAR missions and patrol regattas and marine events, often in conjunction with regular Coast Guard units. Auxiliary members have no law enforcement powers. When such authority is needed, a Coast Guard officer or petty officer will be embarked on the auxiliary vessel, which will then fly the regular Coast Guard ensign.

Figure 1.5   A Coast Guard Auxiliary instructor teaches knot tying in a boating safety course. *Courtesy USCG*

OTHER SAR RESOURCES

Most serious maritime SAR is handled by the Coast Guard but a substantial number of small-boat accidents are taken care of by other rescuers. These generally occur on inland waters where Coast Guard facilities are not readily available or where nearby boaters or state and local authorities have rapid access to the scene. The small-boat operator with some understanding of who to call and how the SAR system works can receive rapid and competent help in most parts of the United States and its adjacent waters. This help may involve the other armed forces, state and local public safety agencies, commercial and private salvors, the merchant marine, and various federal agencies. These can be alerted by a call to the Coast Guard or a local public safety (police or fire) agency. A major resource is the presence of other small-boat operators who are ready and eager to assist a fellow sailor in trouble if they are made aware of his or her plight.

By coordinating the use of these facilities through a network of treaties and agreements, protection can be afforded not only to coastal and inland sailors but to air crews and mariners over much of the world's oceans.

2
Presailing Preparations

Most experienced sailors agree that the planning and preparations before departure are among the biggest factors in a successful trip. At sea there are no supply and service facilities, and tasks that are simple alongside a dock become extremely difficult in heavy weather. Do everything possible ahead of time.

The extent of preparations will depend on the proposed length of the voyage and the operating environment. A three-week voyage may require days or even weeks of preparation, but an afternoon sail on the river should take less than an hour. Likewise, briefing of a new crew or first-time guests is required, whereas old hands who have sailed together often on the boat may need only a nod of the head or a brief reminder. Finally, there is usually more time to instruct people during some emergencies in protected waters than offshore and briefings may be modified accordingly.

Preparations involve four distinct phases, which should be accomplished in this approximate order.

1. Check that the boat's routine maintenance is up-to-date and systems are A-OK.
2. Before the crew boards, inspect or test any essential systems that may possibly require further servicing and could cause a time delay. Use a preboarding checklist. Load perishable provi-

sions and file a float plan (itinerary) only when reasonably sure of
your departure time.

3. Brief the crew on ship routine and emergency duties.
Carry out prestart check.

4. Start engines and complete departure check.

To prevent oversights, written checklists should be used.
Such a practice is not a sign of approaching senility but a professional approach used by seamen who operate complex machinery daily. It is even more essential for the amateur sailor who uses
his or her boat infrequently and is apt to be rusty on procedures.
In addition to the departure checklists, special checklists should
be compiled for securing the boat for long or short periods, sunset and sunrise routines, and heavy weather. Checklists also en-
hance the safety of persons going aloft, refueling, and towing. For
protection and ease of handling, mount the checklists between
thin plexiglass sheets. Checklists will have to be developed by
each skipper based on operating outlook and the type and size of
boat. A small checklist of a few essential items may be adequate
for a small outboard, but the contents of an adequate checklist
increase dramatically with the size and complexity of the boat,
and such lists are even more essential in the larger ones. Appendix D contains illustrative checklists for a 45-foot sloop. It is
easier to delete items from a large checklist than to add them to
an incomplete one.

ROUTINE MAINTENANCE

A planned maintenance program not only is essential for safety
but helps prevent costly breakdowns and repairs. Most small-
boat sailors do some or all of their own maintenance, bringing in
outside technicians only for difficult or specialized work. Doing
maintenance personally is not only highly satisfying, enjoyable,
and economical, but if something goes wrong at sea, the skipper
is more familiar with the boat's hardware.

Routine engine maintenance is based on the hours of operating time and is usually prescribed in the manufacturer's operat-

ing manual. Preventative maintenance and repairs, however, are dependent on regular inspections.

PREVENTATIVE MAINTENANCE AND INSPECTIONS

The Hull

The primary aim of hull maintenance is the preservation of the hull's watertight integrity and secondarily its appearance. Fiberglass boats, especially smaller ones and those kept in dry stowage, require very little hull maintenance. Larger boats require more care, especially the through-hull valves, seacocks, and hoses leading from them to various parts of the boat. Seacocks must be checked for soundness, corrosion, and ease of operation; they need lubrication as required. Check that all hose clamps that may be below the waterline at normal angles of heel are made of stainless steel and doubled and that all clamps anywhere on the hose are tight and in good condition. Check hoses leading from the through hulls at least yearly for wear, breakdown, or leaks. Insure that a tapered soft wooden plug is fastened adjacent to each through hull for use in case of leaks.

Make frequent visual inspections of the bilge area for any signs of corrosion, blemishes, or bulging of any surfaces. Clean the bilge of debris, which can quickly clog and incapacitate the best bilge pump. Note any shifting of bulkheads or cabin soles, or sticking doors that could be caused by such a shift.

Check the gelcoat for radial cracks resulting from stress; check for any cracks in the laminate. Fiberglass is much harder to inspect properly than wood is, since most of the defects are hidden by fiberglass material. Check for delamination at exposed edges and for chips in the gelcoat.

Check through bolts and major nuts for corrosion and tightness. Check keel bolts, and if necessary, arrange for an X ray. If evidence of electrolytic corrosion and wasting is found, call in an expert to examine the boat. Check the security of lifelines and stanchions.

The underwater body and keel should be inspected for

damage, wear, and blisters when the boat is hauled, and repairs should be made before applying new antifouling paint. The propeller and shaft should be inspected and the sacrificial zinc protectors replaced if necessary. The rudder and rudder fittings should be checked for wear or damage. Between haulouts, opportunities should be taken while cruising to inspect the underwater hull using a snorkel and face mask. Cleaning with a rough towel or a nylon brush will help maintain the boat's proper performance and appearance and will extend the intervals between haulouts.

The Engine

In planning routine and preventative maintenance, consult the manufacturer's handbook, which should always be kept aboard the boat. Some manufacturers issue a more comprehensive shop manual for use by repair personnel or those skippers wishing to carry out more advanced engine repair work themselves. Consult the engine dealer or distributor for advice on maintenance and repairs not covered in the manuals. Much of the engine maintenance can be done with ordinary mechanical know-how if the handbook is followed.

Fuel System

Sample the Raycor filter periodically before starting for evidence of fuel contamination. Periodic checks of the entire fuel system, including the refueling connection and hose, fuel tank, shutoff valves, hose, and filters are essential for safety as well as smooth engine operation. Any smell of gasoline or visual evidence of leakage must be immediately pinpointed and the engine *must not be operated until the leak is repaired* and the boat ventilated. These inspections have been made even more urgent by the federal ban on lead additives in gasoline. Lead has been replaced by alcohol compounds, which work well in boosting the octane rating but are very corrosive and destructive to the rubber hose and metal components of some fuel systems. This corrosion is accelerated when the boat stands idle for long periods, which is common with most pleasure craft.

Diesel fuel leaks must also be promptly uncovered and repaired though they are not as dangerous as gasoline leaks. Oil and fuel must not be allowed to accumulate in drip pans or bilges. This accumulation can be kept to a minimum by putting sanitary napkins or absorbent diapers at the low point of the pan or beneath the leak. Change them as required and clean up oil with a degreaser spray.

It is the manufacturer's responsibility to install a powered ventilation system on certain types of boats, but the operator must ensure that the system continues to work properly. Even if yours is an older boat, built before these requirements, keep your existing ventilation system in top operating condition.

Standing and Running Rigging and Sails

Standing and running rigging and sails are as essential for a sailboat as an engine is for a powerboat, and failure of the standing rigging can result in loss of the mast. Stays and shrouds should be carefully examined for broken wire strands, or fish hooks. Most failures, however, occur in the terminal connecting fittings rather than the wire cable. Swaged terminal fittings should be examined periodically with a magnifying glass and then checked with a dye penetrant and developer if any doubt exists. The dye may be either visible or fluorescent under ultraviolet light. Possible weak points like threads should be checked, especially to see that ample ends of shank are screwed into the barrel at each end of a turnbuckle. Cotter pins should be used to prevent a turnbuckle from backing off.

Clevis and cotter pins should be checked for wear. In an emergency, pulling the clevis pins is the quickest way to release standing rigging. To facilitate this, cut the cotter pin that secures the clevis pin so that one-quarter inch protrudes after insertion. File this smooth and open the cotter pin at a 20-degree spread to allow pulling it quickly in an emergency. Halyards and sheets should be checked for chafing and occasionally reversed to equalize wear.

At least yearly, and before long voyages, send a knowledgeable person aloft in a bosun's chair to inspect both upper and lower portions of the standing and running rigging, hardware, and spreaders. Check all sails for signs of chafing, broken stitching, and tears well before leaving, to permit time for repairs. Spots prone to chafing, such as the contact point between spreaders and the foresail, should be reinforced with a patch of heavy material to absorb the wear. Batten pockets are very prone to wear, and the batten must be tied or sewed in. In an emergency, tears along seams or in the sail material may be patched under way with sail tape or stitching. Periodically, the sail should be taken to a qualified sailmaker for inspection and repaired as necessary. Check the storm sails; they are so rarely used that they may be overlooked.

Electrical System

The complexity of the electrical system usually increases with the size of the boat. A malfunctioning electrical circuit not only is a potential fire hazard but can affect the operation of many other systems because of loss of electrical power or the corrosion from electrolysis. A check to determine any amperage drain with all systems shut off may provide an early indication of trouble; ideally there should be no current flow. Any significant leakage must be located and corrected. A yearly visual inspection should be made of all wiring and connections to locate chafing, worn or oil-soaked wire, and loose connections. This check should also include inspection of the batteries and alternator, as well as the AC shore connection and auxiliary power systems.

Battery Care and Use

Compared with other equipment on the boat, the batteries are relatively short lived, but the timing of their demise is unpredictable. Failure to deliver the expected electrical power may result from a number of factors. Some are easily correctable, but others may require battery replacement. Relatively simple tests can pinpoint the likely problem.

A day before sailing, switch off the battery charger and allow the intended starting battery to discharge under load to about 75 percent of full charge. (Even a faulty battery, coming off a full charge, may give good performance for a short period. Once under load, however, its performance will drop rapidly.)

Start the engine using this battery alone to check its performance under the high starting current load. After the engine start, note the alternator charge. The single battery start is important, for when batteries are used in parallel (selector on *Both*), a good battery will mask the poor performance of a bad one. If each battery when used singly gives the engine a good start, the batteries are probably in good shape and can be brought back to full charge with confidence.

If a battery fails to properly turn over the engine, several things could be wrong. The power cable connections to the battery should be checked first. Remove the connector from the battery posts and clean off all corrosion with a wire brush and sandpaper. Replace and tighten the connectors and apply a light coat of grease or other protection.

The importance of good electrical contact, especially with heavy power loads, cannot be overemphasized. For example, the starter motor on your engine is rated at 3,000 watts, and with clean tight battery contacts, resistance is only 0.048 ohm in the circuit and the current flow is 250 amperes. Because of corrosion and vibration, some looseness develops in the terminal connectors to the battery, which results in an increase of 0.01 ohm in resistance. With the total resistance now increased from 0.048 to 0.058 ohm, only 207 amperes flow to the starter resulting in a starting power of 2,484 watts instead of 3,000 watts. Furthermore, because of the poor contact, not all of this power is applied at the motor; 408 watts of power are dissipated at the poor connection, resulting in only 2,076 watts going to the motor, barely enough to turn over the engine. Yet the increased resistance that caused the trouble is only 0.01 ohm. The wasted power will be evidenced by very high heat at the poor connection, and such spots can often be located by feeling for heat after use. Poor starting performance is often blamed on the battery when poor terminal contacts are the actual culprit.

If cleaning the contacts does not solve the starting problem, make sure the battery is properly charged and that the electrolyte level is up. The state of charge can be determined by a voltage reading on an expanded scale voltmeter or multimeter, or by a reading of electrolyte density with a hydrometer. If the battery is fully charged, the reading should be between 1,250 and 1,300

(1.25 and 1.30 grams/cc). If all cells show a reading below this, the battery probably only needs a long charge. But if one cell reads low, while the others read normal, that cell is probably dead or has a high resistance, and the battery is probably failing. If this occurs, check the voltage again after the battery has been under sustained load; a drop of 1–2 volts will confirm a dead cell. Gas formation and bubbling of the electrolyte when the battery is under load will further pinpoint the bad cell.

Batteries fail for a number of reasons, but the leading one is excessive deep cycling, that is, near exhaustion of the battery charge. This should be avoided by keeping the batteries well charged, and by monitoring the battery voltages to detect droppage early and shifting the load to another battery when the first becomes low.

Overcharging is a second major cause of battery failure. Though shore power converters and alternators have regulators to limit the charging voltage to values between 13.8 and 14.2 volts, a higher reading may indicate a malfunctioning regulator and an overcharge. The small portable chargers and trickle chargers usually do not have regulators. Although high currents charging nearly empty batteries do no harm, when the charge rises above 70 percent, some of the current is used to decompose water. This process with the attendant gas formation and bubbling is normal in the final stages of charging a battery, but if charging is continued beyond full charge, a rapid loss of electrolytes occurs, contributing eventually to failure of the battery. If overcharging is suspected, frequent checks of electrolyte level should be made and the regulator of the charging source adjusted or replaced if indicated.

A battery in *early* failure may be used as a power source when high amps are not required and may be used in parallel with a strong battery without ill effects. The linkage of a good and poor battery will result in a redistribution of the power between them. If they are charged in parallel, however, the good battery will charge while the weak one will begin gassing. When this occurs, not only will charging of the bank cease, but the electrolyte will boil off at a fast rate, the demand on the alternator will remain high, and the bad battery may become very hot to the touch; it should be immediately switched or cut out of the circuit. When this occurs and the hydrometer shows a low reading on a cell even after a good charge, or a voltage drop occurs with a short application of load, it is best to take the battery to a shop for testing and probable replacement.

Ground Tackle

Check the anchor rodes during normal use for wear or chafing of the chain or line; also check the security of the shackles and pins, which must be safety wired. If wear appears near one end of the anchor line, reversing it will provide many more years of safe wear. Check scope markers on the rode.

Electronics

The cause of malfunctions in the radio, loran, global positioning system, knotmeter, fathometer, or other electronic instruments can sometimes be located by continuity checks for breaks or grounds in the power supply and wiring leads. Malfunctions within the equipment will usually require shop or factory servicing.

Steering

Inspect the cable and chain control leads from the wheel to the rudder quadrant, as well as their turning sheaves. Adjust the tension when required and lubricate well. Check terminal fastenings for tightness. Bolts and screws can work loose in a system that is in constant use under way. At least once yearly, try out the emergency tiller while at dock or anchor to refresh your memory and check that the tiller will still slip on. Check the autopilot or steering vane as prescribed by the manufacturer.

Bilge Pumps

If your boat has one of those common, nagging chronic leaks, it will be easy to check the operation of the bilge pumps. If you are fortunate enough to have a boat that almost never makes water, wash down the bilge with a freshwater hose and check each pump individually while pumping the bilge dry. Do not pump oily waters in the coastal areas: the penalties for oil pollution are heavy, including fines, civil penalties up to $25,000, and imprisonment. Use a portable hand pump to pump oily bilge water into buckets, or soak it up in disposable diapers, paper toweling, or other absorbent material and dispose of it in an authorized oil disposal dump. Bilge pumps will not function long with a dirty or debris-filled bilge, and an in-line strainer should be installed between the bilge suction point and a diaphragm pump. If the flow of the bilge pump is inadequate, check the strainer first.

Safety Gear
Carry a plentiful or even redundant supply of safety gear, not just the minimum required by law. Inspect fire extinguishers and detectors as specified by the manufacturer and keep a current inspection card on the bottles. Visually inspect PFDs, which should be labeled with the vessel's name, and attached equipment. Check the EPIRB as prescribed by the manufacturer, and insure it is turned off before restowing. Check man overboard lights, pole, and horseshoe. Have the life raft inspected and repacked as recommended by the manufacturer, using a qualified professional firm. Some racing rules require annual inspections, and the Coast Guard requirement for commercial vessels is also yearly. See that abandon-ship equipment is readily accessible, not outdated, and in good condition.

First Aid Chest and Manual
Check that the inventory of the first aid chest is current and in good condition, and that medications' shelf lives have not expired. Be sure that a medical instruction manual is on board.

Navigation Gear
Check the inventory of charts and publications for the area in which the boat will be cruising. Allow some margin, as weather or other circumstances may force a boat out of the planned area and "off the chart." In larger or far-ranging boats, publications could include items such as *Tide Tables* and *Tidal Current Tables*, *Navigation Rules*, an area cruising guide, and a *List of Lights* (see Appendix F). A reliable clock or watch with corrected time, a sextant, a nautical almanac, and sight reduction tables are

needed by celestial navigators, whether they are far offshore or honing their skills in coastal waters. Most navigators require instruments such as dividers, plotting rulers, time/distance/speed calculator, and a bearing compass. Insure that the compass and standby compass (a bearing compass will do) are reasonably accurate and their error is known. Check all navigation, instrument, and compass lights. Check flashlights and spot lights and insure that spare batteries are available. Smaller boats in coastal waters will have much smaller navigational inventories because of space limitations and reduced requirements.

Stoves and Heaters

Check stoves and heaters according to the manufacturer's instruction manual. If a leak is suspected in a liquified petroleum gas (LPG), or propane; compressed natural gas (CNG); or alcohol system, correct it immediately after first shutting off the supply tank and ventilating the boat. Shut off fuel tanks when leaving the boat for extended periods.

CORRECTING DISCREPANCIES

When engine problems occur that are not covered in the routine or preventative maintenance schedule, they should be promptly corrected, especially if they are related to safety. If some of these require correction by a qualified mechanic, the owner should take the opportunity to observe how it is done and see the engine as it is opened up. Most mechanics are glad to show you; if not, think about getting a more cooperative one. Bleeding the air from a diesel fuel system is simple when you watch the process demonstrated by a qualified mechanic but more difficult when you read about it in a maintenance manual.

To insure that nothing is overlooked, keep a hard-cover account book and enter the material problems encountered during each trip. As they are corrected, enter a notation of the corrective action. This CSMP (current ship maintenance projects) notebook should also contain a record of fuel and oil use; this consumption versus engine hours is vital in keeping track of your fuel state. Many skippers also use this book to diagram the various damage control features such as through-hull fittings, bilge and water pump systems, electrical wiring, toilet fittings, and so on. The CSMP book is also valuable in dealing with insurance and legal matters should a material failure or loss occur.

SPARE PARTS

Each skipper should put together a spare parts kit and a tool kit suitable for his or her operating needs. Some manufacturers provide a recommended list of parts and tools in their engine manuals. From millions of hours of operating experience, engine manufacturers can predict with considerable accuracy what failures will occur, and the spare parts and tools needed to make repairs. If any items are used, they must be replaced promptly on return to port. A parts and tool inventory for a diesel engine used in coastal cruising should include:

manufacturer's handbook for the engine
seawater pump impeller and gasket
freshwater pump driving belt
alternator driving belt (if separate from water pump drive)
hose clips, assorted
hose, assorted
baling wire spool
electrical insulating tape
duct tape
jointing compound
battery hydrometer
magnet
vise grip pliers
pliers
screw drivers, assorted
self-gripping wrench
socket wrench set
slip joint pliers
hacksaw with spare blades
hammer
files, assorted

spare engine lube oil for complete refill
spare transmission oil
spare fuel filter element for each filter
engine starter fluid, one can
electric wiring, assorted spools
light bulbs, assorted
electric wire connectors, assorted
electric multimeter

Boats using gasoline engines should also carry a spare set of spark plugs, points, a plug wrench, condenser, rotor and cap, and coil and coil wire.

Although not strictly a spare part, a fully charged spare battery should be carried by a skipper going very far from home. This "Skipper's Reserve" battery should not be used by anyone else. A boat's main batteries can, through improper power usage, get so low that the engine cannot be electrically cranked to start and recharge them. The spare battery, with attached jump cable or an installed separate switching system, is for that primary purpose. This spare is especially important for sailboats using electric power for long periods with little or no engine alternator charging, or for any boat during long periods at anchor. A daily battery charge and proper use of batteries, of course, will prevent a lot of grief.

Equipment Manuals and Instructions
Most equipment will have a manufacturer's handbook or instruction pamphlet on operation, maintenance, and repairs. All of these should be kept and carried on board, together with copies of any warranty papers, serial numbers of equipment, and dates of purchase.

Stowage and Security
Make sure that all cabinet doors can be fastened so that they stay closed while the boat is heeling. Provide retainers such as bungee cords or netting for gear stowed on shelves. Nothing will ruin a day quicker than a lower deck adrift in loose and broken gear,

especially when it is also soaked with catsup, syrup, paint, or spilled coffee. Loose gear can also cause injuries.

Stowage Plan

Stow seldom-used gear and spare parts out of the way; they must be accessible, however, and their location known without a long search. This is best done with an alphabetically arranged stowage list.

LOADING THE BOAT

The equipment to be carried and the provisions and supplies will be different for each boat and crew, but on a trip of any kind something is always left behind. To minimize this risk, a running list should be started well before departure. Items may be checked off as loaded, and others added to the list as needed. Such an informal list will differ with each trip, even with the same boat and crew. A written list is always more reliable than a mental one.

OPERATING CHECKLISTS

Once the boat is loaded, it is well to check certain items before the crew boards. The preboarding, before starting, and start engine checklists are shown in Appendix C. Specialty checklists for securing after arrival, sunset and sunrise routines, and heavy weather are also shown. Because of its inherent danger, a refueling checklist is recommended. Some may also wish to prepare checklists for potentially risky evolutions such as towing or going aloft. Those in hurricane areas should have a hurricane planning checklist (see Appendix C).

FLOAT PLAN

Before going out on any trip in unprotected waters or out of sight of land or people, it is essential to make out a float plan, or itinerary, giving information on the boat, its occupants and route, and the expected return time or arrival time at another destination. The float plan should contain specific instructions as to when and what authorities should be notified if the boat is overdue. Leave it with a responsible party ashore. Do not try to file a float plan with the Coast Guard, which does not have the resources to handle the thousands of voyages that occur daily. If a float plan is always filed with a person who knows the boat well, it may be verbal but must be clearly understood.

On 30 May 1986, the 32-foot boat *Lora Lee* with three people aboard capsized ten miles southeast of Kodiak Island, Alaska. The crew had just started transmitting a Mayday signal when the boat turned over and radio contact was lost before the distress position could be given. All three people had on survival suits when entering the water. The skipper, moreover, had previously advised people ashore of his plans. When this information was provided to the Coast Guard, an HH-3F helicopter from Kodiak rescued all three men several hours after the sinking.

By contrast, four Miami residents had cleared with no one before heading out for a day's fishing. When their boat broke up and sank, they were forced into the water with only their lifejackets and some cushions from the boat. No one even knew they were missing or overdue. They were spotted fifty-seven hours later in the Gulf Stream twenty-three miles off Jupiter Inlet, Florida, by crew members of the CGC *Tampa*. The cutter was not looking for them but was en route to its home port from a Caribbean deployment. The survival of the members of the fishing party was a matter of luck only.

Appendix A contains a suggested float plan. First fill out the data in the first section, "Boat Description." Then duplicate the forms with boat characteristics already filled in, saving considerable time in making out later float plans.

The use of a float plan cannot be too strongly emphasized. Should an accident occur where no distress call can be made (a common occurrence), a float plan or EPIRB can provide the quickest means of alerting help: the float plan is more reliable but slower. I must also emphasize the absolute necessity of closing out or cancelling the float plan on arrival, or amending it if a change in plans has occurred. The Coast Guard will help you do this if you request it.

CREW BRIEFING

Before getting under way, it is good seamanship and common courtesy to brief a new crew or guests on how the boat operates and the normal routines to be observed. Such an explanation makes for a more congenial and cooperative company. Common-sense precautions and safety procedures can prevent accidents, but people who are not intimately familiar with the sea and boats may have to be advised of them. Should an accident occur, failure to have done so may suggest the skipper or owner displayed negligence and disregard for the well-being of persons who were less knowledgeable than he or she about the possible risks. The crew briefing may be oral but the repetition as crew changes occur may get old. Some skippers hand out a written briefing for crew and guests, then answer any questions they may have. The extent of the briefing will depend on the anticipated length and type of cruise as well as the familiarity of the crew with the boat and skipper.

A vital part of the briefing for the crew involves each person's duties in an emergency. A typical emergency bill for a sail auxiliary is shown in Appendix B. This bill is designed for a four-member crew, but with slight modification will work as well for crews of different sizes. Note that duties and equipment to be provided are assigned by numbers. When the crew is on board, the skipper should assign an emergency number to each person. The emergency bill should be posted prominently in an accessible place where each crew member can read it and memorize his or her duties and the location of equipment. If an excess number of people are aboard, supernumeraries can be assigned to assist the first four crew members in their duties. If shorthanded, some may have to do double duty. After the crew has had a chance to read the bill, the skipper or mate should answer any questions. The skipper should make clear which person will take command should he or she be incapacitated or injured.

Carry out the crew briefings in a matter-of-fact manner that will not frighten any who may be apprehensive yet insist that all hands observe the safety precautions and know their emergency assignments. One sailor/aviator friend always concludes his briefing with the remark, "I wore a parachute for over twenty years, but I only needed it once!"

WHY BOTHER?

All of these presailing preparations may seem unnecessary to some. Of course the effort involved will depend on the boat type and equipment and on the planned length and route of the trip. The law is often limited in protecting a person against his or her own mistakes, but it has awesome power of protecting others from the actions or neglect of an individual.

The owner/operator of a pleasure craft has a duty to his or her crew and guests to exercise reasonable care for their safety. Such care is defined as that which a reasonable and prudent person would exercise under similar conditions. Failure to meet this obligation becomes grounds for legal tort (injury) action if it is a direct cause of harm to another person or person's property.

The exposure of the average boat owner to personal civil liability has also been increased by the litigation fever of recent years. "Pirates are no longer a threat on our coasts," one boat-owning attorney said, only partially in jest: "Today the aggressive tort claim attorneys seeking large awards are not pirates. They are privateers. Their actions are legal and their letters of marque (that is, licenses) are issued by the state."

The absence of criminal penalties will be of little consolation to a boat owner whose operation of a defective or unseaworthy boat results in harm to guests or others, leading to the imposition by an outraged jury of a huge award for *punitive* damages not covered by the owner's insurance (often limited solely to *compensatory* damages).

A boat owner is liable for his or her failure to correct not only dangerous conditions of which he or she was aware but possibly even those conditions of which he or she was unaware but should have known about if he or she had exercised reasonable care and properly inspected the boat and equipment.

Liability attaches to the negligent and reckless operation of a boat as well as to material failings. This includes exceeding speed limits and disregard of navigation rules and safety regulations. Failure to obey these is usually considered to be negligence per se without consideration of the reasonableness of the laws or the circumstances of the accident.

3
Disabled and Adrift

Two of every three recreational boats assisted by the Coast Guard are disabled or adrift, usually from engine trouble or, far less often, steering mishaps. Engine failure is an ever present risk but one that can usually be minimized and dealt with. This requires a multiprong approach, starting with the uses a boat is subjected to. Even an experienced operator in a well-found and maintained boat can force a boat into an environment beyond its capability, in which a small problem can lead to greater ones and occasionally to disaster.

Though the possibility of the failure of a single engine is always there, the likelihood of two failing at the same time is far less. In theory, if the probability of failure in a certain type of engine is 10 percent during a given time span, the probability of the failure of its twin engine during the same time period from other than a common cause is only 1 percent. The probability of prolonged simultaneous engine and sail (wind) failure is even less. If a boat is to be frequently used in an environment where engine failure could lead to serious consequences, a twin-engine boat is obviously safer. Engine failure offshore where severe weather can create large seas or where currents such as the Gulf Stream can carry disabled boats hundreds of miles can transform a minor engine or steering breakdown into a distress case requiring a massive search and costing hundreds of thousands of dollars. Since not everyone wants or can afford two engines, the single-engine disadvantage can be minimized by carrying a reliable radio or traveling in company with another boat in exposed waters.

In late August 1986, a twenty-seven-year-old man departed Shrub Cay alone for a two-hour trip to Walkers Key in the Bahamas, a routine run for his 21-foot boat. Troubles started with a thunderstorm, then a broken steering wheel, and climaxed with an empty reserve fuel tank. At the mercy of prevailing winds and current, the boat was swept out to sea. Six weeks later, on 5 October, he was sighted by a pleasure boat sixty miles off Charleston, South Carolina. Suffering from dehydration and hypothermia, the man sat up as the rescuers came alongside and deliriously asked for a beer. He had survived in an open boat for the entire period on raw fish and two cans of beer! He was removed by helicopter to a hospital, where he recovered uneventfully. Even a small fault can mean big trouble if an engine fails for any reason, even on a short run.

FUEL STATE

Each year hundreds of otherwise responsible people embarrass themselves and upset others by mismanaging or running out of fuel. Some are victimized by faulty gauges, whereas others may suffer fuel leaks or tank contamination. But most of the problem is a result of carelessness or procrastination in fuel management.

Every skipper should know the hourly fuel consumption of his or her engine within close limits. Boats are usually run at the same RPM, and if a record is made of the amount of fuel consumed versus the number of engine hours indicated on the engine counter, a very precise record of use and fuel state can be established. By noting the number of hours run since topping off the tanks and multiplying by the hourly consumption rate, the amount of fuel used is established. Subtracting this amount from the tank capacity shows the amount of fuel remaining and serves as a cross-check on the fuel gauge. Some boats have a fuel tank dipstick as a third check.

A check on fuel is as essential on short trips near shore as it is on longer forays. On 28 March 1988, two young men left Anclote Key, Florida, in a 14-foot outboard boat for the short run to the mainland. Despite the many boats in this busy area, they disappeared. A Coast Guard search was terminated with negative results after three days. Ten days after calling off the search, the boat was discovered by the commercial fishing boat *Apollo* over fifty miles north of the point at which it disappeared. Nineteen-year-old Timothy Daniels of Hudson, Florida, was badly sunburned and drifting in and out of consciousness when he was found. His twenty-five-year-old companion had died only hours before they were rescued. They had run out of gas during the short three-mile run from the key to the mainland.

A boat's preboarding checklist should begin with a check of fuel quantity. If there is any doubt about the adequacy of the fuel supply on board for the proposed trip, fuel should be added and a spare tank carried if necessary. A good rule is to allow one-third of the fuel for the outbound leg, one-third for the return, and one-third for reserve. Lubricating and transmission oils must also be checked and an adequate reserve carried.

Fuel reserves can be deceptive with some tank installations that lose fuel suction if the boat is rolling heavily and the fuel is down to 5 to 10 percent of tank capacity. When this occurs, air is taken into the fuel lines and the engine stops. A gasoline engine may be quickly restarted, but a diesel fuel system must be bled of air before restarting—a frustrating procedure with a hot engine and a rolling boat.

The combination of low fuel level and heavy boat motion can also stir up contaminants that may have settled to the tank bottom. Mixed with the small amount of remaining fuel, this debris and bacteria can clog the filters and fuel system and cause the engine to stop. This kind of engine failure will usually require a tank cleanup and a change of fuel filters.

REFUELING PROCEDURES

Precautions that should be observed every time that a boat is refueled are shown in the refueling checklist in Appendix C.

CHECKING THE ENGINE OPERATION

After getting under way with the engine under load, again check it for normal operation and instrument readings. If problems develop or the engine operates abnormally, either locate the trouble and fix it or determine that it is not significant and will not worsen. If neither action is possible, it is prudent to turn back. Veteran seamen and aviators will confirm that big troubles usually start, not with a bang, but with a seemingly small problem.

EMERGENCY MEASURES

Some problems can be quickly diagnosed and repaired under way or the boat jury-rigged to allow a return to dock under its own power.

1. If the engine will not start initially, check to see that the fuel valve is On. If it is on and open, next check the level of fuel in the tanks. If the fuel tank is empty or very low, there are probably contaminants in the filters and fuel lines. Check the fuel filters before restarting. With diesels, bleed the fuel system of air before restarting.

2. If a diesel engine stops, the problem is usually lack of fuel. Check to see that there is fuel in the tank and that fuel cutoff valves are fully open. If so, next check the Raycor (primary) filter. If the fuel and filter are dirty, replace the filter. Then check the other fuel filters and replace any dirty ones. If the fuel level in a filter is low, fuel may not be reaching that filter. If the engine RPMs surge before the engine quits, there may be air in the fuel system. Check the fuel-line connections and filters for tightness. Bleed the fuel system of air and attempt a restart.

3. If the engine suddenly begins to labor, or stops with a clunk, there could be a line wrapped around the propeller, such as from a crab pot. If the engine runs smoothly in neutral but labors or stalls in gear, this is most likely the problem. Always suspect this first. Do the same if the steering becomes stiff.

4. If the engine is producing a great deal of smoke, check the engine air-intake filter. It may be clogged with foreign matter sucked from the engine compartment, restricting the air intake

and causing incomplete combustion. Cleaning the filter will remedy the problem. An engine overload caused by excessive propeller fouling or a line around the prop shaft can also cause black smoke, as well as overheating.

5. If the engine temperature gauge indicates overheating, before shutting down the engine take a quick look at the overboard exhaust water discharge. Then note the tachometer and voltmeter.

If the tachometer is out or the voltmeter does not show a normal charge, the alternator is not functioning. Because the alternator and freshwater coolant pump in many installations are driven by the same drive belt, check this first. Tighten it, or if broken, replace it with a spare.

If the exhaust water discharge is absent or diminished, and the drive belt to the alternator and coolant pump is OK, the problem is probably a lack of sea cooling water flow. Check at the seacock and the seawater filter trap for possible clogging. Close the seacock and clean the filter if necessary. If it seems satisfactory, next check the seawater pump impeller. Leaving the seawater intake closed, remove the impeller cover. If the impeller has failed or has damaged blades, replace it with a spare, replace the cover, open the seacock, and restart the engine. Recheck the exhaust water discharge. If this is adequate, the problem has probably been resolved. If exhaust water discharge is still poor, the heat exchanger is probably clogged, and will have to be cleaned—a laborious job.

If adequate seawater and freshwater coolant flow does not resolve the overheating problem, remove the engine coolant thermostat. If a faulty thermostat was the problem, the engine can run safely without it until a replacement can be installed.

Whatever the cause of the overheating, always check the coolant level before restarting the engine. Overheating can cause boiling and loss of coolant.

ENGINE FLUID LEAKS

When a leak in the fuel system of a gasoline engine is detected, *immediately* stop the engine and start the bilge blowers to rid the bilges of fumes. *Do not restart* until the leak has been repaired and the boat well ventilated and clear of any gasoline fumes.

If a serious leak occurs in a diesel high-pressure fuel pipe and cannot be stopped by tightening the joints, disconnect the pipe and direct the flow into a can or other receptacle and run the engine carefully on the remaining cylinders. Never attempt to flatten the pipe because that will ruin the fuel injection pump. Leaks in low-pressure fuel pipes can be temporarily repaired by the use of duct tape, hose, and clips. Coolant leaks can normally be dealt with in the same manner.

ENGINE PROBLEM GUIDES

If the above emergency measures do not resolve the problem, a more detailed examination may be required. Every engine manufacturer includes an operator's manual with the engine. Such manuals include sections on maintenance and troubleshooting. These should be consulted in case of engine malfunction.

TROUBLESHOOTING

Before starting an engine examination, first moor or drop an anchor to prevent drifting onto rocks or obstructions while the engine is disabled. Make only one adjustment at a time when troubleshooting. Keep calm, think carefully, and proceed with caution. If you become hot or fatigued, take a break and think through your next step. Most causes of engine problems are simple and curable. If your battery is weak, first advise someone by radio about your predicament before attempting to crank over the engine and possibly exhaust the battery.

STEERING FAILURE

The most common steering failure involves a break in the chain or cable link between the wheel and rudder quadrant. When it happens, the following corrective action may be taken:

1. If the boat is equipped with an autopilot, this may be used for emergency steering, either by autoheading control or by manual control of the autopilot motor driving the rudder quadrant.

2. An emergency tiller may be attached to the rudder or quadrant and the boat hand steered.

3. A jury rig may be fabricated to move the rudder. A small hole drilled beforehand in the upper part of the rudder facilitates this.

4. Anchor or lay to and replace the cable or chain if a spare is available.

5. If the rudder itself is lost or damaged, the above measures will not work. The following steps can be tried:

- Without a rudder, steer by varying the speeds and directions of the twin screws. With a sailboat, steer by adjusting sail trim.
- With only a single screw, trail a warp of line or sail from a bridle to maintain direction. By adjusting the bitter-end loads or the bridle from one quarter to the other, the boat can be turned (see figure 3.1).
- Use any available material to jury-rig a rudder.

Warning: Do not try to maneuver through a difficult inlet or breakwater or close a lee shore with impaired steering. Advise the Coast Guard of your situation and follow their instructions.

SAIL AND RIGGING FAILURES

In nearly all cases, even after a complete rigging and sail loss following a dismasting, a sailboat in coastal waters, *after the crew has cleared away the debris and insured that the screw is clear,* can proceed to port under power. Thus, it makes little sense to worry about recovering the mast or jury-rigging a sail. If engine power is available, it is not necessary and the boat could be further damaged or people injured by an unnecessary or quixotic attempt to make repairs. We will therefore describe (see chapter 11) only damage control steps to try to prevent the initial loss of the mast in the event of standing rigging failure.

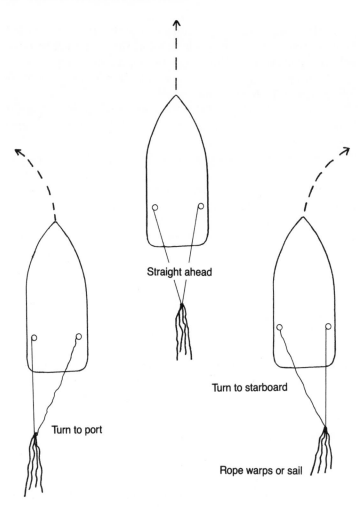

Figure 3.1   Emergency steering rig using trailing warps

The offshore sailor far from help is in a different predicament, and if the boat is also without communications, a jury-rig attempt may be the only possible salvation. John Hughes, a twenty-six-year-old Canadian skipper sailing a 41-foot boat in the 1987 BOC Challenge, covered 4,400 miles under jury rig after being dismasted 1,500 miles southeast of New Zealand. During the forty-five-day trip, described by Hughes as a "private hell," he sailed the crippled boat around Cape Horn, where it was knocked down badly, and then went on to the Falkland Islands for a new mast. Although the young Canadian's judgment in not heading for the nearest refuge is certainly questionable, because no one else was aware of his problem or was involved, he was risking no one other than himself, and the feat of seamanship and perseverance was remarkable.

The situation of the British sailing vessel *Moly* was a bit different, for it involved other people. On 18 November 1987, the Spanish merchant vessel *Pilar* came upon the dismasted *Moly* with one man aboard. The sailor had jury-rigged his sails and declined help. On 20 November, the case was reopened when the crippled boat did not arrive at Bermuda. Four days into the alert, the sailboat was sighted again by the SS *Bardu* 290 miles northeast of Bermuda. Again the lone sailor declined help, though he asked that his position be relayed to a friend. When another two weeks went by with no word, Bermuda SAR authorities officially listed the small boat as overdue. Finally on 19 December, over four weeks after the first sighting, the *Moly* was again located by the SS *New Flame*, 120 miles northeast of Bermuda. Perhaps recalling the legend of the *Flying Dutchman*, which roamed the seas never reaching port, the lone sailor finally accepted help and went aboard the *New Flame*, which disembarked him in London. The *Moly* was left to the sea, and a customary notice to mariners issued. Although a sailor's reluctance to abandon his boat is understandable, when carried to extremes such action may occupy the attention of SAR forces for long periods and result in SAR costs far in excess of the boat's value.

There are rare worst-case scenarios where a coastal sailor is without sail or power or unable to steer and also has no communications. Is a jury rig called for? Does the boat have an EPIRB? If so, the EPIRB should be used at this point. If some type of jury rig will enable the skipper to stand further off and get sea room, it can be tried. But with either crippled steering or doubtful propulsion, a sailor should not close the coast or other restricted waters until a tow or escort is at hand. The sea is most dangerous at its edges. During the Route du Rhum Race of 1986, Tony Bullimore, the sole British entrant, found himself in a quandary after losing the outrigger bow on his 60-foot trimaran, *Apricot*. He limped toward Brest, where a towboat was scheduled to meet and tow him to safety. The towboat was late and inadequate for the job, and Bullimore found himself drifting onto the rocks with his crippled boat. He saved himself by scrambling up the rocks in a full gale, but the boat was destroyed.

An objection to do-it-yourself salvage is the risk of worsening your situation by delay in an unprotected environment. In protected waters, there is far less risk and the competent sailor can try to recover damaged gear, improvise a jury rig if needed, and get the boat into a safe haven unassisted. In protected waters, the anchor is always available if the attempt fails.

NONEMERGENCY SAR—A PUBLIC RELATIONS DILEMMA

As already noted, most vessels disabled and adrift are not emergency cases, and many should be able to solve their own problems without outside help. But some, unless promptly aided, can become distress cases. How are we to differentiate between them?

For over two hundred years the Coast Guard has rendered aid to mariners in difficulty whenever it could reasonably do so. This has included:

- Saving of personnel
- Technical assistance and repairs on scene
- Provision of supplies and equipment to effect temporary repairs
- Towing to the nearest port in which emergency repairs can be made

The Coast Guard, however, has also had a long-standing policy to not compete with commercial tow craft and salvors when they could arrive in a reasonable time and were competent to do the job. Conflicts between the Coast Guard and commercial salvors seldom arose. Most commercial salvage involved large vessels, with the disabled vessel's owners or agent making the arrangements for services with the commercial salvage company.

Until the last decade this arrangement did not affect the pleasure boating community. The value of recreational boats was comparatively small, and assistance to them would have been unprofitable for commercial salvors, even assuming that the boat owners were able to pay the high charges. Because the Coast Guard was the only other source of ready help, rescue by the Coast Guard was customary and generations of boat operators came to accept it as their due.

In the early 1980s, privatization of nonemergency SAR was urged by some members of Congress and the Reagan administration. They contended that a boat disabled in protected waters was no more deserving of public help than a motorist broken down on a highway. Call a towboat, they said, just as you call a tow truck for your car.

The argument had considerable validity, especially when a boater's predicament was caused by sheer negligence or even by design. Hundreds of cases yearly involve people who simply do not check their fuel tanks. Others were more devious. At one period when commercial fishermen were in an economic squeeze, some off the New England coast fished until they had a load, then conveniently developed "trouble" and called for a Coast Guard tow, which saved them fuel on the trip in. The frequent tow missions by the cutters became known as the "Saltonstall Shuttle" after the powerful senator from Massachusetts who steadfastly stood up for the fishermen.

But the advocates of commercial tows for nonemergencies overlooked a basic reality—that the plight of a person disabled at sea or in obstructed waters can rapidly worsen, while ashore it seldom changes. In addition, Coast Guard units already deployed for urgent SAR, law enforcement, and other missions realized little savings (other than fuel) by not undertaking routine SAR, which in the past was considered excellent training for the real thing.

The Coast Guard, under pressure from the administration and Congress, acquiesced in the new nonemergency SAR policy, and small towboat operators sprang up in areas of heavy boat activity to meet the anticipated demand. Many Coast Guard people, accustomed to assisting anyone in trouble, acting first and asking questions later, were troubled by this change of mission and by the complaints of small-boat sailors who felt abandoned by the service on which they had always relied. These complaints often changed to hostility when boat owners discovered that commercial charges of $500 for a ten-mile tow were common. Many small-boat owners perceived this new policy as inspired by the Coast Guard, which they felt was no longer sensitive to the needs of the boating public. This public image was not helped by the service's heavy involvement in interdicting drug traffic, leading many to think the Coast Guard had abandoned its traditional helping role to become the drug cops of the sea.

To top off this growing disaffection, a less-than-valiant Congress imposed a "user tax" on boat operators and directed the Coast Guard to collect it or threaten those who didn't pay with heavy fines and imprisonment. None of the money was destined for the Coast Guard, and in reality the user tax was nothing but a disguised general tax increase on boat owners, regarded by many as an affluent group. In a relatively short period the white-hat image of the Coast Guard, earned over decades of service to mariners everywhere, began turning black.

A boat calling for help in a legitimate emergency is little remembered by other boaters after being helped by the Coast Guard in the usual manner. But a nonemergency, no matter how trivial, attracts the attention of everyone listening on their radio to the boater if he or she protests enough about the lack of service. This is an unusual event and therefore notable. As a veteran of hundreds of air and sea rescues, I am no different. I immediately notice when help is refused someone, for I have long been accustomed to the Coast Guard helping anyone with problems.

In the midst of this political maneuvering, the Coast Guard crews on the firing line attempted to do their duty. Day after day, hundreds of decisions had to be made. Is it a real emergency? Do we handle this or do we call a commercial tower? Whatever their decision, the men and women on watch had better be right.

Some do even better than that. On the evening of 27 May 1991,

Boatswain Mate Charles Turner and Seaman Ken Brown at the Coast Guard Station at Fort Myers Beach, Florida, received a call from the yacht *Wanderer* reporting the 32-foot sailing vessel *Maui Moon* disabled and in need of assistance thirty miles off Fort Myers. They immediately became suspicious when the sailboat actually requested commercial rather than Coast Guard help and checked their intelligence files, which revealed that the boat was under current surveillance. When the *Maui Moon* was towed into port, a Coast Guard boarding team and police divers were waiting. The divers located two cylinders containing two hundred kilos of cocaine attached to the boat's underwater hull. The drug runner apparently planned the tow, hoping that his presence at the end of a towline would throw the Coast Guard off the scent. He could not, however, muster the chutzpah to ask the Coast Guard to make the tow.

The fears of recreational boaters that they will not be aided are largely unfounded, for the Coast Guard still takes full responsibility for SAR operations anytime life or property are in danger. When no emergency exists and the situation appears stable, the Coast Guard will help the boater find assistance from other nearby boats, including Coast Guard Auxiliary vessels or commercial sources. If none of these are available within a reasonable period (normally one hour), the Coast Guard will then use its own boats, even in a nonemergency situation.

Furthermore, even when a commercial towboat arrives to assist, the pleasure boat owner is not obliged to use it. If the owner refuses the help, however, a Coast Guard unit is not obliged to assist as long as lives are not at risk. If the situation worsens so that lives are in danger, the Coast Guard will then send one of its own units.

The present policy appears to meet the needs of most small-boat sailors and the recent availability of towing insurance at cheap and reasonable rates promises to defuse the issue somewhat. Alas, someone, usually a junior petty officer at a shore station, must still decide what is an emergency and what is not, and the calls can be tough. A wrong decision can cost lives and because of the many risks involved, almost certainly will unless the Coast Guard leans heavily on the side of the boater rather than

Figure 3.2 Though most nonemergency cases are taken care of by other boaters, the Coast Guard still handles most serious maritime cases and those where no other help is nearby. *Courtesy USCG*

the towboat operator. In this matter, what has its record been?

The 1989 SAR summary shows that commercial towboats were used in only 4,663 cases out of 39,000, and less than 400 of these commercial tows turned out to be even moderately serious. By comparison, the Coast Guard Auxiliary, which has traditionally been called on for such nonemergency SAR, participated in 7,420 cases, almost double the number assisted by commercial tow boats. Nearly 30,000 of the more serious cases were still handled by regular Coast Guard forces. The hard evidence is that the decisions about who will help are overwhelmingly correct—99 times out of a hundred.

When life is involved, however, even one mistake is too much. The Coast Guard has issued guidance to its watchstanders to this general effect:

When a call for help is received, it will be considered an emergency until you can determine otherwise. If doubts exist, decide in favor of the person asking help. You will never do wrong to act.

If despite all such precautions you receive no response to your request for aid, in a *genuine* emergency you, the boater, have the final say. You can declare an emergency by broadcasting a Mayday call, or an urgent situation by use of a Pan call (fig. 3.2). Either will bring help, but they must not be used lightly, and frivolous use can be a serious federal offense. Only you can decide about your ability to deal with a threatening situation, and the test of how serious is in your own perception of the danger.

4
Fire

Few things are more terrifying than fire at sea, which may force rapid abandonment of a boat and often causes injury or death before escape is possible. An explosion is a possibility, especially with gasoline- or propane-fueled boats, and a hull or engine fire can cause flooding because of the burning away of the hoses leading from through-hull fittings. Even large vessels with adequate equipment and trained crews have a total property loss rate of over 30 percent in major fires, and smaller boats with limited equipment and amateur crews are proportionately higher (see figure 4.1).

Though less than 2 percent of all Coast Guard SAR cases involve fire on pleasure boats, the toll from these cases is severe. In 1986–1990, the Coast Guard reported 2,058 fires and explosions aboard recreational boats. The damages amounted to nearly $35 million, fifty-three people lost their lives, and 913 more were seriously injured. These figures represent only the small portion of cases in which the Coast Guard rendered fire-fighting assistance. Nationally, the American Red Cross estimates there are approximately 7,500 pleasure boat fires and explosions yearly. Ten percent of the boats are total losses.

Fires occur in all types of recreational boats and on protected waters and the high seas as well as at moorings. Any accidental fire on a small boat not extinguished in the first few minutes is a full-blown emergency.

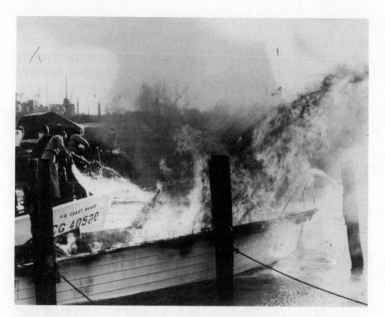

Figure 4.1   Coast Guard boat crew fights a fire on a pleasure boat. Most boat fires progress too rapidly for outside help to arrive in time. *Courtesy USCG*

CAUSES OF SMALL-BOAT FIRES

A common source of boat fires is fuel leakage in the engine compartment or bilge; ignition results from engine heat or spillage onto hot engine parts. In boats with closed engine compartments, the leak may go unnoticed until gasoline pooling causes a major fire or explosion. A small amount of vaporized gasoline in a closed space can produce an explosion if ignited; a cup of gasoline has the explosive potential of several sticks of dynamite. Diesel fuel is far less dangerous but must not be ignored if spillage or leaks occur. Fortunately, the human nose is usually an excellent fume detector and the engine compartment of gasoline-powered boats should be checked by smell before starting the engine.

Electricity is a safe and convenient source of power when properly installed and maintained. With age and wear, aggravated by vibration, moisture, and heat, however, wiring insulation can crack or chafe, exposing bare wires with the risk of fire. Faulty electric motors can also produce sparks and arcing if a winding becomes short-circuited or grounded, or from erratic operation of the brushes. Lack of lubrication can cause a bearing to overheat and ignite other material.

Batteries under charge emit hydrogen gas, which is highly flammable and potentially explosive. Hydrogen is lighter than air and rises; if proper ventilation is not provided, it will collect near the compartment overhead, and a spark can cause an explosion and fire. Battery-cable connections should be checked frequently to ensure tightness. Loose connections result in large power losses and may produce heat and/or sparks when the battery is being charged. Never smoke around a battery. Never connect or disconnect a battery, with the possibility of a spark, until the surrounding space has been thoroughly ventilated. Batteries must have covers to prevent a short circuit and fire in case a metal object falls on the battery.

In April 1987 the new 110-foot Coast Guard patrol boat *Farallon* suffered an explosion and fire while towing the vessel *Linda Patricia*, which she had just seized for suspected drug running. The explosion, which blew a hatch 50 feet into the air, was preceded by a loud hiss and was followed by smoke pouring from the after battery room. The fire was extinguished by CO_2, there were no injuries, and the *Farallon* returned to port under her own power. Investigators found cracked batteries and burned insulation in the battery room. Hydrogen gas from the batteries is believed to have been ignited by air-conditioning machinery.

Many boats are equipped with 110-volt AC electrical systems in order to use AC appliances and battery chargers. The power source may be shore connected, or an auxiliary engine–driven generator may be used while under way. Because of the higher voltages and power, AC is more dangerous than the boat's 12-volt DC system. During a malfunction it is more apt to cause a hot and dangerous fire and may prove lethal if a person touches an exposed shore power circuit while in contact with water. Shore power cable and plugs must be well maintained. Unfortunately, a few people still succeed in forcing 110-volt plugs into 220-volt receptacles, with dire results for the boat's equipment.

Lightning strikes on boats are not commonplace, but nearly all of us know of such cases and even people who were involved. Like shark attacks, they occur just often enough to get our attention. Sailboats with metal mast and standing rigging bonded and connected to a ground such as a radio ground plate or propeller are highly resistant to hull damage from lightning, and safer for people aboard, though electronic gear remains vulnerable (see chapter 8). Power boats with a protective lightning mast or metal radio antenna are also protected to a high degree if properly bonded and grounded.

Overhead power lines also pose a threat to boaters because of the extremely high voltages and power carried. The clearance shown for such power lines over designated channels may be much less outside the channel. Boats being trailered also risk striking power lines. Such contact with a main power line can result in instantaneous death for anyone in contact with a conducting part of the boat.

At sea as ashore, smoking causes many fires. As a strict rule, no smoking should be permitted below decks or on other than the lee side above deck. Smoking around batteries, fuel, or in a bunk should be firmly forbidden.

Most of these fire risks are recognizable as such. But a major percentage of boat fires are caused by stoves and heaters, which because of their common use and our familiarity with them, may not be handled with adequate care.

GALLEY STOVES

The greatest fire hazard on many boats is the galley stove.

Electricity is the safest and most efficient heat source but requires a costly auxiliary generator, for which only the larger boats have adequate space.

Liquified petroleum gas (LPG) is excellent for cooking and refills are available in most ports, but it can be very dangerous unless installed and operated in accordance with strict rules. A leak of LPG, which is heavier than air, can result in an accumulation of highly explosive gas in the bilges and a resultant explosion.

The Coast Guard prohibits LPG on certain passenger-carrying boats.

The use of *compressed natural gas (CNG)*, which is lighter than air and therefore allows the tank to be stowed internally, is now becoming more common. CNG is safer than LPG and outwardly similar, but it is more expensive, has only a fraction of the heat content of an equal volume of LPG, and is not readily available in many places. It is bottled under very high pressures of 2,500 psi.

The most commonly used cooking stove fuel is *alcohol,* which by itself is relatively safe and can be extinguished by water or a wet or fireproof blanket or towel. The pressurized alcohol stove, however, tends to gum up and requires a great deal of patient maintenance. The high-grade alcohol required to minimize these fuel stoppages is also very expensive. *An alcohol stove must not be left unwatched while in use.*

I once violated this rule while cooking breakfast at a marina before an early morning departure. Water was heating on two burners of my alcohol stove, one for coffee and the other to defrost a frozen packaged food. I was called by a friend two slips away to look at a paper, and having nothing in the pots that could burn, I left the burners lit. Several minutes later, I looked over to see smoke coming out of the hatch. Running back, I dropped down the hatch to find the entire starboard side of the center cabin in flames. Having had extensive shipboard fire-fighting training in the service, I grabbed a fifteen-pound CO_2 extinguisher, dropped to my knees, and sprayed the base of the flames until they were extinguished. Holding my breath, I then crawled out of the smoky cabin and through the forward hatch to the deck. It was a near disaster, and I would not do it again, for the heat was so intense in the small cabin that it melted plastic fixtures.

Subsequent investigation by fire experts showed that one flame had been extinguished, and as it cooled, it poured raw alcohol into the pan. This was soon ignited by the other burner and the flames quickly spread. A number of boats have been lost in nearly identical fires. This hazard, peculiar to the pressurized alcohol stove, has been largely eliminated in the newer nonpressurized wick stoves such as the Origo brand. Not only are these wick stoves safer, but they require almost no maintenance, are easy to start, cook well, and use a much cheaper grade of alcohol. With these improvements, alcohol stoves may rise in acceptance with female sailors, who in a recent survey rated alcohol stoves high on their cruise hate lists.

HEATERS

Cabin heaters should not use gasoline as a fuel, and portable kerosene or alcohol heaters should be used only with reservation and caution. They must be an underwriter-approved type.

Built-in electrical heaters are the safest, but away from the dock these require an auxiliary generator for power.

LPG heaters should have an automatic device to shut off the fuel supply if the flame is extinguished; pilot lights must not be used.

Any heater discharging combustion products must be vented through a stovepipe (called a "charley noble" by old sailors) set in well-cooled deck plates or other fire-resistant fitting. If the stovepipe is upwind of an open hatch, a potentially dangerous condition can develop if carbon monoxide is carried into the hatch or a ventilating opening.

Cabin space heaters do not require a stove pipe but must have an adequate air supply in a well-ventilated cabin and must be an underwriter safety-approved model. Because of the possibility of fire as well as carbon monoxide leakage from incomplete combustion or a defective heater, it is a good practice to turn off fuel-type heaters before retiring or sleeping. All portable heaters should be well secured and have an automatic "tilt-switch" to cut off fuel or electricity if upset.

CARBON MONOXIDE

Carbon monoxide, a deadly gas, is invisible, odorless, and tasteless, although some other combustion products associated with it can sometimes be smelled. The gas works quickly and small concentrations can cause serious illness. Heavy concentrations can result in loss of consciousness in minutes and death in less than an hour. Carbon monoxide is very insidious in its effects, and the symptoms closely resemble those of many other illnesses, particularly seasickness. They include headache, dizziness, nausea, increased pulse rate, and shortness of breath. These symptoms worsen as the poisoning progresses, yet many victims lose consciousness before realizing what is happening.

In September 1985, a Coast Guard cutter located a 36-foot cabin cruiser that had been reported overdue. A boarding party went aboard the anchored boat and discovered a husband and wife in the main cabin. On arrival at a hospital, the woman was pronounced dead and the man was comatose and in critical condition. An auxiliary generator was running directly below the main cabin and both people had been poisoned by a carbon monoxide leak from the generator motor's exhaust.

A number of other deaths have been attributed to exhaust gases from generators, engines, and stoves.

Exhaust gases from nearby boats can be carried by wind into ventilators or hatches and collect below deck. In a case in Florida in the 1980s, a family had tied up its boat in a raftup of three other boats, at least two of which were running their auxiliary generators. Some time after retiring, one of the children woke and tried to go to the head, only to discover that he could not move. His cries awakened the rest of the family, all of whom were also suffering from carbon monoxide poisoning, but the family managed to get on deck in fresh air. The source of the gases appeared to be the auxiliary generator exhausts from adjacent boats. The best preventative against such accidents is to secure all engines and stoves before retiring and to keep the living spaces well ventilated.

BUILT-ON AND REQUIRED FIRE PREVENTION DEVICES

Both the Coast Guard and good engineering practices have dictated a number of required design features that must be complied with by boat builders. Because faults in the fuel system are a major cause of fire, special attention has been directed to the system's integrity and construction. These complex technical regulations, promulgated in the Code of Federal Regulations, deal with the fuel tankage, lines, carburetors, pumps, filters, and all aspects of the fuel system.

Fuel system standards for diesel-powered boats are similar to those of gasoline but are modified because of the low volatility and greater safety of diesel fuel. Fuel systems permanently installed in outboards must also conform to these principles. Pressurized gasoline tanks must not be built into or attached permanently to the hull. Caution should be observed when using plastic containers for fuel, and such tanks should carry the approval of a recognized safety agency or fire department.

All gasoline motorboats, except open boats, must have ventilation for engine and fuel tank compartments. Gasoline, especially in its vapor state, is an extremely dangerous explosive, but the danger can be minimized with commonsense precautions. The Coast Guard has required mechanical ventilation blowers on all gasoline-powered boats built after 31 July 1980 (see Appendix E). Blowers should be operated for four minutes before starting the engine, and the operator should check the engine compartments for the smell of gasoline before starting. Diesel vessels are exempt from the ventilation requirements, though many are so equipped in order to evacuate any propane gas from the bilge.

With a leaky gasoline fuel system, an explosion can occur at any time, not just when starting or after fueling. Although air flow through the boat and engines reduces the buildup of fumes, the only positive safeguard is careful inspection and the immediate repair of any gasoline leaks.

A boat's electrical system must comply with the highest standards because of the adverse effects of the marine environment and the stresses encountered. Both the Coast Guard and the American Boat and Yacht Council (ABYC) prescribe safety and design standards including material and construction criteria. A careful examination of a boat's wiring system will give a good indication of the boat's safety, quality, and workmanship.

FIRE PREVENTION AND SUPPRESSION EQUIPMENT

The equipment shown in the table of Appendix E reflects only *minimum* requirements. We strongly recommend at least one B-I type extinguisher in each living compartment, and a fixed automatic Halon extinguisher in an enclosed engine space. We further recommend the inclusion of one or more bailing buckets with lanyards to scoop up seawater. Water should not be used to fight fuel fires other than alcohol, nor should water be used in electrical fires until the power source is cut off.

In addition to the mandatory equipment, the prudent skipper who has either gasoline or propane on board an enclosed boat should consider the use of fume detectors with both visual and audio warnings in the engine space and galley. A basic smoke detection unit is moderately priced, sensitive, and will usually give an early warning of smoke before it is detected by the senses. More sophisticated systems provide flooding, burglary, and electrical alarms. Carbon monoxide detectors are also available and highly advisable in cold climates where engines, auxiliary generators, or heaters may be in use while the boat is closed or poorly ventilated.

THE NATURE OF FIRE

Fire is a chemical reaction known as *combustion*. Combustion is defined as the rapid oxidation of combustible material accompanied by a release of heat and light. For many years the three-sided figure of the fire triangle was used to explain the combustion and extinguishment theory (see figure 4.2). Proper proportions of oxygen, heat, and fuel create a fire, and if any one of the three elements is removed, a fire cannot exist.

Recently, though, a new theory was developed to explain combustion and extinguishment further. Instead of a triangle from plane geometry, the new theory of combustion uses the configuration of a four-sided figure from solid geometry, the tetrahedron, which resembles a pyramid but has a triangular rather than square base (see figure 4.3). One of the four triangular

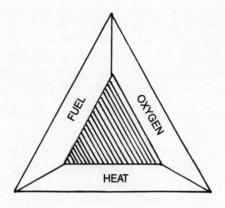

FIRE TRIANGLE

Figure 4.2   Fire triangle. *Courtesy USCG*

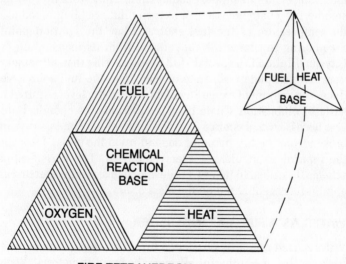

FIRE TETRAHEDRON

Figure 4.3   Fire tetrahedron. *Courtesy USCG*

sides serves as the base and represents the new element in the equation, the chemical chain reaction that takes place during the combustion process. The remaining three standing sides represent heat, fuel, and oxygen. Removal of any one of the four sides makes the pyramid incomplete and results in extinguishment of the fire.*

Classes of Fire

Most boat fires fall into one of three classes. These are named principally after the general properties of their fuel source. Each class requires certain specific types of extinguishing agents. Therefore, before selecting an extinguishing agent, you must know the class of fire with which you are faced. The three classes of fire and a general description of the fuel sources of each are outlined in table 4.1.

Extinguishing Agents

Extinguishing agents put out fires by eliminating one or more elements necessary to support combustion. They work by cooling, smothering, chain breaking, or oxygen dilution. Cooling reduces the temperature of the fuel source below the ignition point. Smothering separates the fuel source from its oxygen supply. Oxygen dilution is a special kind of smothering that, although it does not completely separate oxygen from the fuel source, reduces the amount of oxygen available below the level required to sustain combustion. Chain breaking disrupts the chemical process necessary to sustain a fire. The element or elements that are broken from the fire pyramid depend upon the class of fire and the type of extinguishing agent employed. The classification scheme described in table 4.1 is designed to assist in selecting an appropriate agent based on the class of fire.

WATER AS A FIRE EXTINGUISHER

Water is used primarily on Class A fires. The application of water has a cooling or smothering effect on the burning material. Water

---

*Information about combustion and the accompanying figures courtesy *USCG Auxiliary Boat Crew Qualifications Manual,* 1984.

Table 4.1   Class of Fire, Fuel Source, and Method of Extinguishment

Class	Fuel Source	Method of Fire Extinguishment
A	Fires involving common combustible materials. Fuel sources within this class include: wood and wood based materials, cloth, paper, rubber, and certain plastics.	Water is used in a cooling or quenching effect to reduce the temperature of the burning material below its ignition temperature.
B	Fires involving flammable or combustible liquids, flammable gases, greases, and similar products.	The smothering or blanketing effect of oxygen exclusion is the most effective. Other extinguishing methods include removal of fuel and temperature reduction.
C	Fires involving energized electrical equipment, conductors, or appliances.	This fire can sometimes be controlled by a nonconducting extinguishing agent. The safest procedure is always to attempt to deenergize high-voltage circuits and treat as Class A or B.

should not be used on Class B fires (except alcohol) or on Class C fires until after the power source has been disconnected. Because the flow volume in most boat freshwater systems is low, use bailing buckets with hand lines to scoop up seawater.

PORTABLE FIRE EXTINGUISHERS

Portable fire extinguishers are the most common and usually the only type of fire-fighting equipment found aboard small boats. They are available in many types and sizes. *They contain only a limited supply of extinguishing agent, and should be directed at the base of the fire early, before the small fire can build.* The extinguishing agents are CO_2, Halon 1211, or dry chemical—which is the most common. Even though portable fire extinguishers are simple to use, it is important to insure that all your crew know how.

FIXED EXTINGUISHING SYSTEMS

Recreational vessels of closed construction, especially large yachts, may be fitted with fixed extinguishing systems. These are normally of the Halon 1301 or CO_2 type. They may be discharged automatically or manually. The length of time the discharge will last depends upon the capacity of the installed system.

FIRE EXTINGUISHER AGENTS

Fire extinguishers for boats are described in terms of their contents—the actual extinguishing agent.

Dry Chemical

This type of extinguisher is widely used because of its convenience and relatively low cost. The cylinder contains a dry chemical in powdered form together with a propellant gas under pressure. Coast Guard regulations require that such extinguishers be equipped with a gauge or indicator to show that normal gas pressure exists within the extinguisher. This extinguisher, though economical, is messy, and if used, a cleanup job must follow.

Carbon Dioxide

Some boats carry portable carbon dioxide extinguishers that leave no messy residue to clean up and they cannot harm the interior of engines as some chemicals do. Carbon dioxide extinguishers may also be used where a fixed system is installed in an engine compartment, operated either manually or automatically by heat-sensitive detectors. An engine will stop after CO_2 is discharged in the compartment.

Carbon dioxide extinguishers consist of a cylinder containing this gas under high pressure, a valve, and a discharge nozzle at the end of a short hose. The state of charge of a CO_2 extinguisher can be checked only by weighing the cylinder and comparing this figure with the one stamped on or near the valve.

CAUTION

Precautions must be taken when CO_2 is discharged within a confined space. It displaces the oxygen needed to sustain life yet cannot be detected by sight or smell even at lethal levels. A pre-discharge alarm is desirable on automatic fixed CO_2 systems to alert persons and allow time to evacuate the spaces.

Halon 1211/1301

Extinguishment of a fire with Halon is accomplished by the inhibition of the chain reaction that occurs in the combustion process. Halon is effective on Class B and C fires and may also be used on small Class A fires. It is especially useful on electrical and electronic equipment fires because since it is a gas, little or no residue is left to be cleaned up. When Halon is discharged on a fire, toxic products are formed, but they are so acidic that any person exposed to the gases will not usually breathe a lethal amount. Halon will not adversely affect diesel engines, but the engine should be shut down immediately to avoid dissipating the Halon.

Aqueous Film-Forming Foam (AFFF)

Aqueous film-forming foam is effective on Class B fires. Foam is essentially a blanket of bubbles, and extinguishment is accomplished by smothering the fire. Since the foam solution is lighter than the flammable liquids it is used on, it will float on top, preventing oxygen from reaching the fuel source. When foam is used, it must cover the entire surface of the burning liquid. Foam is primarily used by large vessels and is particularly effective when used by SAR or fire units in extinguishing oil fires.

Nonacceptable Types

Vaporizing-liquid extinguishers, such as those containing carbon tetrachloride and chlorobromomethane, are effective in fighting fires but produce highly toxic gases. They are not approved for use on motorboats and should not be carried as excess equipment because of the danger to the health or even life of a user in a confined space.

MAINTENANCE OF FIRE EXTINGUISHERS

All types of hand-portable fire extinguishers and semiportable and fixed fire-extinguishing systems must be approved by the Coast Guard. Such extinguishers and extinguishing systems will have a metal nameplate attached with information as to the manufacturer, type, and capacity. A sticker or tag should show the date of the latest inspection.

Fire-extinguishing systems should be checked annually and more often if recommended by the manufacturer. Portable fire extinguishers should be checked at least every three months; even monthly visual examinations are not too frequent.

Pressurized dry-chemical extinguishers have a gauge that should be checked for an indication of adequate pressure—the needle in the center or green area of the scale. Do not, however, merely read the gauge; tap it lightly to make sure it is not stuck at a safe indication. If it drops to a lower reading, have it recharged. Even if the gauge reads in the acceptable range, take the unit out of its bracket and shake it a bit to loosen the dry chemical inside to keep it from settling and hardening. Do not test by triggering a short burst of powder. The valve probably will not reset fully, and the pressure will slowly leak off.

Carbon dioxide extinguishers must be checked annually by weight. Any seals on the valve trigger must be unbroken to indicate that the bottle has not been used. Portable units and built-in systems have a weight stamped at the valve. If the total weight is down by 10 percent, the cylinder must be recharged. Weighing is normally the only check for CO_2 fire extinguishers, but it must be done accurately. If a sensitive portable scale is not available, the extinguishers should be weighed at a fire equipment dealer. Bathroom scales are not accurate enough. Built-in systems are also best checked by a professional serviceperson with special knowledge and equipment.

Automatic systems using Halon 1301 are also checked by weighing; a loss of just a few ounces is significant. At the same time, check the valve for corrosion.

It is good practice to discharge one of the portable units each year on a rotation basis. This can be used for practice by putting out an actual small practice fire ashore in a metal pan or tub. Never unscrew the hose from a CO_2 cylinder and then discharge it openly. The intense cold can cause hand injuries.

Make sure that when fire extinguishers are removed for testing or practice discharge they are serviced by a competent shop and reinstalled or replaced as soon as possible, certainly before getting under way.

FIRE-FIGHTING PROCEDURES

Despite strict fire prevention measures, fires still occur. A fire afloat can prove far more serious than one ashore for a number of reasons:

1. A small boat is an inflammable object because of liquid fuel, woodwork, paint, and cushions, so that fire may spread faster than in a building.

2. Smoke fumes and intense heat build up far more rapidly in the small confines of a boat and can become lethal in minutes.

3. Fire can force occupants overboard within minutes and into an equally life-threatening survival situation.

4. Boats are often far from or inaccessible to fire-fighting facilities.

In fighting a boat fire, time is the critical factor. Most fires if attacked within two minutes of ignition can be quickly contained. A delayed reaction often results in a fire getting out of control in the first five minutes. Your fire-fighting plan must therefore include:

1. Presailing briefing of crew on emergency duties and location of equipment. There is no time after a fire starts.

2. Early-warning alarm (smoke detectors) installed and working. An installed heat-activated extinguishing system in closed compartments is also an early-acting option.

3. In event of fire, stop the engines immediately to prevent exhaust of the automatic Halon gases or intake of more fuel. If possible, shut off fuel valves and electricity and turn off blowers.

Immediately clear compartments of all people not actually engaged in fighting the fire. As heat rises, the coolest smoke-free areas will be low in the compartment. Crawl on your hands and knees with your nose close to the deck if in trouble. If the main companionway is fire involved, exit through a hatch in another compartment.

4. Attack the fire immediately *at its source*, using portable extinguishers and water buckets (if indicated). If you must open a hatch to discharge a portable extinguisher, beware of the possibility of burning your hands or singeing your face. As fresh air enters the compartment, it will feed the fire and cause it to blow up in your face. The best method of opening a hatch is to stand to the hinged side of the hatch, and, with gloved or protected hands, pull the hatch open. If you have a closed engine compartment without a fixed system, it is a good idea to provide a small hole with a pivoted cover in the hatch, through which a portable extinguisher may be discharged.

5. Contain the fire and prevent its spread. Turn the boat to a heading on which smoke and flames are carried away from the crew and the vessel. Close the hatches and doors of all compartments where no people remain. An airtight compartment may quickly extinguish a flame because of the deprivation of oxygen. If the vessel is equipped with an automatic extinguishing system, ensure that it is discharging. If the system is manually operated, actuate it and check to ensure it is discharging.

6. If in doubt about the automatic system function, use portable bottles to attack the flames.

7. Initiate a Mayday call to alert other vessels in the vicinity. A fire at sea is a real emergency to any sailor!

8. All crew members should don PFDs and those not actually engaged in fire fighting should move to a topside clear area.

9. Get a life raft or dinghy with abandon-ship gear ready to go over the side, and inflate it if necessary. Life rafts or dinghies on deck are vulnerable to fire damage.

10. If the fire is too big or out of control, abandon ship. Explosion of the fuel tank is a real danger. The safety of personnel is the first priority.

OUTSIDE HELP

Little outside help should be expected in fighting a boat fire because of the time element. Land fire companies can only help if the boat is alongside a dock, and even then time is required to lay out hose on long docks. Coast Guard and fire department boats are unlikely to arrive in time to prevent loss or serious damage, and helicopters have little fire suppression capability. Other small boats are not likely to have any more equipment than the boat afire. Under way, the time and distance factors will probably preclude any effective outside help in saving the boat. The fire must be fought by the crew and equipment already on the boat! In so doing, remember the explosion potential if flames reach a gasoline tank.

OVERHAUL AND CLEAN UP

Once the fire is extinguished, insure that it does not flare up again. Allow the extinguishing agent, especially CO_2, to dissipate before entering the compartment. Burned mattresses and cushions are best thrown overboard because of the threat of lingering sparks. When the fire is completely extinguished, ventilate the boat. Check the damaged area for flooding, because flames can burn hoses leading from the through hulls. Do not restart the engine unless the engine and fuel systems were not involved in the fire. Turn on only essential electrical circuits, such as radio power, and observe carefully for signs of shorts or malfunctions. If smoldering continues behind paneling and bulkheads, tear out sections as necessary to extinguish it. Keep the Coast Guard or others assisting advised of your latest condition and intentions.

5
Grounding

Most people who sail on coastal or inland waters can expect to periodically go aground. Shoal areas are often only a few feet from a deep channel and frequently change as a result of storms, currents, and silting. Depths vary with the state of the tide. Ponce de Leon Inlet on the Florida east coast experiences all of these and in a seven-year period in the 1980s, 287 vessels were lost or grounded there. Running aground in a small boat is not in itself a mark of incompetence and on a soft mud or sand bottom in protected waters is more vexing than dangerous. If the first attempts to get off fail, time and tide will eventually free the boat (see figure 5.1).

Grounding, however, can occasionally prove serious. Running onto a steep rocky shore can be disastrous, as can impacting a rocky reef or coral head. Even a soft bottom is no place to be if the boat is working in a seaway or on an exposed shore. Any type of bottom can cause damage and personal injuries if struck at high speed, and numerous fast motorboats have lost propellers, shafts, and rudders or ripped open their hulls from such impact forces. In aggravated groundings, a decision must be reached whether to try to get off immediately without outside help or to request emergency assistance. The crew should also make preparations to abandon ship should it become necessary.

Figure 5.1 Though only a few feet outside the channel marker, this cruising sailor has no choice but to await the next high tide. The sailboat is in no danger on the muddy bottom.

INITIAL REACTIONS

When a boat touches ground, instantly take off ahead power. If the shoal area is to leeward, drop any sails; otherwise, they are best slacked or backed. If the impact was moderate, try a short burst of backing power, making the logical assumption that if water was under the keel just before hitting, it will still be there if the track is promptly retraced. (Many people attempt to bull their way out ahead in the hope that deeper water may lie there; usually it doesn't and the boat is only forced harder aground.) Attempts to back off with power should be fairly brief, because sand and debris can be ingested into the engine water cooling system from the reverse water flow. Damage to deep spade rudders may occur going either ahead or astern, and careful planning and soundings are required in freeing boats with such a vulnerable rudder.

With small shallow-draft boats, the quickest and easiest solution may be to go over the side and push it off, but shoes and protective clothing should be worn.

Deep-draft single-keel sailboats require special handling after grounding. If the boat has a centerboard down, it should be promptly retracted to prevent further damage, and this action alone may be enough to free the boat. If not, move the crew as far to one side as possible to careen the boat and lift the keel off the bottom (fig. 5.2). If the wind is right, backing the sails will increase the heel as well as force the boat aft. When the boat is well heeled, use the engine to back off.

If the impact was hard, immediately check for hull damage or leaks before attempting to work free. If a leak is found, deal with it as discussed in chapter 6, "Flooding," and decide whether it is even advisable to try to free the boat. A badly holed boat may be better off aground than in deep water. But if it is working or pounding in a seaway or on a hard bottom, the leak will probably be enlarged, and the odds may be better afloat. In either case, a call should be made to the Coast Guard to report your situation. A high-capacity pump may be required to keep the boat afloat after it is free. Although the Coast Guard does not routinely engage in salvage work, it will provide emergency assistance to prevent imminent loss of the boat, or help arrange commercial assistance.

GETTING OFF

If the initial attempts to free the boat fail, size up the situation. Time is not usually a factor unless the tide is falling fast or conditions are worsening. Get a good fix and plot it on a large-scale detailed chart. Next take soundings around and out from the boat using a leadline, boat hook, or merely a cord with a small weight and a marker on the cord indicating the boat's draft. Calculate the present state of the tide and the depths to be expected at high and low tides. With this data, a more informed decision as to how to get off can be reached.

With a rising tide, simply waiting is usually best, provided the wind and current are setting off the shoal. If not, anchors must be laid out to prevent the boat being set further onto the shoal. With a rising tide on a lee shore, this step must not be delayed.

During a northeaster in the Florida Keys in 1985, I watched a nearby 41-foot ketch drag aground on a lee shore. The obviously green crew took neither action nor advice, and as the tide rose, heightened even more by the wind direction, the boat was driven further toward the shore. When the wind and tide abated, the boat sat high up on the mud flat, isolated from both solid land and deep water and remained there until commercial salvors freed it the following day. Though the soft bottom prevented any hull damage, the delay and high salvage costs could have been averted with a couple of well-placed anchors or a call for help to the many nearby boats.

A kedge anchor led out to deeper water with a long scope will help free the boat (fig. 5.3). As the tide rises, keep tension on the line with a large winch and the boat will eventually move easily off the shoal. Sails rigged properly can assist, but a watch must be maintained on deck to prevent driving aground again when the boat floats free.

DRYING OUT

If low tide will occur before the boat can be freed, deep-keel narrow boats may encounter problems with large tidal ranges. Though most sailing vessels will careen far over before flooding into the cockpit, special precautions must be taken by closing all ports, through hulls, and hatches to prevent flooding through these openings at large angles of heel. Protective boards, fenders or mattresses may have to be used to avoid hull damage should the boat heel excessively on a hard irregular bottom.

In an incident in December 1987, a 45-foot schooner drawing over 7 feet went aground on a falling tide inside an east Florida harbor having a 6- to 8-foot tidal range. The highly experienced skipper, on a circumnavigation, decided to await high tide. Near low water, however, the boat, which had remained precariously balanced in an upright position, suddenly fell over on its side when people moved about, striking the hard sand and oyster-shell bottom. A three-foot gash was torn in the side and the boat

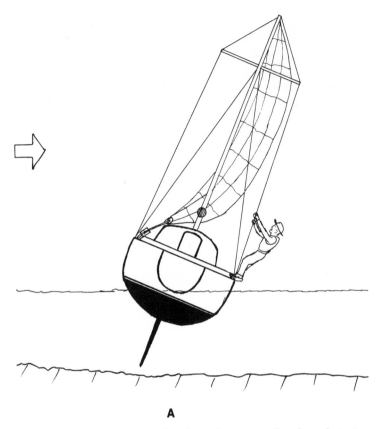

A

Figure 5.2   A. A crew member leans far out on the shrouds to increase the heel produced by the backed foresail. Heeling is most effective with deep-keel boats; sails can be used when the wind is blowing off the shoal area. B. A crew member uses a boom rigged out perpendicular to the center line to produce a greater moment.

flooded. Though not a common occurrence, this event demonstrated that hidden dangers can exist in seemingly benign conditions.

OUTSIDE HELP

If a passerby offers to help, having the boat pass close aboard at high speed may create enough wake to work the boat free, pro-

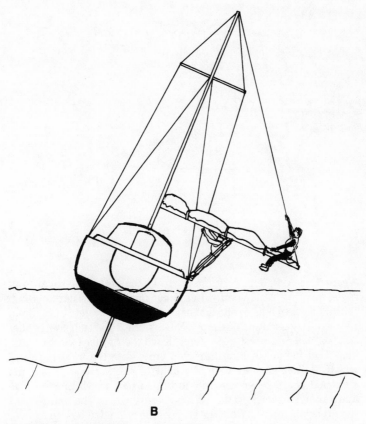

B

(**Figure 5.2,** continued)

vided that the forces are setting off the shoals and the boat is not
too hard aground (see figure 5.4). If another boat offers a tow, proceed with *caution*. The snapping of a small tow line or fitting can
be very dangerous to people on both boats. If the boat is hard
aground on a rocky bottom, attempting to pull it off with a powerful towboat may cause severe damage to the bottom, rudder, and
propeller. A stern pull must be used cautiously when the
grounded boat has a deep spade rudder without skeg, and the
rudder in any case must be lashed firmly amidships. Do not attempt to pivot a long keel boat off a shoal by pulling the towline
at right angle to the bow, because keel damage can result (fig. 5.5).

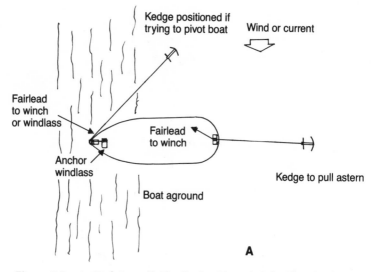

Figure 5.3   A. Kedging off. If a fin keel boat has hit the shoal at an angle, pivoting the bow off with a kedge may be the easiest method. With a long keel boat or one that has hit the shoal straight on, a direct stern pull is usually indicated. For a stern pull, lash the rudder amidships. For a pivoting attempt, leave the rudder free. In either case, lead the kedge line through a fairlead to the most powerful winch. B. Kedging off with the help of another boat. Plant the grounded boat's kedge upwind and upcurrent and lead the kedge line through fairleads to the most powerful winch. The pulling boat should lead a towline from the stern of the grounded boat to its own quarter-attachment point, which will allow the towing boat to swing its stern to counter the current. In very strong current, the towing boat may also drop an anchor upcurrent to facilitate control.

A fin keel boat will pivot much more easily. In general, towing should be deferred until near high tide, or until the boat shows signs of movement with a rising tide. Detailed towing procedures and some legal aspects of towing and salvage are covered in chapter 15.

If the first attempts and the passage of a high tide fail to free the boat, help can be requested from the Coast Guard, which will

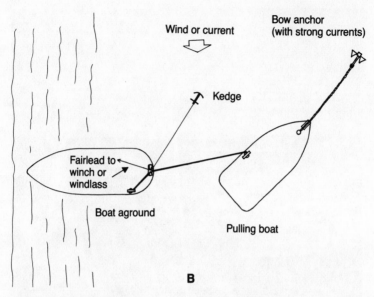

Wind or current

Bow anchor
(with strong currents)

Kedge

Fairlead to
winch or
windlass

Boat aground

Pulling boat

B

(**Figure 5.3,** continued)

probably suggest nearby commercial facilities. If none are available, Coast Guard help may be sent when operations permit. Salvage of vessels in no immediate danger has a low SAR priority.

SALVAGE

If salvage is attempted, cooperate with the Coast Guard or commercial salvors on the scene. Their experience in such situations is usually much greater than that of the crew in distress. Do not hesitate, however, to point out factors that concern you and about which they may be unaware. Owners of an insured boat have an obligation to take all reasonable steps to prevent further damage to a grounded or disabled vessel, and the costs are normally reimbursable until such time as the insurer takes over responsibility for salvage negotiations.

Once afloat after a hard grounding, check immediately for any flooding. At the first opportunity, dive under the boat to

Figure 5.4   Passing boats are a ready source of help, and most offer it gladly. *Courtesy USCG*

check for damage to the keel, skeg, and rudder. Have the rudder cycled while you watch under water. Check the through hulls for mud clogging: it will be easier to clear now than after it is ingested into the engine intake.

ABANDONING GROUNDED BOATS

Occasionally, a boat aground in surf or on a rocky shore must be abandoned immediately (see figure 5.6). In such circumstances, a distress call should be transmitted at once and preparations made to save the crew. Because of the danger to other vessels attempting to assist in rough shoal waters, helicopter evacuation is usually preferable.

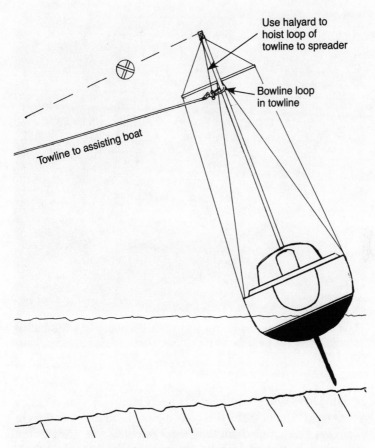

Figure 5.5 Heeling with a pull from another boat. The towline can be made fast directly to the mainsail halyard, but this may damage the halyard masthead sheaves. Avoid this by positioning the towline lower on the mast, using the halyard only to raise it into position, with all the resultant strain being taken by the towline.

The dangers in trying a surface rescue from a grounded boat in a hostile environment must not be underestimated. In the fall of 1987, the 50-foot ketch *Captain Kenneth and Lady Gail* went onto the rocks off the end of Coronado Island, Baja California, and sank soon afterward. The 27-foot sloop *Sonrisa* then at-

Figure 5.6 Grounding in the surf on a lee shore is a full-blown emergency, as the predicament of this shrimper demonstrates. *Courtesy USCG*

tempted to rescue the survivors but was swept onto the rocks by the sea and impaled. The two crew members off the sloop fought their way to shore, where they were rescued by a Coast Guard helicopter. In the meanwhile, a third boat, the *Mikimbi*, broadcast the Mayday call and rescued the crew of the sunken ketch. The Coast Guard then hauled the *Sonrisa* off the rocks, and it was towed back to San Diego by the CGC *Point Brower*. Fortunately, despite darkness, treacherous seas, and cold water, no persons were lost.

PREVENTION OF GROUNDING

Prevention is preferable to even the best cure. To prevent grounding:

• Have a detailed chart of the area and maintain an accurate course plot.

• Check the boat's position frequently when near land or aids to navigation. Observe the color and action of the water for signs of shoaling.

• Keep the fathometer (or leadline) going and monitor it closely in shoal waters. If it has a depth-warning feature, set it at an appropriate warning depth.

• Check the tide tables and be aware of the state of the tide. When anchoring, make allowance for the tidal stage and swinging of the boat.

• Act with caution near inlets or junctions of waterways. Watch for strong currents and shoaling from tidal silting. Use a chart to minimize confusion where the ICW (Intracoastal Waterway) markers merge with ocean inlet buoys or markers.

• Do not follow other boats blindly or assume that they know more about the area than you do.

• When in doubt about your position or the location of shoals or hazards, *Stop!* Decide what to do, then proceed slowly.

Make every attempt to get the boat off without calling for Coast Guard or commercial help. The Coast Guard does not do salvage work except in unusual circumstances when no other help is available; a commercial tow off the shoals is typically $10 per foot of boat plus the regular towing charges. If the boat is so hard aground that salvage may be needed, contact your insurance underwriter for advice.

6

Flooding

Many boats develop leaks, most of which are a nuisance rather than a danger. Frustrated owners experiment with leak stoppers, regular pumpouts, bilge alarms, automatically activated bilge pumps, and frequent visual checks. Finally, the boat may be hauled for a yard inspection and work to halt the leaks. Such leaks are a cross to bear but are seldom dangerous.

Leaks that threaten to exceed the boat and crew's pumping capacity or that persist and worsen over a long period, however, can cause the boat to flood or even founder. They can be caused by material failure, weather, or accident.

SOURCES OF FLOODING

The most common material failure involves through-hull fittings or the hose or piping leading from them. The larger the boat, the more through hulls, and these must be inspected and maintained. They include:

Head seawater intake
Head discharge
Wash basin drain
Galley sink drain
Shower sump drain

Engine-cooling water suction and discharge
Bilge-pump discharges
Bait-box pump water supply and drain
Cockpit drains
Prop-shaft stuffing box
Rudder-post packing gland
Boat plug (small boats)
Knot-meter sensor
Open hatches, portholes, and ventilators

This is an intimidating list of vulnerable spots, and during heavy weather or when the boat is left unattended for long periods, through hulls not in use are better closed off.

Some flooding through these openings may involve not material failure but inadequate design. When a boat heels, fittings near the waterline become more deeply submerged, and the sumps, bilge pumps, or heads that they serve are also below the waterline. The resultant siphoning of the seawater back into the boat can cause serious flooding unless promptly detected and stopped. The best preventative is to lead the hose from the head or bilge pump through a high loop and then down to the through hull. If the top of the loop is always above the outside water level, siphoning will not occur. If the loop cannot be extended high enough because of the boat's interior configuration, the installation of a one-way check valve will work, as will the more expensive alternative of a positive-displacement pump. The pump can, however, develop a leak or backflow with age and wear. A check valve can also stick but will usually clear with a sharp rap from a hammer.

The most likely cause of failure in through-hull seacocks or gate valves is *galvanic and electrolytic corrosion*. The latter, also called *stray current corrosion*, can seriously damage and weaken a metal fitting in a matter of days, whereas galvanic action proceeds slowly over months or years. Both involve the interaction of dissimilar metals in an electrolyte (seawater), but the more rapid and dangerous electrolytic corrosion is powered by the presence of an electric current, often a stray current resulting from poor wiring work. This can be partially avoided by using only metals suitable for a marine environment, avoiding contact between metals that are incompatible on the galvanic scale, and installing wiring carefully.

If all through-hull fittings, struts, shafts, and so on are electrically connected by an internal bonding system, check the wiring annually. Note where connections are made to the fitting or other metal part. Electrical connections in the bilge are subject to corrosion and the development of poor contacts with high electrical resistance.

A visual check of the bonding system may disclose faults, but an electrical expert with special equipment is needed for a thorough evaluation. Signs of corrosion at connections between bonding wires and through-hull fittings may indicate the need for a complete electrical test.

Because of possible electrolytic (stray-current) corrosion, a bonding system with poor connections may be worse than no system at all. Electrolysis can and does cause weakening of through-hull fittings and underwater hardware that can result in serious safety hazards (see figure 6.1).

Another major source of stray currents is shore AC power. The ground wire in a shore power connector ties each boat to every other boat at the dock. Any boat with a galvanic or electrolytic problem will tend to dissipate the zincs and other underwater metals of other boats at the dock. Other than the difficult remedy of finding and fixing the sick boat, solutions involve the use of a ground fault circuit interrupter (many modern built-in battery chargers have such fault isolators), an isolation transformer, or silicon diodes. Most boat owners will not go to this cost and bother unless the through-hull fittings and underwater metals show pitting, discoloration, and other positive signs of corrosion. If suspect, they can be sounded with a hammer. If sound, they should give off a *tink* sound. A *clunk* could mean one is failing. Sound all fittings annually, but if rapid progress of electrolytic corrosion is detected, prompt and positive action is required to prevent a serious failure and perhaps loss of the boat.

An earlier warning is usually afforded by the rapid wasting of the boat's protective zinc anodes. If a marked wasting is noted within weeks or months of installation, conditions for rapid cor-

Figure 6.1 Electrolytic corrosion on a three-month-old propeller.

rosion most likely exist and will accelerate as erosion of the zinc progresses. If other boats along the dock also experience rapid zinc loss, the problem could lie either with your own boat or with others. If a dockwide problem is suspected, an expert technician should be brought in to analyze and correct the problem. Do not disable the shore ground wire in an attempt to avoid corrosion; it has a vital safety function. Should you decide to tackle the problem without outside help, obtain a practical reference on the subject, such as *The 12-Volt Bible for Boats* (see Appendix F), which is indispensable on any yacht.

In addition to the through-hull valves, failures can occur in the hoses or pipes leading to the various systems. These hoses are vulnerable to fire, vibration, and chafing and can slip loose unless double clamped (mandatory below the waterline). Fortunately, repairs can be easily made if spare hose and parts are carried; in many cases a soft wood tapered plug secured adjacent to each through hull will provide adequate first aid until a permanent fix can be made.

Other common sources of leaks are the seams of wooden boats, corroded keel bolts, the rudder-post gland, and the prop-shaft stuffing box. A slow drip (two drops per minute) from the stuffing box is of no immediate concern. If the dripping increases, however, the packing should be tightened (but not to excess) or replaced. Such a leak, especially one that drips when the boat is at anchor with the screw stopped, can prove dangerous over an extended period. Moored boats without regular or automatic pumpouts have sunk from this cause. Others have sunk after the batteries were exhausted by the automatic pump, or the pump ran dry and burned out after a float switch stuck.

Human error and weather also contribute to flooding losses: a common situation is a knockdown by heavy seas, or in protected waters by heavy winds. Small open boats with limited stability, or a small enclosed boat with its main companionway opening well below deck level or with open port holes, are the most vulnerable. Water entering the cockpit will down flood into the bilges unless hatches are closed and boards in. Larger boats with higher freeboard and hatches at the centerline and upper deck level have no such problems. Grounding on rocks or coral, or collision with large floating objects or whales, may also cause serious holing. An increasing concern of cruising sailors is the large number of containers washed overboard from container ships. Although one can avoid some such collisions with good lookouts, at night there is no way to see an unlit and mostly submerged drifting object.

RAPIDITY OF FLOODING

If flooding occurs, what quantity of water are we dealing with? The volume will depend on the size of the opening and its depth below water. A typical 1½-inch diameter seacock located two feet beneath the waterline will admit 62 gallons per minute (gpm), while the same valve four feet down and under higher water pressure will allow 87 gallons per minute. A 5-inch by 10-inch gash in the bottom after a grounding allows 985 gallons per minute at the four-foot depth. Since even the best small-boat electric bilge pumps and high-volume hand pumps have a capacity of perhaps

30 gpm each, a boat with four pumps would be initially fighting a losing battle with a large through-hull fitting or hose leak and would be quickly swamped by a larger structural tear. As the water rises, plugging or even locating the leak becomes more difficult.

The outlook is not as bleak if we can reduce the size of the hole from inside with materials such as towels, sails and sail bags, blankets, and cushions, backed by plywood, which is readily available by using the various stowage covers beneath bunks and lounges. Even if these plugging materials are only partially effective, the flooding volume can be reduced. As the water level inside the hull rises, moreover, the water-pressure differential between the inside and outside of the hull is decreased, as is the resultant flooding rate.

In the case of a 1½-inch hole four feet below the waterline, the initial flooding is 87 gpm. But when the water inside the hull rises above the hole, the pressure head is reduced and the flooding slows. Depending on the inherent buoyancy of the boat, the flooding may eventually be reduced to a volume that the pumps can handle, and the water will rise no further. If the boat has enough built-in flotation, this point of zero net flooding will be reached even without the help of pumps. Failure to understand this possibility has been the cause of numerous premature abandonments. Many small wooden and fiberglass boats will float when fully flooded or the flooding will slow until the volume can be handled by pumps.

An example occurred on 24 August 1986, when the CGC *Steadfast* approached the 44-foot Canadian sailing vessel *Corabia II* in the Windward Passage and prepared to put a boarding party aboard to inspect the yacht for possible contraband and drugs. At this point, the two crewmen began waving the Canadian flag upside down, jumped into a small inflatable raft, and began to drift away. With her decks nearly awash, the *Corabia II* was obviously sinking (see figure 6.2).

The boarding team, backed up quickly by the rescue party from the *Steadfast*, climbed aboard with one of the cutter's 140-gpm portable pumps. With the water six feet deep below decks, the inrush of water had obviously lessened until it could be han-

Figure 6.2   Boarding and rescue parties from the Coast Guard cutter *Steadfast* work to save the drug boat *Corabia II* after it was apparently sabotaged by the crew. *Courtesy USCG*

dled by the pump. Two more pumps with an added capacity of 390 gpm were brought on board by the cutter's rescue and assistance team, and a ruptured (possibly cut) saltwater intake hose to the engine was plugged. With three pumps working, the water level began dropping. Fortunately, none of the 178 packages of compressed marijuana floating around in the boat ruptured to clog the pumps, and their buoyancy may even have helped the water level. Four hours later the sailing vessel, nearly dry, was under way for Guantanamo Bay, Cuba, with a Coast Guard crew, escorted by the *Steadfast* with the two former yacht crewmen as prisoners. The save had been made possible by using enough pumping capacity to exceed the inflow of water, which had been steadily decreasing in rate as the depth of water in the boat increased. Had it not, the boat would have sunk before the source of flooding was discovered. When the hole was located and plugged, the portable pumps quickly emptied the boat of water.

Most boats have little or no positive buoyancy when flooded and will go down before the water rises to a point where the water pressure within the hull equals that outside. If a leak or flooding occurs, the sequence of action must be:

- Quick detection or awareness
- Start all pumps
- Stop or reduce the inflow
- Repair or plug the hole
- When pumped out, repair the flooding damage

DETECTION OF FLOODING

A minor squabble has developed between sailors who advocate regular *visual inspection of the bilges* and those who swear by a *bilge warning system* as the best guarantee against flooding. Let's settle this once and for all—*you must do both.*

A first axiom of good seamanship is frequent and regular visual checks of the bilge, but humans do forget. Yet even the most careful visual checks may not detect rapid flooding, starting between inspections, until the source of flooding is inaccessible beneath the water surface.

The use of a bilge float switch to actuate the bilge pump automatically is an obvious help here, but pumps fail or clog, and water can rise faster than the pump can handle it. Many bilge pumps operate so quietly that they are very difficult to hear amid the sounds of motoring or sailing. How can you detect immediately a rise in bilge water?

The answer is simple and inexpensive: *Install an audio and visual alarm.*

I went to my local auto parts store and purchased a small 12-volt automobile horn for $12.50 and a small red light fixture for $3.15 and installed them in parallel with the bilge pump. The horn is in the upper bilge compartment for convenience, and the light is on the cockpit panel. Any time the bilge float switch is actuated, the horn sounds and the pump and light come on. The installation is simple, requiring less than an hour (see figure 6.3). Skippers who do not wish to design their own can buy a ready-built alarm system. On my previous boat, normal condensation and a sneaky small leak actuated the bilge pump once or twice daily. It ran for twenty seconds to pump down to the cutoff point. If it ran longer or more often, I was quickly alerted that I was taking on more water than usual or that the pump was not working properly.

Some skippers prefer a two-pump system, with a low-volume bilge pump actuated by a float switch low in the bilge to handle the normal condensation and small leaks; this pump has no warning system. If water cannot be handled by the small pump, a high-capacity pump with its float switch mounted several inches higher and connected to a warning horn and light is provided. This has the advantage of sounding the warning system only when the water has gotten beyond the capacity of the small pump and does not disturb the crew during routine pumpouts. This system, however, can conceal the fact that the small pump may be overworking and draining the batteries without the skipper's knowledge. Both systems have their pros and cons, but I prefer to know when any bilge pump is working.

My own bargain installation has twice saved me considerable grief. In a stiff blow off the Abacos, with the boat heeled well over, the alarm came on repeatedly at two-minute intervals, shutting off each time after the normal twenty-second pumpout. We were obviously taking water. A check below soon revealed that as a result of the excessive heel, we were siphoning water back through the bilge-pump discharge as soon as the submerged pump cut off. Reducing sail and heel quickly solved that problem, and the later installation of a one-way check valve provided a permanent cure (the overhead loop of the discharge hose in that boat could not be raised high enough to handle all heeling).

A more serious event occurred two years later. Following a yard installation of a new prop shaft, I proceeded ninety miles to my port of departure. After provisioning, we stood out the channel under power. Once clear of the breakwater, I checked below to find all secure, cut the engine, and hoisted sails. Ten minutes

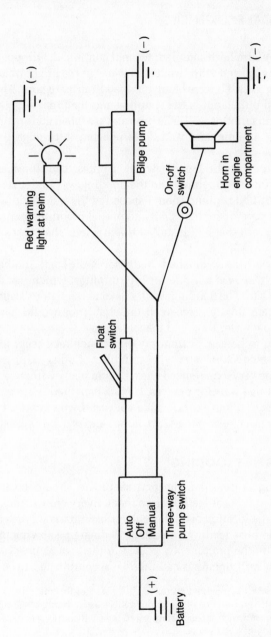

Figure 6.3 The author's homemade bilge alarm system was inexpensive and simple to install. It requires no power except when the pump is on. It shuts down when the float switch drops to a normal position. The pump can be run manually, without the alarm going off, or automatically, without the horn. From John Waters, "Early Warning for the Bilge," *Sail Magazine*, June 1985. Courtesy Sail Magazine

later the bilge alarm horn sounded; when it continued, I dropped below and was greeted with two feet of water in the bilge. Water was streaming in as if it were being pumped from a fire hose. The prop shaft had pulled out of the coupling and the inner zinc retaining ring had failed as well. The prop and shaft had gone to the bottom of the Atlantic, and water was pouring in through the shaft tube.*

I jammed one of the tapered wooden plugs, kept for such emergencies, into the opening, and the flooding was under control. The faithful bilge pump soon disposed of the water, and we sailed back to port for another shaft and prop. I promptly mailed the bill to the yard that had installed the previous shaft just six days earlier.

The bilge warning system had clearly saved the boat. Another visual bilge check was not due for fifty minutes, which would have been too late. The flooding was far beyond the pumps' capability, and when finally discovered the shaft tube would have been well below water level and inaccessible.

The lesson to be gained from my experience may seem too obvious, yet on checking later with a number of other skippers, including some very experienced ones, I found many without audio or visual bilge warning devices. Having benefited twice and been saved once in four years, I am a convert. I won't cast off a line without a last check of the bilge pumps and warning system.

STOPPING THE FLOODING

When flooding is detected, the first suspicion should be the through hulls and hoses leading from them. Every crew member should know the location of all through hulls with a good idea of the piping and hose leading from them. A diagram showing the locations should be prominently posted in the boat. A check of all the regular hull openings can then be accomplished in sec-

---

*A sacrificial zinc ring, mounted on the shaft forward of the shaft packing gland, will usually prevent loss of the shaft. In this case, it didn't. My failure to check that the yard workers had safety-wired the shaft coupling bolts was neglect that nearly cost me a boat.

onds. In most cases of hose failure, the flooding can be stopped by closing the seacock. The seacocks and gate valves should be lubricated as prescribed by the manufacturers and manipulated periodically so that they close easily and do not stick. Every through hull should have a tapered soft wood plug tied to the seacock for instant use. A plug inserted in the opening will swell and remain firmly seated. The plug that I drove into the shaft tube with my fist required fifteen minutes of work with a chisel to get out when the boat was hauled. This says something about the security of the swollen plug as well as the power of adrenaline and fright.

A fracture in a seacock or gate valve is far more dangerous than a hose rupture and may require a larger plug from the damage control kit or the use of towels, blankets, or boards to reduce the inflow. Remember that flow is related to the depth of the fitting. Putting the vessel on a tack to raise the opening will decrease the water pressure and flow, while slowing the boat will reduce water pressure and flooding from damaged areas in the bow.

Because larger boats have many hull openings, it is good practice in heavy weather to shut off seacocks not in use. Use only one head and sink and close off the galley, basins, and head if they are to leeward with heavy heeling.

SEACOCKS AND GATE VALVES

Solid bronze through-bolted seacocks are best for use below the waterline, though they do require some maintenance, are subject to electrolytic and galvanic corrosion, and are expensive. They are strong and reliable, however, and turn off with a quarter throw of the lever. The cheapest alternative is the gate valve, which requires many turns to close, and if the stem fails, which is a common mishap with a sticky valve, the valve is out of use. If you have gate valves below the waterline, you should consider replacing them with ball valves, which turn on or off with a quarter turn, have no vulnerable interior parts, and require no maintenance beyond regular use. Like gate valves, they must be freeze-proofed in cold climates. Plastic seacocks have no corro-sion problems, but they are not as resistant to impact damage.

BILGE PUMPS

The most common kind of electric bilge pump installed on small boats is the submersible type. It is reliable, economical in power drain, and easy to install, but it is easily clogged by debris and can be damaged if run dry too long. It can also siphon seawater into the boat at high angles of heel if improperly installed. The electric diaphragm pump can handle debris better, but it is mounted higher in the boat, and a pinpoint leak in the suction hose will affect its efficiency. A matchstick sucked up and jammed in one of its valves can disable it. It is wise to put a strainer in the uptake hose. Though the strainer can also become clogged, it is much easier to clear than the pump, which must be disassembled.

No pump is any better than its power supply, which is depen-dent on charged batteries and intact wires. Furthermore, any electrical system is vulnerable to flooding damage. It is essential to back up an electric pump with a manual one, or vice versa, depending on preference for manual or powered pumps.

Manual pumps are either of the piston cylinder or the di-aphragm type. The piston model is handy but clogs easily on de-bris. Diaphragm pumps handle debris well, can move large vol-umes of water, and are also easier to operate for long periods because of their short stroke. A few boats use a mechanical pump driven by a belt takeoff from the engine. The installation is diffi-cult in most crowded engine compartments and works only if the engine does.

A makeshift variation of engine pumping involves the emer-gency use of the seawater impeller pump used to provide engine-cooling water. By closing off the intake seacock and breaking the hose at that point, the cooling water pump can be used to draw and pump bilge water through the cooling system and overboard. Whether time will permit this is highly questionable. Some long-range cruisers have anticipated this problem by inserting a two-way diverter valve in the cooling water intake line, allowing suction to be shifted from the sea to the bilge with the throw of a lever. The bilge suction of this rig must be provided with a suitable strainer or strum box, and it must be regularly cleaned. There is also a real danger of fouling the engine heat exchanger, even during testing.

Any type of pump seems to have a high failure rate under adverse conditions, which unfortunately is when they are most needed. This proved to be the case with the 86-foot staysail schooner *Mariah* in late October 1980. Before leaving New York for a trip south, the bilges were flushed using all four pumps to insure that they were working properly. All checked OK. One day out, the boat ran into rapidly worsening weather, and the hull, which was more than fifty years old, began to leak as it worked in the heavy seas. When the electric bilge pump could no longer keep up with the water, the Whale Gusher on deck was activated, but its capacity was limited. The 50-gpm Jabsco pump, which operated off the main diesel engine, was then activated. It failed within a couple of minutes, was repaired, and again failed. Then the big gun, a 75-gpm pump operated by its own one-cylinder diesel engine, was started, but it wouldn't prime, perhaps because of the seas now building to over ten feet. With the wind over 50 knots, the *Mariah* turned for Cape May, New Jersey, two hundred miles away.

The crew began bailing with buckets, which they continued to do for over thirty hours, lending credence to the old saying, "A frightened man with a bucket is a first-rate pump replacement." Within the first five hours, however, the water had risen a foot over the floorboards, and a Mayday call was sent. A Coast Guard C-130 turboprop Hercules arrived first. Over the next several hours, three attempts to drop pumps to the disabled vessel failed because the exhausted boat crew was unable to retrieve the containers from the rough thirty-foot seas. A helicopter was dispatched with more pumps, but after reaching the scene, where hurricane force winds now howled, the helicopter crew gave up the attempt to lower a pump and elected instead to save the crew in a desperate forty-minute rescue effort. The first two persons were hoisted by the helicopter, which was then relieved by the CGC *Alert*. The cutter then launched a 19-foot rigid hull Avon inflatable and took off the remaining crew from the yacht. With the last survivors removed, the *Alert* proceeded to another distressed boat, one of several in the storm. During the night the *Mariah* went down.

MANUAL OR POWERED PUMPS?

The *Mariah* case raised several points about the use of bilge pumps. The failure of all four pumps despite reportedly thorough tests before leaving port is disturbing and certainly unlikely though real in this case. Traditionalists strongly advocate primary reliance on hand-operated pumps, citing the failure rate of powered devices and battery exhaustion. With the *Mariah*, the failure of an electric pump, another driven off the main engine, and the big 75-gmp pump driven by its own engine certainly presented a problem. But the manual pump failed as well, and the crew then had to resort to a bucket brigade. Just as batteries give out, so do human beings, and the *Mariah's* crew was soon so exhausted from the manual labor of dewatering that they were unable to retrieve three different powered pumps dropped to them by rescue aircraft.

A manual pump operated by a very short-handed crew will lose its operating power as quickly as or more quickly than one operated from batteries, especially if a little care is taken to keep the batteries charged up. With a larger crew able to take turns at the pumps, I would opt for a high-capacity hand pump over any powered type for serious work, while still carrying out routine low-volume bilge pumping with the more convenient electric pump. Manual and electric pumps are both vulnerable to trash and debris, so bilge cleanliness and suitable strainers are major factors in pump reliability. Few pumps, powered or manual, moreover, live up to their claimed pumping volume.

PORTABLE AND DROPPABLE PUMPS

Though not successful in the *Mariah* case, the portable gasoline-powered pump is an often-used alternative. The Coast Guard uses them frequently to dewater boats, but few pleasure boats carry one. Delivered by boat, by helicopter, or dropped by parachute (see figure 6.4), they are packaged in a floatable container and come complete with hose, gasoline, and operating instructions. This type of pump not only is simple to operate but handles an impressive volume of water. If flooding is severe, additional pumps are provided in Coast Guard SAR operations.

Shortly after noon, 4 January 1986, a man on the 40-foot fishing boat *Alaska* in the Juan de Fuca Strait west of Port Angeles, Washington, reported a loss of steering and flooding. Twenty minutes later a helicopter from Coast Guard Air Station, Port Angeles, arrived with the first portable pump. Within another hour, the Coast Guard had two pumps in operation on the disabled boat, but accumulations of garbage below decks eventually clogged them. Within five hours of the call for help, a Coast Guard cutter, two Coast Guard small boats, a helicopter, and another fishing boat were at the scene, and a total of three pumps and two eductors were keeping ahead of the incoming water. Though winds increased to 40 knots and seas to seven feet, the boat was safely towed into port. It seems clear that the failure of so many pumps

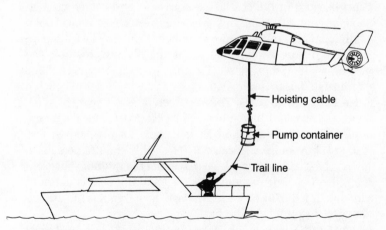

Figure 6.4 Lowering a portable pump from a helicopter. The trail line should be used by the boat crew to guide it to the proper spot. In heavy seas it is best to lower the container into the water alongside to avoid damage to the boat as it rises and falls. *Courtesy USCG*

was attributable to ingested debris from a dirty bilge, which turned a minor problem into a sizable rescue effort.

In an emergency we must not overlook the value of strong backs and plastic buckets. Remember that several buckets can be stowed in about the same space as one. With a capacity of nearly three gallons, a bucket of water every twelve seconds will equal the capacity of an average electric or manual diaphragm bilge pump. Since each full bucket, weighing 20 pounds, must be lifted from the bilge area to topside or a sink, however, this bailing method is feasible only with enough hands and the use of a chain-bucket brigade. With a very limited crew, their energies are better used in survival preparations if the water continues to rise.

BUILT-IN FLOTATION

A final alternative is the provision of flotation systems in small craft. This can include inflatable air bags, a watertight compartment, or closed-cell foam built into or stowed in the boat. Air bags are expensive and require stowage space. The design of most fiberglass boats does not permit truly watertight compartments because of the cost of passing hose and cables through glands in the bulkhead and providing watertight doors. Such subdivision also relies on the crew being able to close all compartments before flooding, which is not always possible. The most nearly foolproof approach is the provision of polyurethane foam in the design and construction stages in order to provide added buoyancy to boats. This has been done for years by some manufacturers. Wellington Boats of Jacksonville, Florida, for example, offers foam flotation as an option on their boats, and nearly all buyers have selected it. This adds about 4 percent to the base boat cost and uses up 6 percent of the interior space, but the tradeoff is a virtually unsinkable boat. If a boat is not built with flotation during its building stage, however, it is not cost effective to install it as a retrofit.

Most small boats under 20 feet built since 31 July 1972 must by federal law have basic built-in flotation for some part of the boat to remain afloat when swamped, but they are not required to remain upright or to support clear of the water the number of passengers authorized for that size boat. In 1978, the requirements were further strengthened to require that outboard motorboats under 20 feet have horizontal flotation capability, so that occupants can climb back in after swamping. Metal plates must be attached to each boat stipulating the carrying capacity.

MAJOR FLOODING

A large hole in the underwater hull resulting from a collision or grounding is critical and probably terminal. As discussed before, any material that will staunch or reduce the inflow should be used as an interior patch. Some ocean cruisers operating in distant waters carry a prefabricated square collision mat made of awning material or canvas. These have been used with good results in serious holing accidents by experienced cruising crews. A makeshift collision mat can be rigged by attaching lines to the corners of a square of awning material or a small jib. It must be worked outside the hull until it is over the hole. Rigging it may require a couple of swimmers and is perhaps beyond the capability of the average family crew (see figure 6.5).

With a very large hole and heavy flooding, the chance of plugging the hole is remote, and the crew had best use the little remaining time to prepare to abandon ship. A distress call should be made, equipment assembled on deck, and a raft or dinghy launched early as a precautionary step but not cast off until the boat is about to go down. If near shore, consider running the boat aground to facilitate later salvage.

SUMMARY

If moderate flooding or leakage occurs, chances are that it can be controlled with preplanned damage-control measures and installed pumps and equipment. If not, the danger will become quickly apparent. Call for help immediately, and complete preparations for abandoning ship if that becomes necessary.

When portable pumps are delivered by the SAR team, get them in operation and advise rescuers if additional pumps or personnel are needed. These pumps are sealed in waterproof

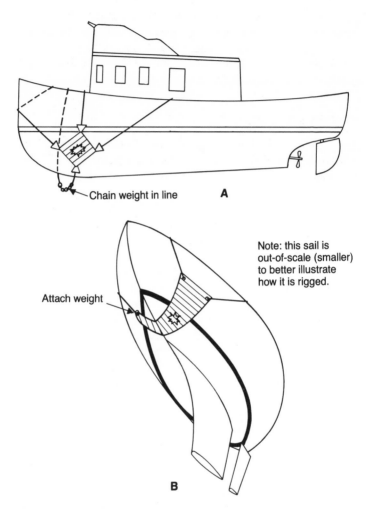

Chain weight in line   **A**

Note: this sail is
out-of-scale (smaller)
to better illustrate
how it is rigged.

Attach weight

B

Figure 6.5 Makeshift collision mats. A few long-range cruising
boats carry a prepared square collision mat of sailcloth or canvas,
with lines attached to eyes at each corner and a chain weight in the
lower line. If time permits, such a mat can be rigged from any piece
of canvas or awning cloth as shown in A, or a small storm jib rigged
as shown in B. But with a sizable hole below the waterline that cannot be plugged internally, time is better used to call for help and prepare to abandon ship.

containers complete with hose, fuel, and a plastic instruction sheet in English and Spanish. They can be delivered by helicopter or boat or parachuted from fixed-wing aircraft.

Do not abandon ship prematurely. The resistance of even a small boat to sinking was once again demonstrated in September 1986, when the trawler *Muriel Kiff* began flooding off Atlantic City, New Jersey. Air-droppable pumps were delivered by Falcon jets and an HH-3 helicopter from Air Station, Cape Cod. Still unable to reduce the flooding, the four-man crew abandoned ship, were picked up by a fishing vessel, and then transferred to the Spanish *Laxe dos Picos*. The cutter *Cape Horn* later arrived on the scene, pumped out the abandoned trawler, and towed it to Manasquan Inlet. The flooding was later determined to have been from a cracked bilge-pump fitting.

7
Collision

Collisions cause half of all significant boating accidents and are exceeded as a cause of death only by capsizing or falling overboard. Collisions with fixed or floating objects are more common than collisions with other boats but usually produce less damage and fewer fatalities.

Despite more than a century of effort by the maritime nations to develop and enforce foolproof rules to prevent collisions between vessels, they still occur with alarming frequency. Even the great technological advances in radar, navigation, and communications have failed to prevent collisions involving superbly equipped and presumably well-operated ships. Small pleasure craft are even more susceptible to such mishaps and also have an appalling record of hitting fixed objects.

On 11 April 1985, the large modernized carrier USS *Coral Sea* collided with the Ecuadorian tanker *Napo* in the Caribbean Sea, even though the warship had originally contacted the tanker at a range of twenty-three miles in favorable weather conditions. Equipped with every modern navigation, communication, and detection device, and with hundreds of trained personnel on duty, the two ships collided, resulting in millions of dollars in damages to both vessels and the relief and reprimand of five of the carrier's officers. It was one more in a long series of accidents involving large modern vessels that would seem to be well protected from such hazards by advanced technology and experienced crews.

At the other end of the scale are small-boat sailors, by comparison scantily equipped and always short handed. They too have their share of collisions, ranging from merely hard knocks at the start of a race to the ill-fated 1986 single-handed Route du Rhum Race from Saint Malo to Guadeloupe, where four out of thirty-three competitors were involved in collisions at sea.

Most collisions between boats can be attributed to lack of alertness or reckless operation, with alcohol contributing heavily to both. These are followed closely by ignorance of the Rules of the Road and excessive speed, which is abetted by the production and sale of ever faster and more overpowered boats (see figure 7.1). All of these factors involve human rather than material failings or natural causes (fog and visibility are exceptions).

RULES OF THE ROAD

Regulations to prevent collisions at sea were first promulgated by Great Britain in 1863 and by the United States the following year. The first International Rules of the Road were developed in 1889. The most recent update came in 1977, based on the changes made by the Convention on the International Regulations for Preventing Collisions at Sea, 1972 (72 COLREGS). In 1983 further regulations were issued by the United States to reduce the number of differences between the International Rules and its own Inland Rules. These rules have the full effect of both treaty and statutes and are periodically amended by regulations.

It is essential that anyone sailing on navigable waters have a reasonable familiarity with these rules, and serious sailors and professionals should have a thorough understanding.

Though they appear formidable at first glance, the rules follow a logical rationale and are not difficult to comprehend. The five main parts of the rules are:

A.   General
B.   Steering and Sailing Rules
C.   Lights and Shapes

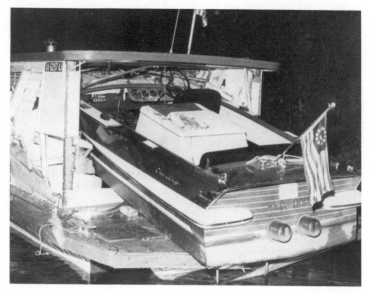

Figure 7.1 This speeding 15-foot motorboat overhauled and crashed into the slower houseboat on a river in West Virginia, killing one and injuring eight. Observing the Rules of the Road could have prevented the accident. *Courtesy USCG*

    D.   Sound and Light Signals
    E.   Exemptions

These principal sections are followed by various annexes, explanations, and interpretations.

    Since most small-boat operators are found on inland waters, they should first master the Inland Rules; if offshore cruising is planned, the differences between the Inland and International rules should then be reviewed. *Chapman's Piloting, Seamanship, and Small-Boat Handling* contains excellent (though not complete) overviews with an emphasis on the Inland Rules (see Appendix G). Once this overview has been digested, a definitive reference is the Coast Guard publication, *Navigation Rules, International—Inland* (COMDTINST. M16672.2A). This official publication is available at low cost from most marine book stores or the Government Printing Office and is required by law to be carried on all U.S. vessels over 12 meters (39.4 feet) in length. A handy cockpit aid for the small-boat sailor is a plastic, water-proof device, *Quick Reference Navigation Rules*, produced by Davis Instruments and available at many marine hardware dealers for about $5.00. This easy-to-use illustrated memory aid contains most of the information needed by the small-boat sailor to comply with the rules, assuming he or she has gone over the basic text at least once.

CAUSES OF COLLISIONS

Though the Rules of the Road are specific and logical, collisions still occur as a result of:

1. Lack of alertness and failure to maintain a lookout, the primary cause
2. Poor visibility and failure to have or use radar aids
3. High speeds and reckless operation of boats
4. Failure to comply with or ignorance of the Rules of the Road
5. Failure to recognize the meaning of lights and signals indicating vessels with restricted maneuverability or tows
6. Chance encounters with floating or submerged objects or marine life
7. Failure to properly navigate and stay in marked channels or safe waters
8. Crowded boating areas

Small-boat skippers must recognize that though they may technically have the right of way, the reality is that a large ship bearing down may not have seen a small boat or may be unable to maneuver clear because of a narrow channel or momentum. Since a tanker-yacht collision is a one-sided contest and even the wake from a near miss is dangerous, the small boat is well advised to leave the arena entirely to the big boy (see figure 7.2).

On 20 August 1986, for example, the large Yugoslavian freighter *Jablanica* collided with a 35-foot U.S. fishing vessel

Figure 7.2   A view to avoid at all cost: a freighter head-on.

Razal Brothers in northern Lake Michigan. The fishing boat sank immediately, and the freighter recovered one person, who was air-evacuated to a hospital by helicopter and pronounced dead on arrival. The boat and the bodies of the other two crewmen were located three days later by divers.

Though the decision to avoid a large ship should be obvious, many collisions between small boats of similar tonnage are caused by too strict an interpretation of the rights of the privileged (stand on) vessel. In the early stages of a meeting or crossing the privileged vessel has a duty to maintain course and speed. But if both vessels continue on collision courses, and the burdened (give way) vessel has not given way, the privileged vessel is then clearly required to avoid a crash with the burdened vessel by Rule 2 of both the International and Inland rules, which says in essence:

Once either skipper perceives that a collision may be imminent, one or both had better do something to avoid it and not stand on legal privilege.

The courts have repeatedly held that a privileged vessel that continued to hold course and speed after realizing that a collision was imminent is a contributing party to the accident, having violated Rule 2. Insurance underwriters report that 10 percent of all marine claims are for collision damages, usually both parties are at fault, and lack of vigilance is the common cause of collision.

On sighting another vessel that may pass close, any ship, whether privileged or burdened, should:

A.   If available, use a radar and a reflector.
B.   Take a series of bearings. If the boat's bearings change fore or aft, the other boat will clear. If the bearings remain steady, it is on a collision course with you. If this is the case:
    1. Sound the proper passing or helm signal by horn.
    2. Make an obvious, unmistakable change of course as signaled. Leave no doubt as to your intentions.
    3. Continue taking bearings until the other boat passes clear.
    4. If the other boat's course or intentions aren't clear, contact the vessel on VHF/FM Channel 16 to clarify the matter. If unable to make contact, or if the threat is imminent, sound a warning signal of five or more short blasts on the horn and immediately take evasive action or stop.

At night, avoid heading directly at another vessel. The changing lights presented by a yawing small boat are very confusing. Take a course that will clearly present either your red, green, or stern light to the other vessel until clear. If the situation appears threatening, play a strong light on your sail or superstructure and use a searchlight, other lights, or flares to attract the other vessel's attention. Many highly automated freighters and jumbo tankers run with small crews, and some watchstanders could be nodding off in a seemingly empty sea. Merchant vessels do not continuously monitor the radar as is the practice in warships, but rely on periodic checks by the watchkeepers. Small boats are difficult to see on radar, especially in rough weather.

Small boats must steer clear of less maneuverable craft such as tugs with tows, dredges, vessels disabled or not under command, and commercial trawlers and draggers with gear down. (Note: Trolling sport fishing boats have no inherent rights other than those conferred on any powered vessel by relative position.) The inherently privileged vessels like those listed above show special shapes and signals by day and lights by night. As they are difficult to remember, keep a reference publication or a Davis Quick Reference nearby as a refresher. Most of these vessels can be contacted on Channel 16.

Special vigilance must be maintained at night when it is hard to see nets, dredging gear, and the towlines between tugs and barges (see figure 7.3). Deaths and serious accidents occur yearly because of such collisions. When identified by their special lights or markings, these privileged vessels should be given a wide margin.

Though collisions between boats are the costliest in lives and amount of damage, a substantial number, many fatal, are caused

Figure 7.3   A tug towing or pushing a long string of barges can be a grave hazard at night or in fog unless its special lights and signals are recognized.

by boats hitting fixed objects such as bridges, docks, buoys, and particularly the large unlighted day beacons seen on the ICW and rivers. Careful navigation, slower speeds, and use of searchlights at night near unlighted objects would have prevented most of these. Unfortunately, alcohol, with its accompanying lack of judgment and caution, too often interferes with these elementary precautions.

Constant vigilance is essential but difficult over long periods with short-handed crews, whose attention may also be diverted by other activities. On sailboats, the view ahead is too often obstructed by the mast, cabin, or foresails (fig. 7.4). A helmsman who is sitting down may have trouble seeing. It is wise to post an additional lookout forward and for the helmsman to yaw periodically to check the area ahead for other boats or objects. Because of the large number of navigation aids, obstructions, and other

Figure 7.4 Sailboats, especially when heeled under sail, have a blind area ahead. The big day-marker just emerging from the blind spot behind the sail can be a dangerous obstruction when not seen or kept in sight.

boats, cruising on inland waterways involves a far greater risk of collision than the open ocean, and a higher level of vigilance is required in this seemingly safer environment. Few events are more startling or frightening than seeing a large buoy or beacon suddenly loom just ahead after having been concealed in the boat's blindspot or behind a sail.

Partially submerged objects are difficult to detect at any time and nearly impossible at night. On 4 September 1986, the sole crewmember of a 47-foot racing sloop *Air Force* reported that he was abandoning ship into a life raft 130 miles northeast of Bermuda. The *Air Force* was on the first leg of a single-handed voyage around the world when it hit a submerged object. The impact was so severe that the operator was knocked unconscious and suffered a back injury. When the electric and manual bilge pumps could not keep up with the resultant flooding, the survivor, now conscious, donned a survival suit, made the distress call, and abandoned ship. A Coast Guard HU-25 Falcon jet from Cape Cod located the survivor's EPIRB signal in less than ninety minutes, and he was picked up by a navy helicopter from Bermuda and released from the hospital the following day. Investigators believe his boat may have struck a partially submerged cargo container. Many of these are lost each year from large container ships in heavy weather and are a threat to all boats traveling offshore.

Despite the claims of some supporters, long-distance single-handed racing and cruising is hazardous, not only to the individual but to others he or she might encounter on the water. Keeping a proper lookout at all times if a sailor is alone is impossible and clearly a violation of International Rules. A solution would be to heave to before sleeping or leaving the deck for long periods, but few solo sailors do so in good weather.

HOT RODDERS AND ECCENTRICS

Probably no other activity so arouses experienced sailors as the reckless operation of overpowered fast boats in crowded or confined areas. As an old seaplane pilot, I hold firmly to the belief that nothing should be going faster than 50 knots on the water unless it is ready to become airborne. A big fast boat approaching head on at high speed is an alarming sight, and so is a boat following close behind a water skier, where a fall means instant disaster.

Law enforcement has not been successful in controlling this menace. There are few posted speed limits, and judges have been reluctant to convict offenders on a sometimes vague charge of reckless operation. The Coast Guard, because of its heavy enforcement duties at sea, maintains that enforcing such laws on inland waters is primarily a responsibility of the states.

Reckless or negligent operation of a vessel, however, may lead to the imposition of civil penalties by the Coast Guard. Grossly negligent operation of a boat is a criminal offense subject to fines of up to $5,000, imprisonment for a year, or both. Actions that carried to extremes may result in such heavy penalties include:

- Operating a boat in a swimming area
- Operating a boat while under the influence of alcohol or drugs
- Excessive speed in the vicinity of other boats or in dangerous waters
- Hazardous waterskiing practices
- Riding on the bow, seatback, gunwale, or transom

The increased death rate attributable solely to reckless boating practices has brought on stronger punitive reactions from the public. In November 1987, an 800-horsepower high-speed boat operated by a Miami man, Armando Marquez, 27, ran through a large crowd of boaters at anchor listening to a concert near Key Biscayne, Florida. A small inflatable dinghy occupied by two men was struck by the speeding 41-foot boat and one of them was killed. Though Marquez was tested and found to be sober, he was indicted under Florida's new boating homicide law and after conviction sentenced to five years' imprisonment.

Criminal proceedings, in the absence of an accident or injuries, are not common. A Coast Guard boarding officer who observes a boat being operated in an unsafe condition specifically defined by law or regulation, and who determines that an especially hazardous condition exists, may direct the operator to take immediate steps to correct the condition, including returning to port. This is preventative safety rather than a punitive step. Termination of unsafe use may be imposed for:

- Insufficient number of CG approved personal flotation devices (PFDs)
- Insufficient number of or inadequate fire extinguishers
- Overloaded condition
- Improper navigation light display
- Fuel leakage
- Fuel in bilges
- Improper ventilation
- Improper backfire flame control
- Hazardous inlet/entrance conditions (Thirteenth Coast Guard District [Pacific Northwest Coast] only)
- Manifestly unsafe voyage

An operator who refuses to terminate the unsafe use of a boat can be cited for failure to comply with the directions of the Coast Guard boarding officer, as well as for the specific violations that were the basis for the termination order.

On 12 June 1986, the Coast Guard Station at Ocean City, Maryland, learned that a 52-year-old man intended to sail from Ocean City to Spain alone on a 16-foot Hobie Cat. He had stocked the boat with 13 gallons of fresh water, a hand-held compass, a VHF/FM radio, two flashlights, an inflatable raft, and food for four weeks. The day the craft departed Ocean City, a station boat crew promptly boarded it and cited the operator for failure to carry a life jacket and visual distress signals. The craft then resumed its voyage for a few hours until the Fifth District commander determined the voyage to be "manifestly unsafe." A Cape May Air Station H-52 helicopter relocated the vessel and vectored a boat to the scene. The voyage was terminated without incident and the craft towed to port where the operator was directed not to resume the voyage.

An even more bizarre case occurred off the West Coast, where a man was intercepted by the Coast Guard and forced to return to shore after sailing for Hawaii in a modified bath tub. Both of these cases were obviously unsafe. Others are not as clear-cut. A scheduled two-day sailing race was started off Florida despite Coast Guard misgivings and resulted in a number of emergencies because of the severe weather conditions. The Thirteenth Coast Guard District, which includes the Pacific Northwest Coast with its treacherous bars and inlets, has statutory authority to prevent boats going out when conditions are deemed unsafe. This authority, however, does not apply to inbound vessels that may choose to transit the bars against the advice of the Coast Guard while seeking shelter. In a "save ship" situation, the captain of a vessel in distress has nearly absolute power and authority in the actions he or she may take.

Lest a Big Brother attitude seem an unwarranted intrusion on boaters' freedom, remember that the men and women of the Coast Guard who have to go out and rescue them also have rights, as do the taxpayers who must pay the high costs of a large SAR operation.

ALCOHOL, BOATS, AND DRUNKS

Boating has long been idealized as a last resort for privacy in an overcrowded world, and boaters have assumed the right to do as they please. Until the dramatic growth in water recreation in recent years, this picture was fairly accurate. But with more people on the water, conflicts arise between the rights of an individual and those of others using the water. One result has been the increasing regulation of pleasure boating by federal and state governments.

Special attention is now being focused on the misuse of alcohol by boat operators. Although some of this effort is an offshoot of the movement against vehicular driving while intoxicated (DWI), much has resulted from studies showing the high correlation between intoxication and boating accidents, regularly demonstrated by severe boat accidents. Some 1,000 people die yearly in such accidents, 90 percent of them by drowning. The probability of death and injury in such accidents is doubled when alcohol is involved.

110 SMALL BOAT EMERGENCIES

A landmark study by the California Department of Waterways disclosed that in this largest boating state, 59 percent of boating fatalities were alcohol-related. As a result, legislation was passed defining a blood alcohol level of .10 percent as legally drunk, and .05 to .10 percent as evidence that the operator was under the influence of alcohol. Most states as well as the federal government now have similar laws prohibiting the operation of a vessel while under the influence of alcohol and other drugs, and some states have included an implied consent clause, similar to that for driving, that allows testing for blood alcohol content.

Another five-year study in four states showed that 31 percent of those killed in boat accidents had greater than .10 percent blood alcohol level, and an added 51 percent had .04 to .10 percent, a level known to cause impairment. The Red Cross reports that 30 percent of all boat occupants admit drinking. (See table 7.1.)

Statistics alone do not give the same picture as do actual occurrences. In April 1988, a 25-foot sports fishing boat powered by two 200-horsepower engines ran onto the darkened jetty at the

Table 7.1 Blood Alcohol Levels by Body Weight and Consumption

	APPROXIMATE BLOOD ALCOHOL (%)								
	Body Weight (lbs)								
No. of Drinks	100	120	140	160	180	200	220	240	
1[a]	.04[b]	.03	.03	.02	.02	.02	.02	.02	BE
2	.08	.06	.05	.05	.04	.04	.03	.03	CAREFUL
3	.11	.09	.08	.07	.06	.06	.05	.05	
4	.15	.12	.11	.09	.08	.08	.07	.06	OPERATION
5	.19	.16	.13	.12	.11	.09	.09	.08	IMPAIRED
6	.23	.19	.16	.14	.13	.11	.10	.09	
7	.26	.22	.19	.16	.15	.13	.12	.11	DO NOT
8	.30	.25	.21	.19	.17	.15	.14	.13	OPERATE
9	.34	.28	.24	.21	.19	.17	.15	.14	
10	.38	.31	.27	.23	.21	.19	.17	.16	

SOURCE: Based on table prepared by the National Safety Council, 8–87.
[a]One drink is 1.25 oz. of 80 proof liquor, 12 oz. of beer, or 4 oz. of table wine.
[b]Substract .01% for each 40 minutes of drinking.

entrance of Miami harbor at high speed, killing the operator, a 36-year-old man from Miami Beach, and two young sailors in the British navy. Another British sailor, a 31-year-old cook on the HMS *Ambuscade*, survived. All four men had been drinking at a Miami River bar until 3:00 A.M., when the American boatman offered to take his three new British friends back to their ship in his boat. The one survivor and the three bodies were found by a Coast Guard boat after witnesses reported hearing a crash and calls for help in the dark. All the bodies had a high blood alcohol content.

In similar alcohol-related accidents, near Jacksonville, Florida, five men were killed in two accidents when their boats hit docks; three others were killed when their boat hit a bridge; another was killed when his boat hit a large channel buoy (see figure 7.5). All four accidents occurred after midnight and involved alcohol. Seven people died and nineteen others were injured in three separate boating accidents near Beaumont, Texas, in 1987. All of the accidents involved alcohol.

Figure 7.5   Damage after hitting a fixed object at high speed. *Courtesy USCG*

It seems likely that the recent trend of charging vehicular manslaughter and even murder in deaths involving DWI will be extended to the boating community. Because the operation of a boat usually involves as great a need for alertness as operating a car, and the stresses of the marine environment augment the effects of alcohol, there is little rationale for differing between land and sea situations involving alcohol. Marine enforcement agencies can conduct boardings and inspections with fewer restrictions than can their shore-based contemporaries (who must have probable cause), so the small-boat sailor may soon be as likely to encounter an alcohol test as a motor vehicle operator.

Can there be a compromise between traditional individual rights and those of society? We have three suggestions:

- Have a competent nondrinker ("designated driver") operate the boat under way
- Drink in moderation
- Anchor or tie up before indulging in more alcohol

AVOIDING COLLISION

Prevention of collisions on the water is basically simple and straightforward:

- Keep track of your own position as well as that of other boats, obstructions, and objects near you.
- Keep a sharp visual and listening watch.
- Know and observe the Rules of the Road.
- In reduced visibility, use radar and radar reflectors, reduce speed, and sound the proper signals. If possible, anchor in shallow water where large vessels cannot go.
- If a collision threatens, sound the danger signal (five or more short blasts on the horn), *slow down*, and use any reasonable means of getting the other boat's attention. After sounding a signal, be alert for unusual maneuvers by novice sailors, such as turning in the wrong direction or into greater danger. *If collision seems likely, take any action needed to save your boat.* Do not stubbornly stand on technical privileges or legal rights.
- Do not drink while operating a boat.

8
Heavy Weather

A storm at sea can be exhilarating at first, but eventually the physical and emotional strain of a prolonged blow will wear down even the hardiest mariner. When some crew members become incapacitated or seasick, their duties fall upon the more physically able, compounding their fatigue. Crew mistakes or omissions after the onset of fatigue are a leading cause of weather losses at sea.

Weekend and coastal cruisers in North American waters have far less risk of encountering a full gale or storm if they anticipate and respect the weather, use common sense, and are not too proud to run for the nearest shelter. They cannot, however, avoid all the thunderstorms and squalls common in the warmer months or even in the cooler seasons over warm water and along advancing cold fronts. These intense local storms can prove dangerous to an unprepared crew even in well-protected waters, and though they rarely produce the large waves common with prolonged gales, the winds and lightning can be both frightening and potentially lethal. Dealing with any storm requires advance preparation, and an early awareness of its approach is vital.

Weather over the continental United States tends to move from west to east, though variations occur in the southern states during the summer. These movements are closely monitored by satellites, hundreds of weather-reporting stations and radars, and some seventy forecasting centers and stations operated by the National Weather Service (NWS) of the National Oceanic and Atmospheric Administration (NOAA).

Sailors in our coastal regions have an abundance of weather information, including frequent television and AM/FM radio broadcasts; a system of NWS stations providing continually updated and repeated weather on marine VHF/FM; and numerous Coast Guard and commercial radio stations that provide weather warnings on VHF/FM and single side band (SSB) radio. Daily newspapers carry weather sections and maps, though they vary widely in quality and completeness of information.

The NWS forecasts on VHF/FM can be heard either on the boat's VHF/FM transceiver or on a small hand-size portable available at most radio stores at a modest price (see figure 8.1). There is no excuse in our coastal or inland waters for sailing in ignorance of pending weather. By the time the usual cold front or depression moves into the Atlantic Ocean, it has been observed for a week or more moving cross-country. Though its characteristics may change when it hits the moist maritime region, there should be few surprises.

The Pacific Coast, with its weather moving in from the sea, is a greater problem for forecasters and sailors. The limited number of safe inlets and refuges on the Pacific Coast further increases the risks. Delays in detecting worsening weather can result in dangerous inlet conditions developing before boats can reach shelter. Despite the increasing use of automated offshore weather buoys and orbiting weather satellites, weather forecasting is still as much an art as a science. The experienced meteorologists of the NWS issue more than two million forecasts yearly, but the prudent mariner still adds his or her own allowance as insurance against inaccurate predictions.

To improve their performance, the National Weather Service has announced a billion-dollar modernization program, which will be completed by the mid-1990s. This will involve the closure of nearly half of the service's present 372 weather stations, placing their functions in 160 larger and updated stations. Many of them will have a greater ability to detect wind shears (microbursts) and tornadoes, and they can possibly give as much as

Figure 8.1 A small table-top VHF/FM weather radio can save a lot of grief if monitored before leaving home on an outing.

twenty-minutes warning rather than the five minutes now typically afforded. Data processing will be speeded up by more powerful and up-to-date computers fed from weather stations and one thousand automated and unstaffed surface stations that will collect current weather data and transmit it to computers.

One significant cause of trouble is not ignorance of approaching weather but a deliberate decision to sail into the danger to keep a time schedule or get back to an appointment or job. Boats, especially under sail or in exposed waters, can be very unreliable when people are trying to adhere to a planned agenda.

The tragic disappearance of the 55-foot ketch *HSH*, a favorite myth of Bermuda Triangle buffs, was in no way a result of "strange and mysterious forces" but severe weather and poor decisions. At the time I was commanding the U.S. Coast Guard Air

Detachment and SAR Group, Bermuda. The well-equipped and -maintained *HSH*, owned by a Philadelphia advertising executive and carrying a professional captain and several passengers, had stopped in Bermuda for a short visit before sailing on to the Antilles. The day before its planned departure, I was invited by a mutual friend to meet the party from the *HSH* (which I was told meant Home Sweet Home) to discuss the trip. I asked our aerology people to prepare a weather forecast and weather map. The forecast was grim. January had been a month of storms, and now another deep low that had formed over Louisiana had moved rapidly eastward into the Atlantic. It was no time to go sailing. That night, the owner of the *HSH* agreed, but two of the guests were becoming anxious to get back to the States within ten days for business reasons. I again urged that the weather not be ignored. After a pleasant visit, we walked to the door.

I said jokingly, "I hope that we never have to meet professionally."

The following day, we were startled to receive word from the harbor master that the *HSH* had sailed. Winds were already gusting to gale force. Twenty-four hours later, winds were up to 92 knots in gusts—full hurricane force. About 0930, the Coast Guard radio operator at Bermuda heard a call on 2182 kilocycles from the *HSH*; it was a calm, steady voice: "Coast Guard Bermuda, this is the *HSH*. Over."

The operator quicky answered, but there was no reply. When repeated calls failed to raise the *HSH*, two large Coast Guard cutters at sea to the southeast of Bermuda also called without success. In their area, where the *HSH* should have been, the storm was raging.

When two days passed with no further calls from the *HSH*, we were concerned, but with four actual distress cases in the area, our forces were completely committed. Moreover, in the prevailing weather, a search for so small a vessel would have been nearly hopeless without radio or electronic aids. Nevertheless, the rescue coordination center (RCC) controllers started a drift plot based on the assumption that the *HSH* could have been dismasted the second day out. For the next eight days, the probable drift was plotted, using wind and weather reports from ships at sea.

On the ninth day, we presumed the *HSH* should have arrived in the Antilles, and the Coast Guard at San Juan made a harbor check of the various ports in that area. There was no trace of the vessel. On the tenth day after sailing, a search was started.

This was no simple track-line search from Bermuda to Saint Thomas. With the *HSH*, we were assuming that she was a dismasted drifting hulk. The night before the search began, the drift calculations were again checked, and the enormity of the problem hit us. If the *HSH* was still afloat and dismasted, its most likely position was 870 miles east-southeast of Bermuda, in the trackless wastes of the Sargasso Sea.

To search the area would require six hours of flying each way, leaving only two hours to search in the most likely area, even using the big long-range Martin Mariner seaplanes. Fourteen hours of flying would be required to search for two hours in the distant likely area. The outlook was bleak, but at 0400 the following morning, I took off in the first aircraft.

Fourteen hours later, with less than two hours of fuel remaining, we sighted the welcome lights of Bermuda (see figure 8.2). Search conditions had been terrible, there were no navigational aids in the search area, and the weather was worsening. We estimated detection probability as only 10 percent. For the next three weeks, the search went on as weather permitted, over continually stormy seas. At last it was called off, but was reopened the following week by orders from Washington: the owner of the *HSH* was a friend of the president. After four weeks the case was finally closed. Not a trace of the *HSH* was ever found.

The loss of the *HSH* was a direct result of the decision to sail into a severe oncoming storm, despite strong and specific warnings from knowledgeable professionals. We can only speculate that the decision was influenced by the time schedule of some of the passengers.

FORECAST VERSUS ON-SCENE WEATHER

The proficient sailor should not be dependent solely on broadcast weather reports but should be able to interpret weather from personal observations, which sometimes differ greatly from that predicted. The weather service forecasts average wave heights

Figure 8.2   The author debriefs after a 14-hour search for the *HSH* in mid-Atlantic.

and sustained wind speeds rounded to the nearest 5 knots, but the occasional rogue sea or heavy wind gust may be far greater. Since conditions at the scene may be quite different from the forecast, unexpected severe weather phenomena should be reported by radio to the Coast Guard or a nearby marina for relay to the nearest forecaster.

Chapman's offers an excellent weather overview and there are a number of good, readable books on weather and aerology that go into greater detail (see Appendix F). A few hours spent studying one of these will help the amateur sailor to better understand, recognize, and cope with the boating environment.

THUNDERSTORMS

During any afternoon or early evening in the warmer months, dozens of thunderstorms are active over and near the North American landmass. In the late evening or early morning hours, or in the colder months, thunderstorms occur more often over the relatively warm offshore waters.

Although there has been little success in predicting exactly where these storms will strike, their general area and direction of movement are easily tracked by radar. The chance that a boat moving from point A to B during a day will encounter a thunderstorm is purely random, and there is little point in trying to avoid a storm until it is actually heard or sighted visually or on radar, or weather advisories are received on VHF/FM.

Once the storm is sighted, it is sometimes possible to avoid it even though such storms can move at 20 to 30 knots, whereas many small boats can run at only 5 to 10 knots. Bearings should be taken to determine if the storm will miss or is on a collision course with the boat. Because of the storm's size, however, bearings must be taken of both the left and right side of the storm. If both bearings are moving in the same direction, the storm will probably clear in that direction. If the left bearing is moving left, however, and the right bearing to the right, a part of the storm is on course for the boat.

All thunderstorms are accompanied by lightning. Though few boats are actually hit, enough have been sunk, damaged, or crew members killed or badly injured to make us wary. The greatest threat, however, is from the high winds in and near the storm. (See figure 8.3.)

It is imperative that preparations on board be made well before the storm hits. Thunderstorms can move rapidly and their closure rate is often underestimated, particularly when the main storm body is obscured by other clouds or reduced visibility. The storm's accompanying winds can extend out as far as 2.5 miles from the center with velocities as high as 168 miles per hour. Tornadoes sometimes accompany severe thunderstorm activity and produce winds estimated as high as 300 miles per hour.

Because they are unpredictable, all thunderstorms must be treated with caution until one can determine by actual contact that they do not contain severe weather. Overconfidence or carelessness can occasionally betray a sailor who has weathered a number of such storms. This was the cause of a frightening experience for me.

Both my sailing companion and I had seen our share of the

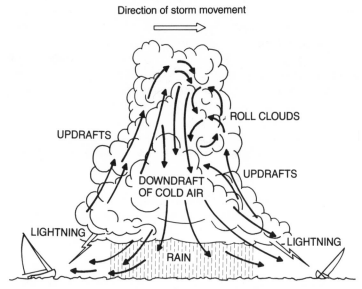

Figure 8.3 Cross section of thunderstorm. Warm, vertically moving moist air currents rise above the freezing level and cool through expansion and release of moisture. Soon, columns of rapidly descending cool air are generated. As these strike the water's surface and fan out horizontally, strong surface winds result, often changing abruptly as the storm moves past.

big ones and were respectful in their presence. When I turned over the watch at midnight, we noted the flashes of lightning over the South Carolina coast some fifteen miles to the west. It was, we concluded, the last flicker of a coastal thunderstorm that would diminish as evening progressed and the land cooled. But, two hours later, I was aroused from a sound sleep by a summons from the deck to find winds up to 25 knots and thunder and lightning about two miles away. The main was quickly hauled down and secured. The wind picked up another 10 knots, and rain began lashing the boat. Taking turns on the genoa furling winch, we began a race against time to get the foresail in. Suddenly the cranking became hard and then stopped. The genoa sheets, flailing in the wind, had wrapped into the furl, and the sail was jammed in the half furled position. To clear it, the sail would have to be played out again and rewound.

But with the next bolt of lightning and nearly instantaneous crash of thunder, the storm hit. Within seconds the wind was screaming in excess of 50 knots, and the boat was heeled about 70 degrees to starboard. Bracing my feet on the lee side (now the bottom) of the cockpit, and hanging onto the pedestal, I looked down at the water only feet away and then at the companionway, left open when I came on deck. They were awfully close together! Throwing the wheel hard to windward, I managed to reach the starter switch, and the diesel roared to life. I threw the transmission ahead, and opened the throttle fully.

Over the roar of the engine and the scream of the wind, the jammed genoa flapped and cracked, and large tears appeared when the lightning flashed. As the sail tore and disintegrated, the full rudder and engine power took effect, the bow came slowly into the wind and the boat fought back up. Fortunately, no waves had developed from the dampening effect of the very high winds and heavy rain. Within five minutes the wind shifted and began dropping, and after that the rain slowly subsided. The whole episode was over quickly, leaving a ruined genoa, a torn bimini, and a wet cabin.

It was a small price to pay, considering what could have occurred. The cockpit drains had worked well and the open companionway had not flooded as the boat rallied from the knockdown. Turning to me, my friend quoted an old aviator's proverb about thunderstorms: "If you keep looking," he said in a quiet voice, "you'll find one you can't fly through."

In retrospect, I had made a number of mistakes, starting with the conclusion that the storm was dying out. A thunderstorm is very unpredictable, and I should have based my planning on what the storm was capable of doing rather than what I thought it would do. This in turn led to late and hurried preparations for the storm and the bimini still up, the furling genoa jammed, and the companionway left open. The tearing away of the jib may well have saved us from heeling further and flooding through the open companionway. The use of engine power was an act of desperation and in this case it worked, though it is certainly not in most books on storm tactics. I could easily have wrapped a trailing line in the screw. I felt properly chastened and resolved to handle a storm situation better next time.

Some two years later, I was at sea with another crew when we sighted the flashing lightning of a squall line to the west. The time of night and the scenario were uncomfortably like those off the South Carolina coast two years before, but this time we were off the central Florida coast. Florida bows to no state in the size of its alligators and thunderstorms. Ten minutes before the storm hit, all the sails had been secured except for a small, partially furled foresail for steerageway and steadying effect; all hatches, ports, and through hulls were closed; and the watchstanders were in foul-weather gear and harness. My wife decided to go below and read a magazine. Before disconnecting the VHF antenna and power leads, I called the Coast Guard Group at Mayport, Florida, and reported the squall line and intense electrical activity, adding that I would call again after the line passed. The radar people at Jax International knew the storm was there, but I wanted the Coast Guard to know that I was too. The vertical streaks of lightning and the fact that my mast was probably the tallest object within twenty miles made me a little insecure.

The storm hit in a near replay of two years before, but this time we were ready. Turning to weather, we steered close to the wind to reduce speed and heel, falling off as needed to maintain steerageway. With winds gusting to perhaps 60 knots and only a tablecloth-sized sail, we ran at speeds as high as 7 knots. Within thirty minutes, the storm had passed. I went below to hook up the VHF and report it to Mayport. The results of this squall had been quite different from those of my previous hit, lending an added bit of credence to the saying that the Lord helps those who help themselves. But the big difference was timely preparation.

WATERSPOUTS

Waterspouts are tornadoes that form or move over the water, although they are less vicious and violent in character than their land cousins. They are often seen over southern and tropical waters on hot summer afternoons, usually in association with rapidly building thunderstorms (see figure 8.4). Off Sale Cay in the Abacos, we once sighted three in one afternoon, but they were moving slowly and soon disappeared. The only victim I have seen was a 35-foot sailboat in a state of disarray, with torn sails haphazardly lashed down, lying in the inner harbor at Ocracoke Island, North Carolina. Noting no activity aboard for some days, I inquired at the nearby Coast Guard station. The boat had been hit in Pamlico Sound by a waterspout some weeks before. The crew had then come into Ocracoke, dropped the hook, and hadn't come back. The experience must have been impressive.

MICROBURSTS

Weather phenomena even more dangerous to small craft than water spouts are microbursts, for they are far more common and

Figure 8.4 Waterspouts beneath thunderstorms, obviously an area to avoid. *Courtesy National Oceanic and Atmospheric Administration*

often hit with little warning. Microbursts are caused by a dome or column of cold air within a thunderstorm, which is heavier than the surrounding warm air and produces a steep pressure gradient and high winds. This rapidly descending column of air is from ½ to 2 miles in diameter and is active for 5 to 15 minutes. As it hits the surface of the water or land, it spreads out in all directions like the spokes of a wheel rather than in the tight circular pattern of a tornado. Winds average about 30 knots with gusts as high as 150 knots and shift radically in direction as the storm passes. At night, they are often confused with tornadoes because of their shifting winds and violence. They occur in the United States predominantly during the spring and summer and are generally associated with towering cumulus clouds or thunderstorms. There are dry microbursts and wet ones, identified by the absence or presence of rain with the storm.

On 1 August 1988, at Andrews Air Force Base near Washington, D.C., the wind from such a disturbance began at 1409 from the northwest. Less than one and a half minutes later, it peaked at 120 knots. It dropped to 2 knots as the center passed, then again peaked from the opposite direction at 84 knots. Only minutes before the microburst, known to pilots as *wind shear*, Air Force One had landed on a dry runway with little wind.

The microburst is often seen in unsettled weather or building cumulus clouds without an associated thunderstorm, and with no opportunity for preparation, events can move so fast that a sailor may be overwhelmed. The only warning may be that it is a dirty-looking day, with possibly a rapid shift and increase of wind, which will be considerably colder than before. The ocean is sometimes flattened beneath the down draft. These violent winds often have no accompanying rains, thunder, or lightning, which differentiate them from the usual high winds of a thunderstorm and are called *white squalls*. Although it is rare for a medium-sized sailboat to be knocked down by a steadily increasing wind if prompt reductions of sail are made, there may be little time for this when a microburst hits.

Because microbursts strike with little warning and are more prevalent than their more obvious cousins such as waterspouts and tornadoes, the sailors must be ever alert during dirty squally weather and ready to take instant action if such a squall is encountered, either with or without the presence of a thunderstorm. Unfortunately, not all sailors are that watchful. In April of 1988 after entering Ponce de Leon Inlet from the ocean, I turned south for an anchorage. Noticing heavy weather forming to the north, I tuned in the nearest NWS VHF station and noted that severe weather warnings were being broadcast. I quickly struck my sails and prepared for a blow. During the next hour, however, I encountered six vessels with full sails heading north toward the dark clouds.

Thinking that the conditions were ripe for downbursts, though no signs of thunderstorms had been seen, I called each boat as we passed to inquire if they were listening to the weather. Only one of the six had bothered! I suggested to each that they at least shorten sail, which most did. That night I learned that a downburst had hit only five miles from our passing point and had overturned a truck and trailer.

With a large sail area up, the boat may be knocked down and flooded through open hatches and ports, and such flooding can be so massive that the boat sinks. After a microburst is encountered, there will be no time to drop the sails. All sheets must be instantly released and allowed to run. If the wind drops, take in the sails and be prepared for the wind to hit suddenly from another direction. When it does, if sails are still up the sheets must again be let to run free.

LOSSES FROM MICROBURSTS

We should not leave the matter of thunderstorms, microbursts, and the freak weather associated with them without touching on the losses of the *Marques* and the *Pride of Baltimore*.

On 5 June 1984 the 88-foot English barque *Marques* was northbound seventy-eight miles off Bermuda under heavily reefed sails. Westerly winds of 35 to 40 knots and seas of 20 feet had made a rough start for the voyage, and the crew had carried out storm precautions. About 0400, the ship was hit by a squall with winds of over 60 knots and knocked down within ten seconds. Less than a minute later it went down with the loss of nineteen people. Only nine survived.

A report in May 1987 following a three-year investigation by the British Department of Transport found that the *Marques* was unseaworthy because of insufficient stability. The report further found that it was not the fault of any person that the barque had insufficient stability to resist the squall, but that in the light of experience and knowledge now available, she would not have been found adequate for operation as a sail-training ship in noncoastal waters. The report also found that the *Marques* was otherwise in a safe and seaworthy condition and in a proper state of repair. With certain reservations, the ship was found by the investigators to have been properly manned and sailed, and human error did not contribute to the disaster.

Less than two years later, the 90-foot American schooner *Pride of Baltimore* was northbound in a position 240 miles north of San Juan, Puerto Rico in 6-foot seas with a beam wind of 20 to 30 knots. Near 1200, having sighted squally weather to windward, the captain ordered all hands on deck to reduce sail. The ship continued under a double-reefed main and a full staysail. Shortly thereafter, without any change in direction, the wind increased to over 65 knots within seconds, knocking down the vessel. A large aft companionway hatch was open and the vessel, lying on its port side, flooded within a minute and sank within five. Four crew members were lost.

Though in both instances the crews were aware of threatening weather, the squalls' impacts and effects were so violent and sudden that no hands on either vessel had time to reach a sheet to release sails, or to bear up. For the same reason, no distress messages could be sent, nor any EPIRBs activated. The life rafts in both cases were torn loose and drifted free on their own and were then luckily grabbed by the survivors.

Two lessons from these latest in a long series of sailing ship storm losses are clear—carrying even reduced sails in the path of an approaching thunderstorm or squall can prove highly dangerous. If a knockdown occurs, the damage is compounded by open hatches or ports. Both of the doomed vessels were replicas of older types of vessel with large hatches and ports, and the down flooding was rapid and catastrophic when they were knocked down with the openings below water. Why they were left open is not known.

Microbursts have also recently claimed a number of non-sailing boats, including a charter boat with the loss of thirteen lives; a showboat with fifteen lost; and a sternwheeler with eleven dead; all were in protected waters. Larger sailing vessels lost to microbursts include the *Albatross* in 1961 and the *Isaac H. Evans* in 1984, the latter in protected waters.

DEFENSIVE MEASURES IN STORMS

Defensive steps, especially with a boat under sail, must be started when a thunderstorm is still some miles away. Though the lightning flash and thunder actually occur simultaneously, the thunder is heard five seconds later for every mile of distance because of the slower speed of sound: that is, thunder heard ten seconds after its flash indicates the lightning is two miles away. All lightning is accompanied by thunder. The so-called heat lightning of summer evenings is simply lightning too far away to be heard. Before a storm arrives, the following must be done on a boat:

1. Take in or drastically reduce sails. Get the main in, secure it well, then the jib. If furling gear is used, the jib can be deferred until the later stages. It will take little time and can be done from the cockpit. Bear in mind, however, that furling gear that normally works well may jam under the stress of high winds unless well maintained.

2. Secure all loose gear topside and below decks, as well as canvas dodgers and biminis. High winds can quickly shred or carry them away.

3. Close all hatches, ventilators, and seacocks not immediately required, and secure the boards or doors to companionways leading below. Small sailboats are especially prone to knockdown and flooding of the cockpit, and an open companionway with a low sill is an invitation to severe flooding. Discon-

nect electronic gear where possible to prevent extensive damage if lightning strikes.

4. Have all crew members don life jackets, and those assigned topside should have foul-weather gear and safety harnesses. Rig a jack line to attach the safety harness lanyards if movement about deck may be required.

5. If conditions permit or require it, anchor or lie to, though neither may be advisable if too near land, as it is impossible to predict the directions of wind in a thunderstorm. If anchored, be prepared to get under way if dragging, or use power to ease the strain on the anchor. In small open boats, rig a drogue to keep the boat end on to the wind and sea. Be wary of using an anchor with a low freeboard boat when high winds, seas, or current are running. If near shore, such small craft are best hauled out.

6. As the storm approaches, send all hands below who are not required on watch. Warn them to remain clear of metal objects if lightning is seen. If under way, place the boat on autopilot or lash the helm to minimize contact with the metal wheel.

7. If conditions become severe, the deck watch should be reduced or ordered below if sea room permits. The primary danger after the storm hits is from high winds and lightning. Thunderstorms are usually of short duration and have neither the time or fetch to build up heavy seas, and heavy rains beat down the seas. With ample sea room, and hatches and sails well secured, there is little real danger to larger or enclosed boats other than from lightning.

LIGHTNING

Like sharks, lightning has been seen by humans as a threat for eons, yet little is known about either. Benjamin Franklin first discovered that lightning was electrical in nature, but studies since that time have produced only two reliable axioms: (1) Lightning will not strike an object in a grounded *metal* cage, and (2) Lightning tends to strike the highest objects on the horizon. This last rule is not, however, inviolate. Lightning also tends to choose paths having the lowest electrical breakdown, a factor that many sailors use as an argument against grounding a boat (thus producing the least resistance to ground). The progrounding advocates, on the other hand, cite the first rule, though a fiberglass or wooden boat is only as safe as the metal grounding framework (cage) installed within it.

The threat of lightning is real enough, especially in the sunbelt with its ubiquitous thunderstorms (see figure 8.5). In 1986, a 44-foot Choey Lee ketch, lying at the same slip now occupied by my boat, was hit by lightning, causing thousands of dollars of damage to the electronics and hull. The owner was most fortunate in having just disconnected his VHF antenna before the strike. The action could have been fatal if the hit had occurred a few seconds sooner. Two years later, a new 43-foot sloop only fifty yards from my slip was hit, totally wiping out the electronics suite.

Figure 8.5 Vertical lightning in a coastal storm. *Courtesy National Oceanic and Atmospheric Administration*

The worst was yet to come, for lightning does strike the same place twice. During the passage of Hurricane Hugo in 1989, my boat, which was well bonded to a ground plate, was hit at exactly the same spot occupied by the *Choey Lee* three years before and with the usual complete destruction of the electronics gear but no hull damage. During this three-year period, three sailboats were hit at the same North Florida marina, and they were the tallest boats there, all with masts over 60 feet. None of the smaller sailboats or power boats were affected.

One cabin cruiser, however, after leaving the protective cover of the tall boats, was struck by lightning in the river. After a loud crash, the skipper, who was down below, found himself flat on the deck with ears ringing and skin tingling. The boat's electronic and electrical gear were wiped out. In the same period, two other cruising sailboats from the club were hit while under way. Strikes at sea are likely to be more severe because storms over water, lacking points to produce discharge, can build up electrical fields five times the strength of those occurring over land.

In summary, of seventy-five boats using the same marina in North Florida, six were hit in a three-year period. Five of the six were sailboats with tall masts. In every hit, the electronics suite was destroyed. Two of the six suffered hull damage, and one person was slightly injured.

LIGHTNING PROTECTION

One can probably minimize the chances of hull damage and personal injury by having a grounding system in the boat. Since few small boats are constructed with an adequate system, it will be up to the owner to install it. A typical grounding system consists of a straight high-capacity electrical conductor from the highest point in the boat to an exposed metal keel, ground plate, or engine propeller shaft (see figure 8.6). Large metal masses such as the engine and fuel tanks should also be included in the grounding to prevent side flashes of lightning within the vessel. Grounding wire should be #8 AWG copper wire or larger, connected firmly with corrosion-resistant hardware rather than solder, which can melt. A metal mast is itself a conductor, so the wire may be attached to its base and on to the ground object.

At anchor, a temporary ground system can be rigged as shown in figure 8.7. A proper ground theoretically protects the boat in an imaginary cone formed by a 45- to 60-degree angle from the highest grounded point on the vessel, usually the top of the main mast. It must be understood, however, that there is no certain protection against the powerful and capricious ways of lightning, and some people feel that the grounding system invites a lightning strike by providing a better path to ground. Well-grounded boats have been hit and their electronics gear severely damaged, but a grounding system should minimize the hull damage and harm to people from a hit.

LOCAL PHENOMENA

Freakish and unpredictable winds may occur as a local phenomenon in coastal areas adjacent to mountains. Known in different locales as williwaws, foehn winds, Chinook winds, Tehuantepecers, and other names, these sudden blows caused by cold air flowing down from the mountains can in minutes increase from a calm to near-hurricane force. Because of this, sailors should be wary of seeking protection close to a mountainous coast with winds coming from the land.

An entirely different action occurs locally in the vicinity of inlets, breakwaters, and restricted channels when strong tidal currents are opposed by fresh or strong prevailing winds. Under these conditions, seas become steep, confused, and dangerous to small boats. The conditions ease dramatically as the tide turns, or the boat clears the entrance and moves out of the current axis. The easiest passage through the bottleneck is with the current and wind both astern; with both ahead, progress is slower, but the seas should not be too rough. The worst conditions are a strong current on the nose with a stiff wind and high waves opposing it. In such conditions, consult your tidal current tables and decide if you should heave to well clear and wait for a change of tidal current. If entrance conditions appear rough, reverse course before entering the bad area. Trying to turn around in heavy breaking seas can invite a capsize.

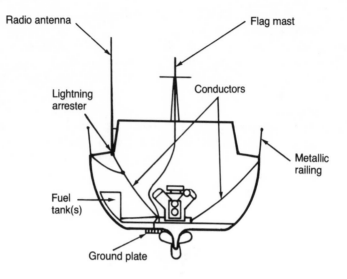

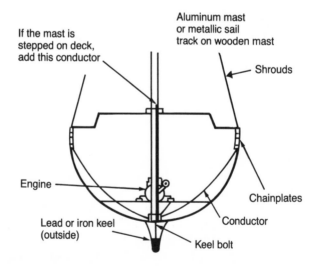

Figure 8.6 A. Bonding a motorboat and sailboat for lightning protection. B. Expected protection zones in properly bonded boats. Nothing, however, will protect attached electronics. *Courtesy USCG*

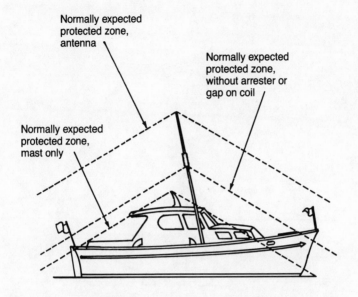

Normally expected protected zone, antenna

Normally expected protected zone, without arrester or gap on coil

Normally expected protected zone, mast only

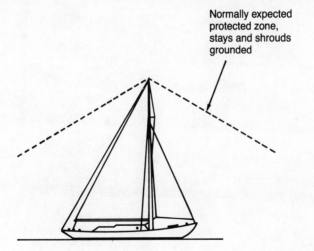

Normally expected protected zone, stays and shrouds grounded

B

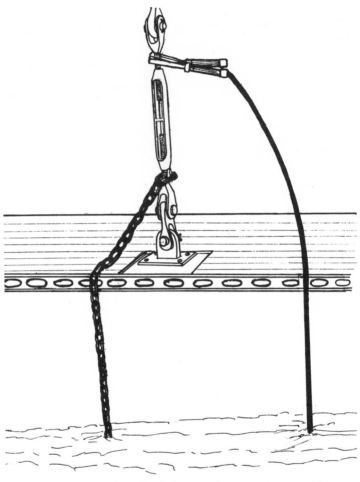

Figure 8.7   Using a length of chain or battery jumper cable as a ground from a shroud or stay to the water while at anchor.

Another dangerous local condition involves steepening and breaking seas as ocean swells move from deep water onto a shoal coastal ledge (see figure 8.8). The potential energy of the oscillating deep-water system is translated into the moving kinetic energy of breaking waves as the sea bottom contour causes a sharp steepening of the swells. This is commonly seen in shoal areas or approaches to inlets when high swells are running. One well-known example of this effect is the outer passage around Whale Cay in the Abacos, where large ocean swells generated by storms hundreds of miles to the north frequently roll in and produce steep dangerous seas in the shoaling water, even on days with little wind. A number of pleasure and commercial boats as well as lives have been lost in these steep plunging seas, known locally as a "rage."

But the most dangerous such areas in our North American waters lie along the Pacific Northwest coast, particularly off the Columbia River bar. Over the years, this treacherous stretch of water has claimed hundreds of ships and lives. On the afternoon

Figure 8.8 Boat entering a rough inlet. The steep seas caused by shoaling water are worsened by wind blowing against the tidal current. *Courtesy USCG*

of 12 January 1961, with gale warnings flying, the Cape Disappointment Coast Guard Station received a report of the 38-foot *Mermaid*, disabled and drifting toward the breakers. A 36-foot heavy-duty motor lifeboat was dispatched but with the worsening weather and light probably did not have the speed to reach the distressed boat in time. A faster but less seaworthy 40-foot utility boat was dispatched to try to keep the boat out of the breakers until the slower heavy-duty boat could arrive.

A larger 52-foot motor lifeboat was also dispatched and arrived at the scene after dark (fig. 8.9). Deeming the bar too dangerous to recross, the big 52-foot lifeboat stood offshore after taking the distressed boat in tow in winds of over 60 knots and 30-foot seas. The 40-foot utility boat, unable to stay at sea, attempted to cross the bar and was capsized. The crew was picked up by the 36-foot motor lifeboat, which then made its way to the Columbia River lightship before having to abandon ship because of damage incurred in the rescue. The disaster was quickly compounded by

Figure 8.9 A 52-foot motor lifeboat in breaking seas near where a sister craft was lost. *Courtesy USCG*

news that the rugged 52-foot motor lifeboat had capsized and sunk, with only one man picked up. Another 36-foot lifeboat from Point Adams took over tow of the *Mermaid*, but the fisherman was soon hit by a series of breakers and disappeared. In that terrible night, the sea claimed two fishermen and five Coast Guardsmen, as well as three Coast Guard boats and the *Mermaid*. It was a chilling demonstration of the power of storm seas in shoal water.

Today, the National Motor Lifeboat School at Cape Disappointment uses these same waters daily to train Coast Guard coxswains and others from many foreign nations how to deal with such killer seas. Though equipment and techniques change, the sea remains the same constant threat.

Such sea conditions also existed when a violent storm hit the northern California coast the night of 2 December 1985, creating 20- to 30-foot seas only three miles off the Golden Gate Bridge. The raging seas tore the pilothouse off the motor yacht *Girlfriend III* and holed the *Wynn D II*. The Coast Guard dispatched a helicopter and a 44-foot motor lifeboat. The rescuers sighted flares fired from both vessels, and headed for them.

Two hundred yards from the *Girlfriend III*, the 44-foot lifeboat was rolled 360 degrees in the dark, quickly recovering as it was designed to do but suffering over $10 thousand in damages. With only the engines still working, the lifeboat limped home, its crew grateful to be alive. An 82-foot patrol boat, a Falcon jet, two more Coast Guard helicopters, and three navy aircraft quickly joined the rescue effort. In a hazardous night operation, Lieutenant Michael Quinn hoisted a man with a crushed vertebra off the *Wynn D II* and took him to a hospital.

CGC *Point Heyer* then launched a rigid-hull inflatable boat (RHIB), which removed the three other men from the *Wynn D II* and brought them to the cutter. Because of the worsening storm, the small cutter was unable to reach the *Girlfriend III*, and the powerful 378-foot cutter *Morgenthau*, whose crew had been hurriedly recalled, sailed from Alameda at 0200. She raced toward the Potato Patch, which got its name in the nineteenth century when vessels with deck cargoes of potatoes spilled thousands of them in rough weather (see figure 8.10). This stretch of shoals

Figure 8.10 The 327-foot Coast Guard Cutter *Taney* fights her way through the huge breaking seas near the Potato Patch off the Golden Gate. Picture a yacht a tenth of the cutter's size in these seas. *Courtesy USCG*

outside the Golden Gate Bridge has claimed more than three hundred ships as victims since 1800.

Two hours after arriving, the *Morgenthau's* searchlights picked up six men clinging to an overturned raft. They had been in and out of the water for nine hours and had been pitched overboard from the raft five times. One man had been swept away during the night. A boat launched from the cutter picked up all the survivors of the *Girlfriend III* in just ten minutes.

Seas can also be disproportionate to the wind strength when

the wind is blowing against the flow of a major fast current such as the Gulf Stream. Hundreds of small-boat sailors cross the stream each year en route to the Bahamas and southern islands, and many of them have developed a firm resolve not to try it again, after experiencing winds over 15 knots against the current. Though the boat may be able to take the steep seas, such conditions can lead to a wet and less than enjoyable day. When winds increase above 15 knots and rise to gale force against the 3- to 4-knot current of the Gulf Stream, sea conditions become highly dangerous as seas steepen and develop a plunging action.

While I served at the Coast Guard Air Station, Miami, from 1958 to 1961, we were often faced with multiple cases of boats in distress after the passage of a strong cold front over the Gulf Stream brought strong northerly winds. One of the best known was the loss off the southern Florida coast of the new 43-foot ocean racing yawl *Revonoc*, owned and skippered by Harvey Conover, a highly skilled and respected deep water sailor. A long air and surface search turned up only one clue—a damaged dinghy. At the time, there was some speculation that the boat had been run down in a collision with a larger ship, but no proof whatsoever emerged. Other knowledgeable sailors theorized that the combination of gale-force winds blowing directly against the strong 4-knot current created killer seas that proved too much for even a seasoned crew in a well-built boat.

OFFSHORE STORMS

Despite all we have said about the improbability of prudent coastal sailors having to ride out a storm offshore, a few may be caught out by an inaccurate forecast, carelessness or procrastination, or blind adherence to a predetermined schedule. The options for a skipper riding out a coastal storm may be limited by wind direction and the proximity of coastal shoals and reefs. Because of a shoaling effect, seas may be steeper and with more pronounced breaking than occurs further offshore. Some such seas are so huge and steep that no defensive tactics can guarantee safety (see figure 8.11).

Figure 8.11   A 44-foot motor lifeboat close into a steep shore on the treacherous Pacific Northwest coast during training exercises at the National Motor Lifeboat School. *Courtesy USCG*

WAVE HEIGHTS

All waves (except tidal) are generated by wind. (See figure 8.12.) The height, speed, and length of offshore waves will depend on:

Wind strength and direction.   The stronger and steadier the wind, the higher will be the resultant waves. Wave height is measured vertically from the trough to the crest.

Duration.   The longer the wind blows, the higher the waves until a maximum height is reached.

Fetch.   The distance over which the wind is acting on the water surface is a major factor. A wind blowing from shore has little fetch in close-in coastal waters, and seas will not become very high regardless of wind speed and duration. On the other hand, steady trade winds acting over hundreds or thousands of miles may produce significant wave systems with only moderate

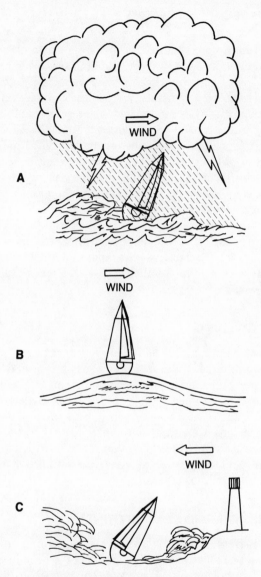

Figure 8.12 Three types of waves from the same storm. A. Storm waves driven by high winds with many whitecaps and some breaking. B. Swells radiating from the storm with little local wind or breaking. C. Plunging and spilling seas as swells move into shoal water. These can be dangerous even on days of calm winds.

wind speeds. Because thunderstorms are local in nature, both fetch and duration are very short, and high seas seldom result.

Since high winds blowing for long periods over great distances are required to generate really big seas, such seas are not common. All these factors are seldom present simultaneously, especially in the coastal area where fetch may be limited, and safety can be sought in a harbor before the seas have time to build to dangerous proportions. This build-up time may be as much as twelve to thirty-six hours. On the negative side, we have noted the severe conditions caused by coastal shoaling, ocean and tidal currents, and local inlet conditions. A pleasure boater should promptly seek shelter before a storm develops fully, after which coastal waters will likely be more dangerous than those further offshore. If unable to reach shelter before the inlets become too hazardous, a boater should alter course and seek deeper water and sea room.

DOWNPOWERING

In nearly all cases a boat, whether under sail or power, will have to be downpowered as the winds and seas increase. It is much easier to reef and shorten sails early than wait until the boat is being overpowered and sails begin to rip or carry away. Driving a vessel hard under sail or power can cause structural damage or failure; even large warships have learned this hard lesson, as the ships of the U.S. Third Fleet did in the disastrous typhoon off the Philippines in December 1944, which cost millions of dollars of damage and hundreds of lives.

BOAT DESIGN AND SEAWORTHINESS

A boat's performance in heavy weather, excepting crew error, will depend largely on the type and size of the boat, its stability, and whether it is under power or sail. The typical 30- to 50-foot-long keeled and sturdy cruising sailboat can deal with nearly any sea if handled by an able crew and downpowered to meet conditions.

Unfortunately, the demand for speed and the intense racing competition in the 1970s resulted in the development of fast, light boats with low freeboard, wide beams to permit carrying a greater sail area, greatly reduced, shallow hull wet areas to lower drag, and high centers of gravity. Though possessing high initial stability, the ultimate stability as the boat heels over is far less than in a traditional cruising boat and is exerted over a more restricted angle of heel (see figure 8.13). Deep spade rudders of high tech but vulnerable design were developed to afford greater control and maneuverability for the often skittish fin-keel racers. Some of these design features were incorporated into stock cruising boats.

The demand for racing performance often overruled safety considerations, and some designers and builders of cruising boats followed the trend. These inherent dangers were tragically exposed in the Fastnet disaster of 1979, when a third of the entrants were knocked down, and eighteen suffered 180-degree rollovers, many had rudder failures, twenty-four boats were abandoned, and five sank with heavy loss of life. Yet the larger, more solidly built boats came through in good shape. Even among the smaller boats (less than 38 feet), those built before 1975 had few problems, but the ones incorporating the new design look suffered badly. Later studies and analysis confirmed that similar accidents were occurring elsewhere and were closely associated with the lighter, beamier, and less stable designs. Numerous boats of this category are still in use, and many recreational sailors are presumably unaware of the dangers of their otherwise handsome boats in adverse conditions.

Anyone sailing one of the beamy and light racing-type boats built in the last ten to fifteen years should examine the matter further before taking one offshore in heavy weather. A book with an excellent coverage of the subject is *Offshore Yachts*, prepared by the Technical Committee of the Cruising Club of America and published by W. W. Norton, New York in 1987. Though detailed and thorough, it can be understood by the average recreational sailor.

Size and Stability

The size of a boat has an important bearing on seaworthiness, an obvious reason being relative scale. An ocean liner, a destroyer, and a 30-foot sloop react entirely differently to a twenty-foot sea;

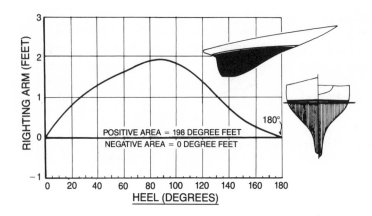

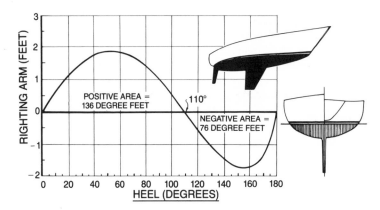

Figure 8.13 Stability curves for very different types of boats. (Top) This narrow, deep, heavy boat could not have a better range of positive stability. (Bottom) Light, beamy, and shallow, this typical IOR (International Offshore Racing Rules) boat of the 1980s has a stability range of only 110 degrees, which is about the point where the mast hits the water. From *Offshore Yachts* (W. W. Norton: New York, 1987), 72. *Courtesy Cruising Club of America*

the larger vessels are the least affected. The larger and heavier a boat, moreover, the more it resists being rolled by a breaking sea, because of its inertia, which is proportional to its mass (size and weight). A body at rest tends to remain at rest and requires a considerable force to start it rolling. The bigger the boat, the greater the force required to roll it, and few sailboats over 60 feet in length capsize. Heavy and high rigging also adds to the inertia and increases resistance to rolling; but it also raises the center of gravity, thereby reducing the righting moment.

Dropping a heavy centerboard lowers the center of gravity and increases the inertia (resistance to roll) by moving weight further from the axis of roll. Some believe that a deployed centerboard tends to trip the boat in a breaking sea, but other studies indicate changes of as much as 30 percent in keel area have little adverse effect, and that the most dangerous tripping factor may be the lee deck edge. A few have expressed fear that in a rollover, the heavy centerboard can fall back on the boat and cause damage. If conditions have advanced to that point, such a happening would seem to be merely an added woe.

Though size is a proved advantage in heavy weather, on sailboats this is often offset by the difficulty of handling the large sail area. Relatively few recreational sailors sail in boats over 50 feet, and the sea constantly reminds us that in dealing with the elemental forces of nature, there are few absolutes, including size (see figure 8.14). Some years ago, I was on board the Coast Guard cutter *Bibb* to coordinate air-ship exercises to the east of Bermuda. A severe storm with huge seas and hurricane-force winds moved into the area and hung on for two days. The 327-foot *Bibb*, a fine sea vessel, had to turn and run before the sea for thirty-six hours after having one of its port boats torn loose and heavily damaged. On the second day, word was received that a small 20-foot boat with two native fishermen was missing. It had last been seen forty miles west of the island just before the storm hit. The *Bibb* and several aircraft searched the storm-tossed seas for several days without success. After docking at Saint George, Bermuda, I told the press, "There isn't a chance that a 20-foot boat with a 12-inch freeboard could have survived. I was out there in

Figure 8.14   A Coast Guard cutter battles a North Atlantic storm and 50-foot seas. Midocean seas show less tendency to break and plunge than do seas in coastal storms. *Courtesy USCG*

the middle of the storm, and it couldn't have stayed afloat ten minutes."

Ten days later, and over two weeks after the storm had hit, a Military Airlift Command (MAC) aircraft en route to the Azores sighted a small sail to the east of Bermuda. A Coast Guard cutter ordered to investigate found the missing fishing boat. For over two weeks, with only rainwater and two cans of pumpkin, the two men had endured hurricane winds, followed by another severe storm, that had carried them from one side of Bermuda, past its treacherous reefs, to the other side. The information that the boat had a 12-inch freeboard turned out to be erroneous—it was only 9 inches.

Sails and Rigging

Regardless of the size of boat, strong rigging is essential in sailing vessels. Good design and workmanship are not enough; careful periodic inspections are required to insure safety and security. Sails properly carried help reduce the vessel's motion in wind conditions; even under bare poles, the combination of wind against the standing rigging and the inertial resistance to roll provides considerable relief from excess motion.

The coastal sailor who is not dedicated to racing will place comfort and room ahead of a large inventory of sails. Usually being short handed, he or she will also be less inclined to make sail changes. If a sailor does not perceive a great risk of unavoidable heavy weather, a storm forestaysail will most likely not be carried; in actual practice such a sail is not used often even by offshore sailors.

One of the most popular recent developments in running rigging has been the furling jib, and increasing use has been made of it for reducing the foresail when required. This has been made practical by the use of multiweight fabrics, especially reinforced to take the loads on partially furled sails in high winds, though furling jibs tend to bag when partially furled. The rig is not really suitable for full storm conditions or prolonged work, but it can be useful for limited periods under more moderate conditions. Another drawback is the position of the partially furled jib—far forward and high above the deck—resulting in greater heeling forces. (See figure 8.15.)

A heavy load is also placed on the light furling line, proportional to the amount of jib still flying. If a shortened-luff jib is to be used with the furler, a pendant must be rigged between the furler's top swivel and the sail head. There is then an angle between swivel and the jib halyard sheave that prevents the swivel from turning properly and can result in a jammed furler. A forestaysail rigged on an inner forestay is much more reliable, but not many such rigs are carried by cruising sailors because of the extra work in tacking with an inner forestay and running backstay, and because sailors perceive such a rig to be of limited use or need.

In using a furling foresail, caution must be exercised, for it

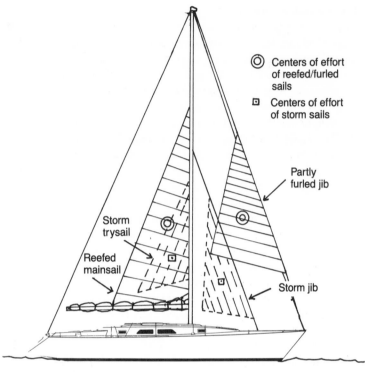

Figure 8.15 Center of effort in storm sails compared with that in a reefed main and furled foresail. Note that a partially furled foresail has a center of effort well forward and above that of a storm jib, and the boat may tend to fall off and run. Likewise, the storm trysail has a lower and more centered effort than does a reefed main. Storm sails cause less heel and yaw than do a shortened main and jib and are generally stronger material. The jib furling line is also vulnerable in prolonged blows.

can jam either from poor maintenance or from heavy stresses. A sailor is often tempted to get in the mainsail first, because it involves more work and exposure. But if the furler jams, as mine did in the knockdown off South Carolina, one must then handle a badly flogging sail on an exposed foredeck.

A conservative sequence as weather worsens is to (1) reduce furling jib, (2) reef main, (3) take in main, and (4) reduce jib to storm dimensions to maintain steerageway, or furl completely and lie ahull.

Downpowering the main sail can be accomplished by putting in one or more reefs or striking it entirely. Trysails are not commonly used by coastal cruising sailors.

In summary, reducing sails in time or taking them in entirely before heavy weather hits not only is essential to the safety of the boat and crew but is a more important factor than the sail inventory or rig.

POWER BOATS IN A SEAWAY

A powerboat, because it has less inherent stability, a higher freeboard, and a vulnerable superstructure with large windows, doors, and cockpit, is not as suitable as an enclosed cabin sailboat for heavy weather. Lacking a deep keel and the stabilizing effect of sails, most powerboats roll heavily. This not only makes them more susceptible to capsizing but quickly brings on seasickness and fatigue, with devastating effects on human performance.

With its greater speed, however, the powerboat can usually flee to a protected anchorage rather than fight the weather. Most high-speed motor boats have planing hulls, derived from the seaplane hulls of the 1930 to 1950 period, featuring a sharp bow profile with a full flat after hull to facilitate planing or "getting on the step." The light weight permits easier planing and higher speeds, so ballast is limited. These light, beamy boats are thus vulnerable to capsizing in heavy beam seas, or broaching in following or quartering ones because of the lift of the broad stern section and the digging in of the deep bow. Broaching is less likely in boats fitted with a substantial skeg to resist skidding and fishtailing in following seas.

Few high-speed planing boats are safe in offshore heavy weather and should quickly seek shelter on the approach of a storm. If a boat is caught out or if entrance conditions make a return to shore inadvisable, it is usually safest to take the seas off the bow at a speed just sufficient to give rudder control. A course parallel to steep seas invites a capsize and must be avoided even if a zig-zag course to either side must be steered to make good a desired course that happens to parallel the seas (see figure 8.16). Running before a sea while varying speed to stay with the waves is a choice that will depend on the type of motorboat, the size and vulnerability of its cockpit and superstructure, and its speed. In small, open outboard motorboats with low transoms, presenting the stern to the sea is inadvisable, and keeping the seas off the bow is perhaps the best of a bad situation. With a powerboat in heavy seas, fuel and engine failure are a constant concern, for without power it will lie beam to the seas with capsizing or structural damage a constant threat.

Figure 8.16 During tests, a 30-foot motor lifeboat takes a heavy breaking sea on the bow and survives. A beam sea would have rolled it over. *Courtesy USCG*

V-shaped or constant deadrise displacement hulls are far safer in rough water, and the more complex cathedral hull designs also have shown promise. Among the most seaworthy powered pleasure boats are the modified trawler types featuring round deep bottoms, sensible superstructures, good stability, ample rudder control, and often a small steadying storm staysail. Many have bilge keels to reduce rolling, and a few larger ones have stabilizers or antiroll devices. Most have a large fuel capacity, an important asset for powerboats, which must at all costs maintain steerageway in heavy weather.

Let us again emphasize the strong point of high-speed motorboats—the ability to run for shelter before a storm hits or entry conditions become hazardous. Their poor sea-keeping qualities in heavy weather are numerous, and even if they survive a major storm, the crew will take a fearful beating, which by definition is not pleasure boating.

Small, open motorboats are even more vulnerable and must seek shelter ahead of threatening weather as a plain matter of survival. Though such boats are sometimes seen fishing thirty to forty miles offshore, it is foolhardy unless the boat is equipped with radio and a constant watch is kept on the weather.

MULTIHULLS

Few subjects are as controversial among offshore sailors as the relative safety of monohulls and multihulls in heavy weather. The controversy centers around the stability of a multihull. It has a tremendous initial stability (although some claim that this imposes severe strains on the rigging), but the righting moment reaches its maximum force at a fairly moderate angle of heel and then rapidly diminishes as the heel further increases. If the large multihull exceeds its recovery angle and capsizes, it is virtually impossible to right without outside help (see figure 8.17). In the inverted position, an intact multihull is nearly unsinkable but offers a precarious refuge. The safety record of multihulls offshore leaves much to be desired.

By contrast, the *well-designed* monohull's righting moment increases until it reaches the 90-degree (knockdown) position,

Figure 8.17   A crew member from the capsized multihull *Gonzo* is hauled by line to a cutter that had been alerted via an EPIRB signal. Though having great initial stability, a large multihull cannot be righted by its crew once it has capsized. *Courtesy USCG*

and even when rolled completely over by a heavy sea, it is able to right itself. This righting capability is most pronounced in deep-hulled and heavily ballasted sailing vessels and least pronounced in shallow draft, beamy vessels with light ballast.

Some multihulls carry masthead flotation chambers as safe-guards against a 180-degree capsize, but the practice is still not widespread. Others use sponsons to increase their ultimate stability. In addition to the lack of ultimate stability, multihulls are subject to structural failure and a greater risk of damage when striking peak seas or floating objects because of their greater speed, which also requires greater alertness on the part of the crew than might be the case in a slower monohull boat.

Experienced multihull sailors are divided as to the best storm tactics, some advocating lying a-hull and others opting for running off. The latter group further differ on whether to run off at high speed or at a slower speed trailing warps or lines. In the coastal region, or at least those sections having gradually shoaling and sandy beaches, in extreme circumstances a multihull can be sailed through the surf and beached. Though this seems a last-ditch measure, the maneuver itself is routine with small sport multihulls on any summer afternoon at the beach.

MONOHULL SAILBOAT STORM TACTICS

The wisest tactic for any coastal sailor in dealing with a major storm is to avoid it. This is practical advice in an area with numerous inlets and refuges, though not always possible well offshore or even along coastal areas having long runs between inlets.

If you find yourself at sea in heavy weather, should you reduce sail and continue; heave to; lie hull to; or run before the weather? Should a sea drogue be used? Will oil ease the breaking sea? No pat answer is possible, since every storm is different and what seems merely a fresh breeze to a deep-water sailor in a sturdy 43-foot ketch with a five-member crew may appear horrifying to a family caught out alone in an open 25-foot boat. The type and construction of the boat may also affect the choice of tactics, as will the experience and physical condition of the crew. A lack of watchstanders may force a skipper to adopt passive tactics prematurely or against his or her best judgment. Finally, five experienced skippers may elect to use five different approaches to the same storm—which probably appears different to each of them.

Fortunately, only a handful of us will ever encounter a "survival storm" in a lifetime of recreational boating. In a sea and aviation career extending over fifty years, I have been through a number of hurricanes at sea and in the air, in large aircraft and ships. But with the exception of short periods of intense activity around thunderstorms, I have seldom in a small boat had to ride out sustained storms with winds above 40 to 45 knots. This is partly the result of my aversion to the extreme discomfort of a fully developed storm, but it also results from careful attention to weather conditions and forecasts and a willingness to change plans as necessary. Even so, a few recreational boaters may be forced to deal with severe weather. Reading and learning from the experience of others can be highly beneficial. Practicing storm tactics in moderate conditions can then afford hands-on training.

The boat, whatever its design, will likely exhibit more endurance than the crew. A slow-moving and worsening storm will wear down any crew physically and spiritually, particularly with the heavy rolling and pitching associated with powerboats. Sailboats are more stable because of the dampening effect of the sails, rigging, and heavy ballast. Whatever the type of boat, the fatigue of the crew can become the greatest danger in severe weather.

Heaving to.   Taking into consideration the need for the crew to rest, one of the best tactics for a sailboat in average blows is to heave to—turning through the wind, backing the jib, and sheeting in the main to maintain a little headway. The boat will ride more comfortably, and with the helm lashed or locked to leeward, most of the crew can get some rest. Most boats when heaved to ride with the seas between 30 and 70 degrees off the weather bow. The boat will move ahead slowly under the drive of the mainsail until the combination of increasing speed and full lee helm cause the boat to turn toward the wind. When this occurs, the mainsail luffs, the boat slows followed by a loss of rudder effect, and the wind on the backed jib takes the bow to leeward. (See figure 8.18.) As the mainsail fills, the cycle is repeated. This constant oscillation shouldn't cause alarm, and the limits can be adjusted by changes in rudder or sail settings. Heaving to should be practiced and understood in moderate conditions, however, to avoid possibly overcontrolling the boat in real storm conditions. A good time to practice is before a meal when all hands wish to sit down together with a minimum of motion.

Heaving to can also be used to hold or loiter in one place while waiting for a favorable tide or rendezvous. To prevent unnecessary strain or holing of the foresail by the spreaders, no more than a 90-percent jib or furled-foresail equivalent should be used.

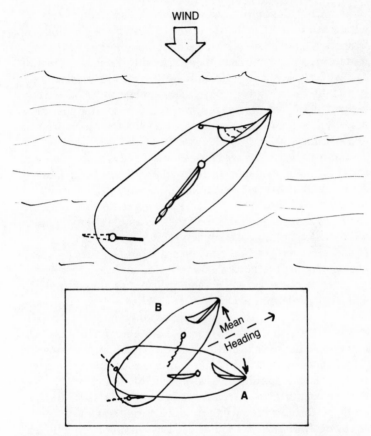

Figure 8.18   Heaving to. 1. Reef main and reduce to storm jib or partially furled foresail. Sheet both in hard. 2. Turn through the wind until jib backs and boat falls off. Apply lee helm to hold the bow up. A. With wind on the beam, the mainsail will fill and drive the boat forward. The rudder will then turn the boat toward the wind. B. As the bow turns into the wind, the mainsail will luff, the boat will slow, and the bow will fall off as the rudder loses its effect. The boat will slowly oscillate between A. and B., making little headway and largely tending itself. The oscillation and mean heading can be affected by the tension on the jib and main sheet and the amount of lee helm.

Running (Scudding). Another tactic is to run before the wind with only a small storm sail or bare poles. In moderate blows, such a course quickly eases the pounding felt during a beat into the wind and seas, though steering becomes more difficult with following seas. In really heavy weather, the boat tends to pick up excess speed, and as seas increase, the boat can be popped by an overtaking sea or broach and in extreme conditions may pitchpole. Trailing warps or a drogue may help slow down and stabilize the boat (see figure 8.19).

Running before the sea also imposes a heavy load on the person at the helm, who must be relieved frequently. With the small crews common to coastal cruisers, this rotation will quickly lead to fatigue and inevitable mistakes in technique and judgment. Lastly, running is feasible only if there is ample sea room downwind, which in the coastal region is often not the case.

Beating into the Sea. When sea room becomes a factor, a course may have to be laid into the wind and sea. This will require active steering, while keeping speed as slow as possible and still maintaining steering control. When a steep or breaking sea is encountered, the bow is aimed directly at the breaking crest, after which it is quickly pulled off to maintain speed. Use of the engine with sails may help in this situation. Beating into a sea will subject the boat and crew to increased impact forces with resultant fatigue and should be avoided if the circumstances allow. A more comfortable alternative is to keep the seas off the bow, while powering with the engine and a reduced sail rig.

Lying Hull To. A simpler but less comfortable tactic for a sailboat is to take in all sails, lash the helm, and lie hull to, allow-

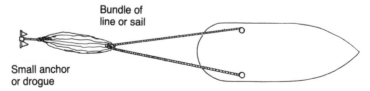

Bundle of
line or sail

Small anchor
or drogue

Figure 8.19 Trailing warps while running before the sea. Note that securing points on the boat are well forward of the rudder post so that the stern may swing freely and avoid a "bound rudder."

ing the boat to take its own heading. Most boats will then ride with seas on or near the beam, depending on rudder angle. Many very experienced sailors believe that a good boat, left alone, will look after itself and its crew. Certainly the numerous documented cases of abandoned vessels surviving in severe conditions lend support to this theory. It is also the simplest action for an exhausted and inexperienced crew to take.

A boat in this position in heavy seas, however, is vulnerable to a knockdown or falling off the top of a crest, especially motorboats or light, beamy racing boats. Under more moderate conditions, the greatest discomfort will be the rolling (see figure 8.20). Even under bare poles, the wind on the rigging will have some steadying effect but less so in lighter winds or the relative shelter of the troughs. With a normally rigged main boom, rolling while lying hull to can result in heavy stress on the topping lift, mainsheet, and main traveler. If a prolonged blow is anticipated under bare poles or a storm trysail, the main boom should be well secured to the boom gallow or the aft end lowered into the cockpit and secured before a gear failure occurs.

Figure 8.20 The schooner *Halcyon*, just after a rollover in a storm off Cape Fear, N.C. The boat is badly damaged, and the lone crew member is in the water as an RHIB from the cutter *Alert* approaches to rescue him. *Courtesy USCG*

(See figure 8.21 for a summary of the four basic choices for sailboats in storm conditions.)

DROGUES AND SEA ANCHORS

None of the above tactics (heaving to, running, beating into the sea, or lying hull to) guarantee security in extreme conditions with breaking or plunging seas. A boat running before the storm can be broached by a big sea and knocked down while in this vulnerable beam-on position. The risk is even greater for the boat that has deliberately been placed beam to the seas while heaved to or lying hull to. Yet fatigue will eventually force nearly any crew into passive tactics after a time. Is there a safe passive course of action?

One method is to deploy a sea anchor or drogue. This is a method often recommended by experienced high-seas cruisers but little heeded or used by recreational sailors. They are not alone. Few of the major ocean-racing associations list sea drogues as mandatory equipment, and none of the boats in the 1979 Fastnet disaster carried one.

The traditional cone-type drogue must be quite large, with a diameter equal to 10 to 15 percent of the boat's length, and strongly constructed in proportion to the boat's displacement. Even so, such drogues exhibited substantial failure rates in recent Coast Guard tests. One problem is that a drogue will not hold a high-bowed boat into the wind. As the boat falls into a beam position, the drogue prevents it giving with the seas and imposes severe strains on the structure. Some sailors have reported success with surplus military cargo parachutes with a diameter equal to 50 percent of the boat's length. Though such chutes do hold the bow into the sea, there is the risk that the boat will be thrown back on its rudder and sustain disabling steering damage. While using a sea drogue in coastal waters, one must also constantly check that ample sea room exists to leeward. (See figure 8.22.)

In practice, few sailors carry a drogue for the following reasons:

1. Breaking wave capsize is relatively rare, and most sailors survive them by lying ahull, heaving to, or running off.

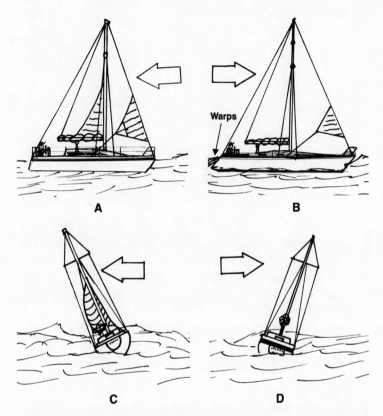

Figure 8.21 The basic choices for a sailboat in worsening weather. A. Depower by reducing or reefing sails. B. Run before the wind and sea with only a small storm jib and trailing warps. Either of these methods will require a helmsman to steer. C. Heave to with helm lashed down; this is the most comfortable stance if sea room permits. D. Lie ahull under bare poles. This is likely to be uncomfortable because of rolling and risks a knockdown or rollover in breaking seas. A well-found boat, however, will usually look after itself if left alone.

2. People do not think they will ever be in survival seas.

3. Most know little about drogues or their effects other than that they are expensive, hard to stow, and probably difficult to deploy.

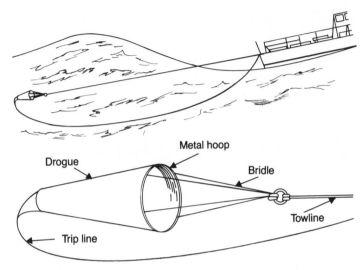

Figure 8.22   A sea drogue is seldom carried by pleasure boaters, and many of those carried by cruising sailors are too small and poorly constructed to be effective.

4. In a survival storm the crew is often tired and disorganized. If the drogue is difficult to deploy, they are unable to handle the job.

Following three years of extensive tests, Coast Guard research engineers have developed a new type of series drogue, consisting of ninety or more 5-inch-diameter sailcloth cones spliced into a ¾-inch braided nylon line with a conventional 25-pound anchor. It is deployed easily over the stern, keeps a constant tension on the line, and is more durable than other types of drogues. The Coast Guard report concluded that the series drogue, which is easily stowed and deployed, offers the best protection in very rough and breaking seas.

OIL ON TROUBLED WATERS

Like the sea anchor, the use of oil to calm rough waters dates far back into maritime history, and there are many cases attesting to its usefulness. I had occasion once to use oil in steep breaking seas while recovering a small boat in the shallow waters of the Yellow Sea off Manchuria and was impressed with the results. The most effective oil is that of animal origin. The spare engine lubricating oil carried on most boats is a substitute of limited value, and most small-craft sailors have neither the room nor the inclination to carry enough animal oil to be useful.

SEA ROOM

Most of the storm tactics discussed above require sea room. If being set on a dangerous lee shore or shoal is a possibility, there may be no choice but to motor or beat to windward, whatever the sea. If the set onto a dangerous shore cannot be checked, a distress call should be transmitted and preparations made to either take a tow or abandon ship. A last resort before going on to a lee shore is to use the anchor, but the chances of anchor gear holding in a heavy open seaway and high wind are slim. Even with heavy chafing gear, rapid rode failure is likely. The leeward drift may be slowed for a while, however, and some time gained for rescue or a possible change in weather.

This was the case with the 41-foot sailboat *Fine Wine*, caught in the backside of Hurricane Danny on 15 August 1985 near Grand Isle, Louisiana. The seven crew members were en route from Fort Myers, Florida, to Galveston, Texas, when according to the skipper, "Poor communications and lack of knowledge got us into the storm." The vessel anchored twice during the storm, but the high seas and 55-mile-per-hour winds broke the anchor lines both times. After the distressed boat was located by an Air Force C-130, a Coast Guard helicopter began hoisting the crew. Despite heavy rolling and a high mast that actually dipped into the shoaling water, three men were safely hoisted. The last four then boarded a small dinghy and pulled away from the *Fine Wine* to make the hoist easier. There were no serious injuries. In this instance, the weather was simply too much for the crew to handle. By dropping anchors, however, even though they parted, they did buy enough time for rescuers to arrive before the boat was set into the surf.

HURRICANES

There is little reason, given the efficient detecting and warning system of the National Weather Service, that any small boat should be caught at sea in a hurricane along the U.S. coast, and no one should ever stay out by choice. Most hurricanes originate far from the U.S. coasts and are tracked for days before becoming a threat. Occasionally, however, they form very close to our coast with little warning. On one occasion I was ferrying an aircraft from Norfolk to Bermuda; on checking the weather before departure I was advised that with the exception of a cold front one hundred miles off Cape Hatteras, there was little significant weather, and that the chances for formation of a tropical storm were slight. After we penetrated the cold front, however, the weather became progressively worse and the seas below appeared to be driven by winds well over 50 knots. Puzzled, we reported this to Bermuda Air Traffic Control and were told, "The weather you have reported is a hurricane that has just been located by a hurricane hunter aircraft." It had formed with almost no warning midway between Norfolk and Bermuda and only three hundred miles from the U.S. coast.

Such a rapidly forming storm was the undoing of a 38-foot sloop and its crew of three on 18 August 1991. They had departed Little River Inlet, South Carolina, on 16 August for a planned four-day delivery trip to Newport, Rhode Island. That same day, a tropical storm with winds of 45 knots formed just off the Bahamas and headed for the U.S. coast. Late that Friday evening the storm was upgraded to hurricane status and designated Bob. (Because of the warnings, I delayed sailing from Mayport, Florida, in my boat until the movement of the storm became clearer.)

As Saturday morning arrived, the doomed sloop was approaching Cape Hatteras, with Bob coming up rapidly from the south. By nightfall, Bob raged 250 miles east of Jacksonville, Florida, with winds over 75 knots. When hurricane warnings were issued for the coast between Cape Fear, North Carolina, and the Virginia Capes, the little sailboat was in the center of the declared danger area. Along that desolate coast, only Morehead City, North Carolina, by now well on the port quarter, or the Virginia Capes, still a day's sail ahead, offered a safe entry and sanctuary. The boat continued on, and on Sunday, Bob hit Cape Hatteras a glancing blow and roared toward the north, with hurricane winds extending well ahead to where the sailboat labored in 40-foot seas and 70-knot winds. In the midst of this, it was hit by a waterspout and dismasted. The two men and one pregnant woman abandoned ship in a life raft with a survival kit, rations, and three gallons of water, most of which were lost when the raft flipped several times.

On 23 August, two days after they were due at Newport, the boat's owner notified the Coast Guard and a search was immediately started. Because of uncertainty as to the lost boat's position, a large expanse of ocean off the mid-Atlantic states had to be searched. On the fifth day of the search, the raft was sighted by a Coast Guard aircraft, and a helicopter from the aircraft carrier USS *America* picked up the survivors. They had lived for ten days on fish and seaweed and had been without water for the last three days. Two survivors were too weak to get into the helicopter hoist sling, and Petty Officer Steve Doerner went into the shark-infested water to attach lines to them.

Having to ride out a hurricane at sea is unlikely in coastal waters, but this case once again shows that it can occur, and great caution must be exercised when tropical storms are anywhere in the area.

Remote as are the chances of encountering a hurricane at sea, many boat owners along our Atlantic and Gulf coasts have learned that boats in port can be hard hit despite advance warnings (see figure 8.23). This is primarily a result of the huge tidal surges of 5 to 25 feet, high winds, and wave action. In areas normally well protected, waves may roll over the land and sea walls at high tidal surge, and other boats dragging can become battering rams. Docks are often submerged and boats ride up on them two and three deep (see figure 8.24). Floating docks can float off their pilings and be swept along with their attached boats. Creeks and narrow bodies of water can experience currents of 10 to 15 knots from tides and rain-swollen runoffs. Faced with this ugly prospect, a boat owner has several options:

- Trailer a small boat to a secure inland location.
- Haul the boat at a marina and lash it down. Many marinas will not allow this because of possible liability for damages.

Figure 8.23   A hurricane in a protected harbor. *Courtesy USCG*

- Secure the boat well at a dock using old tires for fenders. Many marinas will not allow boats to remain during a hurricane because of the possible liabilities for boat losses and the probability of severe dock damage. The marina's policy on this should be ascertained before the hurricane season.
- Secure the boat with multiple lines to a mooring buoy that has an adequate weight anchor and chain, *but only if the chain has been recently inspected*. People can easily inspect their chain anchor rodes, but the chain portion of a mooring buoy is subject to much greater corrosion and because it is beneath the surface, it is seldom examined. In two recent hurricanes, mooring failures were largely a result of the failure of the chain portion of the mooring rather than the rope pendants between the boat and buoy. By contrast, the easily inspected chain of an anchor rode seldom fails.
- Anchor the boat in a protected hurricane hole or bight where the seas have limited fetch, preferably one with good holding ground, a mud or sand lee shore, and normally little current. This should have been selected well in advance and the boat moved there twenty-four to thirty-six hours ahead of storm passage to avoid being crowded out. Anchor as far as possible away

Figure 8.24   Wreckage in a Texas marina after a hurricane. High tides and other boats often cause more damage than wind and waves, making a marina a dubious shelter. *Courtesy Boats/US*

from concentrations of other boats, which are likely to drag and become battering rams. (See figure 8.25.)

• Staying aboard, either at anchor or at the dock, is *not* a viable option. Though a boat with an experienced watch may suffer less damage than when unattended, the human risk is far too great for the average boat owner.

Whichever course of action is chosen, have a prepared hurricane plan similar to that shown in Appendix C, Operating Checklists.

STORM ANCHORING

Anchoring in or ahead of an approaching storm requires planning and continuous alertness, for dangers exist even in a seemingly protected anchorage. One study of two hundred accidents involving world cruising boats revealed that forty-two re-

Figure 8.25 Boats smashed against a railroad embankment at Stonington, Conn., during Hurricane Gloria in 1985. Of fifty boats that went aground, thirty-five parted their rodes because of chafing at the bow roller trough. Similar scenes were repeated during Hurricane Bob in 1991. *Courtesy Paul Stiephaudt*

sulted from a failure of the anchor or rode. Over half of these forty-two boats were later judged to be total losses.

Anchoring ahead of a hurricane is a special case, for there will usually be at least twenty-four to forty-eight hours warning and preparation time, and unlike many cruising situations, the boat does not have to be occupied during the storm. Because of this, somewhat different precautions should be taken. All removable gear, sails, and canvas topside should be stowed below or ashore to reduce wind drag and possible damage. Anything left topside should be firmly secured and lashed down with double ties. Valuable items such as electronics gear and sextants should be removed and stowed ashore to avoid damage by water or lightning. Before leaving the boat, close off all seacocks except the bilge pump exhaust and the cockpit drains. Plug the engine exhaust with a tapered wooden plug to prevent back flooding into the engine. Insert covers or seal off dorades and ventilators.

In severe weather, the working anchors carried by most small boats will probably not hold, even in normally good holding grounds, because the anchor is likely to be broken out by the pitching of the boat in heavy seas. With adequate time to prepare, the holding power of anchors can be greatly boosted by laying two in tandem on each rode. The inboard anchor will keep the chain to the outboard one horizontal, causing it to dig in rather than break out. Numerous boats remain at the dock or hauled out during the passage of a hurricane, and arrangements with their owners or the marina for the temporary use of a couple of anchors and short leads of chain can be made.

With anchor-holding power increased by tandem or multiple anchors, chafing at the point where a rode leads overboard through the anchor roller or bow chock becomes the greatest threat (see figure 8.26). Ample chafing gear should be placed at this point and extended far enough to protect the rode where it may wrap around the bow or bobstay. A split neoprene hose, slipped onto the rode and secured to it by heavy cord, provides good protection.

To buy more time, rig a snubber line on each rode. Using 10 to 15 feet of half-inch stretchy nylon, attach the line to the main rode about seven feet outboard using a rolling hitch. Lead the snubber line back to a securing point separate from that used for the rode. Then ease out the anchor rode until the snubber line is carrying the strain of the anchor. Make it fast, leaving about 2 feet slack in the main rode above the rolling hitch. Next adjust the chafing gear of both lines, so that the now-taut snubber line is protected, as is the main rode should it later have to take the load. Do the same for the other anchor rode. With this setup, assuming the anchors hold, four lines must chafe through or four securing points fail before the boat goes adrift.

Such a double tandem anchor system is seldom possible for recreational sailors running for shelter before a storm, as most will have only two anchors. Because a parted rode permits little time to react (dragging usually does), most sailors prefer two rodes with single anchors rather than two anchors in tandem on a single rode.

Two rodes, of course, increase the risk of fouling as the boat swings and will have to be cleared after the storm passes. If the rodes also have tandem anchors, this can be a back-breaking job, but it is much preferable to a lost boat.

Snubber lines should be rigged any time severe weather is

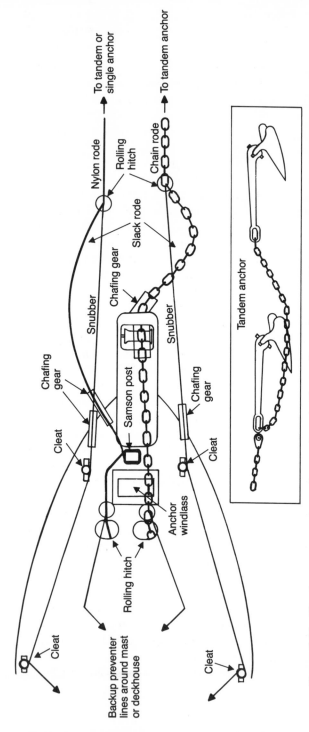

Figure 8.26 Hurricane or severe weather anchor rig. Two rodes and two snubber lines are used, each made fast to two different securing points. Thus four lines or eight securing points must fail before the boat goes adrift. Chafing gear must be rigged on rodes and snubbing lines where they lead over the side and for several feet outboard for protection against chafing on the stem or bob stay. If cleats are of doubtful strength, a strong bridle should be led from them around the mast or deckhouse as a backup.

expected, whatever the rode and anchor makeup. This will buy priceless time should a line part in a crowded or confined anchorage. I was once forced to anchor in a strong current because of engine failure, and the new ⅞-inch nylon rode completely frayed through in less than ten minutes. Fortunately I had a backup line ready, which held until the problem was resolved.

ROPE OR CHAIN?

The most common rode material for small craft is twisted nylon, which is strong, stretchy to absorb surge loads, lightweight, and relatively cheap. It is also much easier to handle if the anchor must be hoisted by hand. It is, however, vulnerable to chafing when under heavy load, and unless it is combined with chain or a riding weight to exert a horizontal pull, it tends to pull upward and break out the anchor. A short length of chain at the anchor end will exert horizontal pull and protect the rode against chafing on a sharp bottom. The rode must be well secured in the bow roller trough or chock by lashings or a bolt to prevent it from coming adrift with resultant damage to the rode and the boat's structure. A snugly fitting bolt also prevents distortion of the roller trough by heavy side pressures.

Chain is much stronger than rope and not as susceptible to wear and chafing. Its lack of stretch and give, however, will tend to break out the anchor with heavy pitching and can also wreck the bow roller fitting. Under severe conditions, snubber lines should be rigged with chain rodes to cushion the shocks.

ANCHOR WATCH

If riding out a storm at anchor, check frequently for dragging and for chafing of the rodes and snubbers. Pay out more scope and use riding weights to keep the anchor from breaking out. Pay out a few feet of line and adjust the chafing gear if chafing is noted. The engine may be used to ease the strain on the anchor rig, taking care not to overrun the anchor.

POSITION IN AN ANCHORAGE

If you have confidence in your ground tackle, a good place to anchor is to windward of a mass of boats and under the lee of the shore. This is not as desirable a location if the weather is squally with drastic and unpredictable wind shifts. But with a predictable or steady wind it has the virtue of being well clear of the main body of boats if they begin to drag in heavy weather. The advantage of such a spot was demonstrated when a summer storm hit Nantucket Island on 18 August 1986. In late afternoon, a 140-foot schooner was observed dragging in the crowded Nantucket Harbor, and a Coast Guard boat was dispatched to help her reset her anchor. As the winds increased to 60 knots, Mayday calls began flooding the Brant Point Coast Guard Station from other boats at anchor that had begun dragging. Some dragged into other boats, while others were taken in tow throughout the night by a hard-working Coast Guard boat crew. One yacht dragged into a dock area and began bouncing off the docked boats before being lassoed by the rescue crew and towed clear. When dawn came, seventy-five boats had been washed up on Nantucket beaches or damaged by the storm. Brant Point Station had received twenty-six Mayday calls and all of them had originated in Nantucket Harbor.

An alternative spot to anchor, if there is room to leeward, is well downwind of the main body. Though this leaves you exposed to any dragger, it does leave you freedom of action, and you will not drag into another boat.

I once anchored to the leeward of a large fleet formation lying off the coast of China in relatively shoal water. During a night of heavy gales, I was twice called to the bridge to get up the anchor and maneuver to reset it. On the third call, an examination of the chart showed no obstructions and the same depth of water for another six miles downwind. I left appropriate night orders with the officer of the deck and turned in for a good night's sleep. By the following morning, we had dragged two miles but were none the worse for wear. In the main anchorage, however, a destroyer had dragged down onto an amphibious ship, catching its chain in the smaller vessel's screw and causing considerable damage. The middle of a pack of dragging and swinging vessels is no place to be, and the upwind or downwind positions help avoid that predicament. Whatever your spot, in heavy weather, vigilance in an anchorage is as essential as at sea.

SUMMARY

The coastal cruiser and those who occasionally go further off-shore must beware of and respect the threat of heavy weather. The threat can be minimized, however, by:

1. Keeping current on existing and forecast weather.

2. If the weather is worsening or forecast to do so, postpone the trip for a day or so; if already under way, promptly seek suitable shelter. On anchoring, carry out heavy-weather preparations.

3. Do not deliberately sail into bad weather just to meet a schedule or be macho. You may find a storm too big.

4. If unable to reach shelter, or if caught by severe local weather, make all storm preparations as early as possible. If on a lee shore or off a breaking bar or inlet, stand off and seek sea room. The ocean is most dangerous at its edges.

5. Depower the boat before conditions worsen and try to minimize crew fatigue. If necessary, alter course for a better ride or heave to. As a last resort, run before the sea or lie hull to if sea room and conditions permit. Consider the use of warps or drogues, preferably trailed over the stern.

6. Do not panic and abandon a storm-beaten boat unless it is sinking. Even a waterlogged boat may be better than a life raft in heavy weather. When rescuers arrive, consult them on further action.

7. When riding out a storm at anchor, remain alert and be prepared to take prompt action if required. Many boating accidents occur at anchor.

9

Man Overboard

Despite the vast improvement in boats and nautical equipment over the centuries, crew members still fall overboard. In the 1980s, this has resulted in the deaths of several highly experienced, world-class racing sailors. Such mishaps are always unexpected and in rough cold waters bring on shock, disorientation, and panic, which quickly incapacitate the victim. Even strong swimmers may have difficulty staying afloat without flotation, so little cooperation should be expected; help must be brought to the victim. Because survival time may be measured in minutes in the worst-case scenario, rescue efforts must be rapid and effective.

Many victims are never sighted again after going over. In heavy seas, with a low height of eye, a person in the water is mostly hidden in the troughs and is very difficult to see; a night sighting is nearly impossible without visual aids or a whistle. So it is essential that the first available crew member be designated as a spotter with the sole duty of keeping the victim or marker buoy and lights in sight.

Even after the victim is located and the boat brought alongside, hoisting the person aboard will prove surprisingly difficult if he or she is exhausted or comatose. Many survivors of naval battles and marine disasters have been lost alongside rescue vessels, despite all the efforts of strong, trained seamen. Pleasure-boat crews, often emotionally upset and some in mediocre physical condition, have to work from unstable platforms with poor leverage and are at a particular disadvantage. Finally, with small crews, a predetermined assignment of duties in event of a man overboard is subject to last-minute change, depending on who has fallen overboard.

Before getting under way, new hands should be briefed on the safety rules existing on the vessel and assigned duties as outlined in the boat's Emergency Bill (Appendix B). Though this may seem to smack of man-of-war routine, it does inspire confidence among the crew, especially novices who may be understandably anxious. *After an accident occurs is no time to brief a crew!*

Don't assume that everyone knows what the old salt knows and does subconsciously:

1. Always hold to a solid structure with one hand.
2. Walk with feet well spaced and knees bent, or in bad weather, crawl.
3. Wear deck shoes with good tread.
4. Avoid walking on a wet deck with bare feet.
5. In heavy weather or darkness, always wear a life jacket and harness clipped to a strong jack line or fixture.
6. Never leave the cockpit to go on deck in bad weather without another hand topside.

We would also discourage standing by the lee rail to urinate in heavy weather, a practice that is reputed to have diminished the male seagoing population over the years.

All children under ten should wear life jackets when they are topside, and small children should be secured by a line when not under the continuous eye of an adult. A simple harness with a short tether fastened to the back may be substituted for a life jacket on hot days. If despite all this, a small child were to fall overboard, a strong swimmer (preferably the father or mother) should have been designated to go over with a personal flotation device (PFD) to assist, but only when OK'ed by the skipper. Then full man-overboard procedures should be followed.

Along with the precautions, use common sense. In protected

waters and benign weather, people can relax. But falling overboard in darkness, cold, and high wind and seas, combined with surprise and shock, can be lethal in minutes, and Coast Guard and police accident records are replete with accounts of healthy and experienced people drowning with help only yards away. If weather conditions worsen, the skipper must decide when to rig jack lines, when to require life jackets or harness, and when to double the watch or take other precautions. Pleasure boating should live up to its name whenever possible, but it should also be safe.

BOAT SAFETY EQUIPMENT

Lifelines and stanchions must not be used as a primary handhold or snap on for the harness lanyard. Most rigs are not stressed for this. Grab rails, as the name implies, exist for that purpose. Either strongly mounted deck padeyes or jack lines should be used to attach the safety harness lanyard. Jack lines are rigged from cockpit to bow on either side. If the lanyard is hooked onto the weather jack line when going forward, a fall will end on deck rather than over the lee side. Some jack lines are made of rope, others of plastic-covered wire, and some of stainless-steel wire. Wire does not, however, have the stretch and cushioning effect of rope in case of a fall. Grab lines or loops can also be placed in key spots on the boat to afford a handhold when needed. Sail tie material is good for this, because it is strong, easy to grip, and holds a knot.

Any boat operating on exposed waters should have ready for immediate launching a horseshoe or ring float, a marker pole, and a floating strobe light, all attached together by floating polypropylene line. Some skippers keep a buoyant seat cushion at the steering station with a watertight electric lantern attached. If a crew member should fall overboard, the person at the helm stands, switches on the lantern, and throws the cushion and lantern over. He or she then pivots aft and throws over the horseshoe, pole, and strobe light. The entire evolution requires about fifteen seconds. The few seconds saved in deploying the first light could be vital and the two lights give a reference range to the individual in the water.

In the cockpit, there should be readily accessible one of the most valuable but most ignored tools to bring a victim alongside—a heaving line. If a boat can be placed within fifty feet of the victim, any reasonably proficient seaman can place a heaving line within reach of the victim. The person can then be hauled in to the place on the boat where you wish to take him or her on board. It is quicker, safer, and easier than any other method of man-overboard rescue. For security, a loop can be made in the end of the line or a floating horse-collar used. The line should float, to assist the victim in grasping it as well as to keep it out of the propeller. To use this centuries-old recovery tool, one needs to know only how to heave a line, which will take ten minutes of instruction from an experienced sailor. A bonus will be a noted improvement in getting lines ashore while docking. A patented heaving line with collar can be purchased commercially, or an equally suitable one made up at home.

The other recovery gear can be quickly adapted from equipment already installed on the boat for other purposes, such as a boarding ladder, swimming or fishing stern platforms, and a vang purchase and mast halyard.

INITIAL ACTIONS

If despite all precautions, someone falls overboard, there is not any *best* way to return and get within heaving-line distance. The methods will vary with conditions, type of boat, size of the crew, weather, and visibility. There are preferred and proved ways, given a certain set of circumstances, but the final results will depend on common sense and good seamanship. The four basic tasks are always the same, however:

- Keep the victim in sight and afloat.
- Return to the person overboard as promptly as possible.
- Get a line on the victim for security.
- Haul the person aboard.

When cruising, the skipper should always mentally picture the proper actions if an overboard accident should occur, and the helmsman should visualize his or her possible actions in the prevailing conditions.

In every case:

1. When a person goes over, shout, "Man Overboard!" Immediately throw over a cushion or other floatable object if available, then follow it with the MOB pole, horseshoe float, and strobe light.

2. When the first person arrives on deck, order him or her to watch the victim's location and point at it continuously. Only then should the boat be turned or stopped. Many boats now have loran or GPS (global positioning system), which enters the present position into the memory with the push of a button. This should be done as soon as possible after someone goes overboard and updated again when the boat returns to the light or the victim's estimated position. Once punched into its memory, the computer will supply a continuing bearing and distance to that position, which can serve as a datum point if a prolonged search is necessary. At least two crew members should know the position storage procedure.

At this point all hands should be on deck and a decision made on how to proceed. If the skipper is the helmsman, he or she will remain at the wheel and give the necessary orders. If not, the skipper must decide whether to rely on the helmsman who is already there and adapted to the weather and light conditions or to take over the helm.

RETURNING TO THE VICTIM

The immediate decision is how to quickly return to the victim, for the person will seldom be able to swim to the boat. Whatever maneuver is used, *Keep It Simple*. Complex evolutions may look good on paper, but to a skipper newly arrived on deck on a black night, they can be confusing. The aim is simply to place the vessel within fifty feet of the survivor as quickly as possible. After sizing up the weather and sea conditions, rely on common sense and good basic seamanship to do this. With boats under power, this will be a straightforward evolution, preferably quickly stopping and backing down, or turning until the victim lies dead ahead.

MOB APPROACHES FOR SAILBOATS

Vessels under sail require more handling, but three basic approaches work well: the "spouse's maneuver" (turning through the wind), beating into the wind, and running downwind (racetrack pattern).

Spouse's Maneuver: Turning through the Wind

Tack through the wind, backing the jib; bring in the main tight; then use full lee helm to stop the boat upwind of and near the victim (see figure 9.1). While thus hove to, the boat's leeway will take it down toward the victim. The engine can be used and the main sheet and rudder trimmed to make small adjustments to the boat's fore or aft motion to keep it drifting toward the swimmer. The engine should be put in neutral or stopped when close. This heaving to maneuver should be practiced by all cruising couples.

A variation of the spouse's maneuver (turning through the wind) is to turn into the wind, start the engine, and drop the sails, making the approach later with power. Be sure after dropping the sails that *all lines are out of the water and the propeller is clear* before engaging the engine.

Beating into the Wind

If the victim has fallen over while the boat is beating into the wind, either the spouse's maneuver or its variation is suitable, since the boat after tacking is already in the desired upwind position and drifting down on the MOB (see figure 9.2). I prefer dousing the sails and using power as required to position the boat, again bearing in mind that lines may be trailing over the side after the sails are down, and they must first be secured to avoid fouling the screw. Leaving the sails up, especially with a small crew, may distract the crew's attention from the victim and may further risk the boat getting in irons or being set rapidly by the sails at a critical point in the pickup.

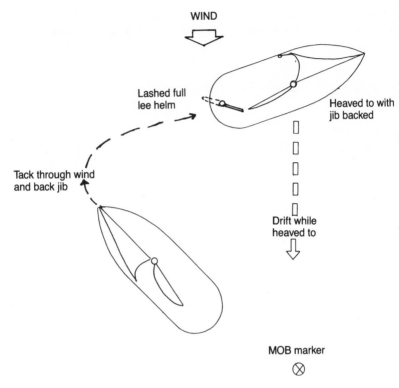

Figure 9.1 The "Spouse's Maneuver" for cruising couples or any two-person crew. If one goes overboard, throw over a marker and float. Then turn through the wind while sheeting in hard on the main and allowing the jib to back. Use full lee helm to prevent the boat falling off too far. With the boat heaved to, it will drift down on the victim until a heaving line can be thrown.

Running Downwind (Racetrack Pattern)

Running before the wind, where the boat is downwind of the victim, a "racetrack" pattern can be used to bring the boat back to a position upwind of the victim (see figure 9.3). As the boat is tacked to make its final approach, the jib should be taken in and the engine started if required. Approaching the pickup point, take in or slack the mainsail. Have a heaving line ready.

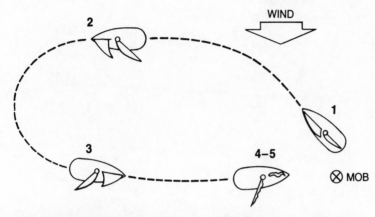

Figure 9.2 Man overboard (MOB) while beating into the wind.
1. Toss overboard MOB rig. 2. Open out on beam reach. 3. Jibe and
start approach. Take in jib. 4. On approach, slack off main to dead
slow.

THE PICKUP POINT

The object of any approach is to stop the boat, under control,
about fifty feet upwind of the victim. As the boat drifts down to
the MOB, a heaving line with a loop in the end, or a sling, can be
thrown to the victim, who is then brought to the boat at the desired pickup station. *Now comes the most difficult part—getting
the victim on board.*

PREPARING THE PICKUP GEAR

While closing the victim, equipment must be readied to get the
individual aboard whatever his or her condition. (See figure 9.4.)

1. Break out the buoyant MOB retrieving line of ½-inch polypropylene stowed in an accessible cockpit locker. This line has a
sling at the end for the victim, and five feet from the sling, a snap
hook to attach the hoisting tackle (if needed). This MOB line
should be at least 50 feet long. Make ready for heaving and secure
the bitter end snap hook temporarily to a cleat or lifeline.

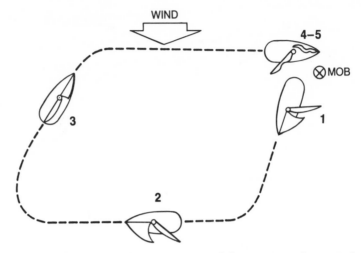

Figure 9.3 Man overboard (MOB) while running downwind: racetrack pattern. Toss over MOB rig. 2. Turn to beam reach. 3. Tack and fall off to a beam reach. Start and idle engine. 4. Place boat upwind, slack sails, and drift down on victim. Or, turn up into wind and luff alongside victim. 5. Throw heaving line or MOB line to victim.

2. In a sailboat, lead down a spare halyard (or the mainsail halyard) and attach it to the hauling (cam cleat) end of the boom vang. Unsnap the other vang snap shackle and attach it temporarily to the lifeline where the victim will be hoisted aboard.

3. Heave round on the halyard until the upper end of the vang (fully extended) is 10 to 12 feet above the deck. The hoisting purchase is now ready if needed.

While this is being done, a strong swimmer should put on a life jacket and a reversed harness attached in the back to 25 to 30 feet of floatable line and be ready to go over the side if necessary. The line must be attached to the boat and preferably attended.

TAKING ABOARD THE ABLE-BODIED SWIMMER

When within range, heave the swimmer the line and sling. With this line to control the swimmer's position, there is less danger of

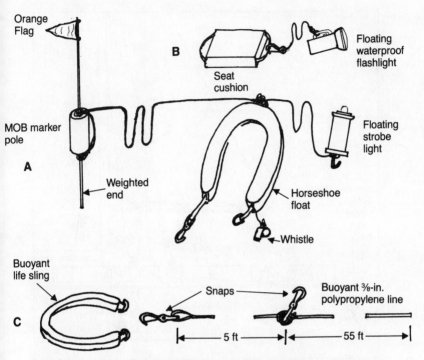

Figure 9.4 Man overboard (MOB) hardware. A. MOB pole attached to a horseshoe life ring and floating strobe light. B. Helmsman's seat cushion with a floating spotlight or flashlight for normal cockpit use, or for the initial marking of a man overboard. C. MOB heaving line with a snap hook at the end and another snap hook 5 feet from end. End hook is attached to the floating life sling. With the victim alongside in the life sling, the other hook is snapped on to the lower end of the hoisting purchase, or temporarily onto a lifeline or other securing point until ready to hoist the victim.

the boat drifting over him or her or the bow or stern conferring a nasty crack. If the victim is able to assist with the rescue, maneuver him or her to a swimming platform or a ladder and be ready to haul on the heaving line to help the person up. If there is no ladder but an adequate number of hands on deck, get several crew members on the line and pull the victim on board. Manually hauling a victim aboard is easier with a line and sling on the vic-

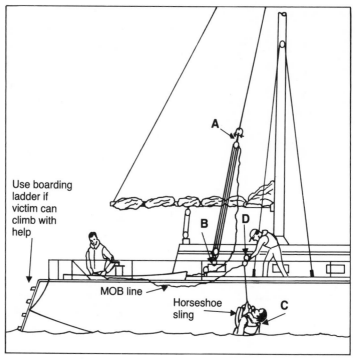

Figure 9.5   Using a purchase to hoist MOB aboard. Approaching the victim: A. Attach a purchase such as the boom vang or Cunningham to the end of a halyard. Hoist the connecting point to a position at least ten feet above the deck. B. Extend the purchase and snap its lower end onto the lifeline, ready for use. C. Throw the MOB horseshoe sling to the victim and pull him or her alongside. (If the victim is unable to get in the sling, a swimmer will have to help.) D. Attach the "five-foot" snap hook onto the lifeline or other securing point to keep the victim afloat alongside until ready to hoist. E. Fasten the "five-foot" snap hook to the lower end of the purchase. F. Heave round on the purchase and lead to a winch if needed. G. When at deck level, bring victim aboard.

tim but very awkward without them because of the lack of grip, space, and leverage. If any delay is expected, bring the victim alongside, haul the person up as high as possible, and take a turn on a cleat to prevent him or her from drifting away or drowning.

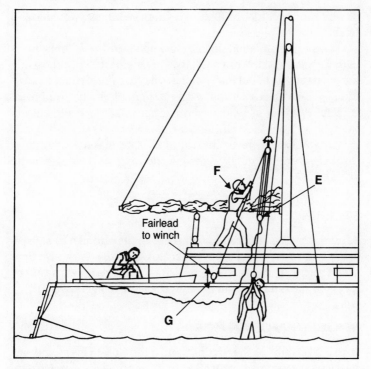

(**Figure 9.5,** continued)

RETRIEVING THE HELPLESS VICTIM

If the victim is unable to get the sling or bowline on, a swimmer may have to go over the side to assist.

With the hoisting gear ready, take the snap hook located several feet up-line from the sling and snap it to the lower hook of the prepared vang purchase. If using a simple heaving line rather than a special MOB line, throw a loop into the heaving line at the same location on the line. Heave round on the vang purchase to lift the victim over the lifeline and on deck. If short-handed, lead the hauling line through a block to a heavy winch. (See figure 9.5.) Drifting down on victims using bowlines with a heaving line is a well-proved technique that was used to save hundreds of lives in the cold, rough waters of the North Atlantic during the bloody convoy battles of 1942–43. Often swimmers were needed to assist the helpless victims.

With a short-handed sailing crew, the readily available mainmast halyard and boom vang provide ample lift. Powerboats do not have such gear, but many do have fishing and swimming platforms, which greatly simplify the recovery of victims overboard.

Engine power may be used during any approach after checking that no lines are trailing over the sides. When a few yards from the victim, however, the engine must be placed in neutral. A turning screw in rough water can be extremely dangerous to swimmers.

SECURING

After the victim is cared for, pick up lights and markers, especially in an area where other boats are operating. Watch for lines that could foul the screw. If a distress or urgent call has been made on the radio, cancel it when the emergency is over.

SEARCHING FOR AN MOB

If you lose sight of the victim, notify the Coast Guard and any boats nearby immediately. Before the arrival of Coast Guard search aircraft, mark the most probable position of the victim (datum point) with easily visible markers, obtain a good navigation fix, and guard VHF/FM Channel 16. Then begin searching using the *sector search* plan if the victim's position is known within close limits, or a *trackline search* if the spot is only known to be somewhere along the boat's earlier track (see chapter 14). When the rescue aircraft calls, give it all your information, then follow the pilot's instructions.

Do not give up! Numerous people have been rescued hours or days after falling overboard, while others seem to have given up or panicked and drowned within minutes. The victim must realize that in heavy seas or swells, he or she may not see the boat even when it is a few hundred yards away and should not lose hope. Searchers should stop their engines periodically to call and listen.

In July 1986, a Falcon jet located a man who had spent ten hours in the water after falling overboard from the F/V *Alaska* eighty miles south of Pensacola, Florida. The jet dropped a raft to the man and then vectored in the cutter *Point Estero* to pick him up little the worse for his ordeal.

In an incident off Cape Canaveral in August 1987, a twenty-one-year-old man from Tampa, Florida, treaded water and floated in the Atlantic without a PFD for twelve hours after being pushed over the side by another crew member during a mutiny on a fishing boat. Despite a bleeding head injury that attracted sharks during the night, he fended them off though he was brushed by some and nosed by one. He was found and picked up at daybreak.

One of the most unusual cases occurred when Franz Strycharczyk, the third engineer on the German freighter *Freiberg*, fell overboard in mid-Atlantic one thousand miles from the nearest land. He was not missed for several hours, at which time the ship reversed course and began searching. In the darkness the ship missed him narrowly, then continued on course searching. Swimming without any flotation, Franz was continually attacked by small pilot fish, who nibbled at his clothing. Seventeen hours after falling overboard, the exhausted swimmer was sighted by Ensign James T. Turman of the CGC *Absecon*, which had responded to the report of man overboard. When a cargo net was lowered to him, the courageous German climbed up under his own power and was soon walking about the deck. He was returned to his own ship, which paid for the stocky, 185-pound engineer with 185 pounds of German delicacies, including Lowenbrau beer.

The ability to survive in the sea seems to be dependent on the will to live as well as on equipment. Some people cling so tenaciously to life that they defy normal probabilities. Those searching for them must not give up hope until there is no possibility left for their recovery.

10
Medical Problems Afloat

Sailors are subject to the same medical problems afloat as they are ashore, plus a few peculiar to the marine environment. Yet some small-boat owners make few provisions for possible medical needs. If the boat is seldom far from an urban area with quick access to shore medical help, this omission may not prove serious. If, however, the boat will operate in isolated waters, adequate planning for dealing with medical emergencies is essential. Remoteness must not be measured just by geographical distance. On one occasion, we were only seventy miles from medical facilities, but we were storm bound for three days in an uninhabited island anchorage during which a crew member developed an excruciatingly painful toothache from an abscess. Fortunately, we had a good medical reference manual and a medical kit containing both antibiotics and pain-killing medication, which provided a satisfactory interim treatment until we reached medical help on the fourth day.

Any medical problems that occur on land can also occur at sea. We will arbitrarily divide these into five categories:

1. *Trauma or injuries*
At sea, we leave behind the auto accidents but assume the risk of falling from the boat's motion—often resulting in sprains, fractures, concussions, lacerations, and bruises. Wearing good deck

shoes prevents some of these accidents, especially toe injuries. Burns from the boat's stove are more common than burns from ranges ashore, and lacerations from anchor tackle and lines are common. Drowning and hypothermia are environmental risks, as are food poisoning and the bites or stings of insects and marine life. Younger people, because they are more daring and active, are more prone to trauma, but the aftereffects are more severe with older persons.

2. *Acute and unpredictable illnesses*
Heart attacks; severe infectious diseases such as pneumonia or flu; and acute abdominal or digestive episodes of various origins are included among possible unpredictable acute diseases. Infections of the ear or genito-urinary tract are common. Severe allergic reactions to foods, medications, and the sting or bite of insects and marine life affect a few people; they should carry medicines to treat such emergencies.

3. *Chronic, recurring, or slowly progressing illnesses*
With the exception of acute diabetic episodes, asthma attacks, and some seizures, these illnesses are not as urgent as trauma and sudden acute illnesses. The patient usually has a history of treatment and should carry prescription medications to treat the ailment. The skipper or designated medic should be told before sailing about an individual's health problem, where the medications are kept, and how they are used.

4. *Seasickness, constipation, diarrhea, sunburn, and emotional upset*
These ailments are common, particularly among people who are unaccustomed to a marine environment, but none of them are likely to prove to be either serious or pressing emergencies (except to the patient).

5. *Dental emergencies*
Dental problems are sometimes more difficult to treat than other medical problems because of the specialized equipment and skills required. Treatment may have to be confined to painkillers and antibiotics until a dentist can be reached.

Generally, only cases of trauma and acute illness need immediate treatment to avoid being life-threatening. After considering the probable cruising areas and locales, and the makeup of the crews, we recommend that the inventory of medical supplies and medical aid training be based on one of the following risk categories (severe weather delays may affect the risk categories):

1. Local day cruising with access to medical facility within 2 to 12 hours. Limited medical supplies similar to those in the home. First-aid training similar to the basic Red Cross course.

2. Coastal cruising. Access to medical facility within 12 to 36 hours. Fairly complete medical supplies. Advanced Red Cross first-aid training.

3. Overseas or remote area cruising. Few medical facilities available and access at least several days and occasionally weeks away. This requires an extensive inventory of medical supplies and advanced training.

MEDICAL AND FIRST-AID TRAINING

The capability and training of the persons who will administer and use the medical supplies will help determine which medical supplies to stock. Arrangements for adequately training the designated medics must have the first priority in the health care of the crew. Drugs are often ineffective unless properly prescribed, and they can be dangerous if misused. In administering medical help, the lay person must abide by the physician's guiding ethic, "Do no harm."

Most sailors will have had some basic first-aid training in school, the armed forces, Red Cross courses, or CPR training. More sophisticated courses are taught by the Red Cross, American Heart Association, and community colleges. One of these courses appropriate to your planned cruising level including actual practice in CPR and the Heimlich maneuver should be completed. Proficiency in CPR and the Heimlich maneuver is a must, for there will be no time to learn either life-saving technique after the need arises. Most other medical treatment can be delayed long enough to consult a reference book or seek outside advice.

RECOMMENDED READING

Classroom instruction should be supplemented by reading and home study. You'll find dozens of books on first aid, home treatment, and medical self-help in your local library and bookstore. In choosing the reading material, consider the following criteria:

1. Is the book outdated? Although basic treatment does not change that fast, the recommended medications and dosages may.
2. Is the format of the book easy for a lay person to read and understand? Is it well illustrated? Is the material well organized and quickly accessible in an emergency? If you have to dig for material and refer to a lot of footnotes, this may not be the book you want.
3. Does the book deal with symptoms and examination as an entry, then move on to a tentative diagnosis and treatment? Beware of books starting out with a disease class and working in the reverse direction. Lay people are not likely to know the overall disease picture, only the visible symptoms.
4. What level of information are you seeking? First aid publications for lay people are quite different from those used by doctors to prepare for medical specialty boards. You should look for a reference that covers medical emergencies and problems with the level of detail you need for the cruising level you plan.

A brief but broad overview is desirable to start the home study. Do not make the mistake of starting with an encyclopedia-sized medical reference that may prove incomprehensible, dull, heavy, and impossible to finish. We recommend as a starter a small and straightforward text written by a physician who is also a sailor, such as: Dr. Michael Cohen's The Healthy Sailor's Book (International Marine Publishing: Camden, Maine, 1983). This book emphasizes prevention rather than cures, and its study of human physiology in a marine environment is invaluable.

At a more advanced level is a book written specifically for use at sea by trained lay people, and a copy of this should be carried on board by coastal and offshore boats: The Ship's Medicine

Chest and Medical Aid at Sea (U.S. Public Health Service: Government Printing Office, 1984). This revised book was designed for the use of the merchant marine on ships not carrying doctors and is written in clear, understandable language. Its sturdy waterproof paper and loose-leaf binder permit insertion of supplementary material and revisions. The various sections cover human anatomy, vital signs and patients' history, diagnosis, and treatment; the section on medications and their ramifications is very complete. For most sailors, this one authoritative and well-illustrated medical reference satisfies all requirements. It may be obtained directly from the Superintendent of Documents, U.S. Government Printing Office, Washington, D.C. 20402. The cost is $44.00.

PROFESSIONAL MEDICAL ADVICE

Even the most intelligent and best-trained lay persons will have questions or be unable to handle some medical problems without professional advice. Such advice can be readily obtained in U.S. coastal waters if in range of a Marine VHF telephone operator or cellular phone system. First call the patient's own physician, who should be familiar with the patient's general health if not his or her specific problem. If the patient's own physician is not available, the partners or associates on call can usually be reached by the physician's telephone answering service.

Second, you may also make a presailing arrangement with an emergency physician's group at your local hospital. This insures that a physician trained in emergency medicine will be present if you call. A third method, which also insures that a physician will be there for your call, is to subscribe to a professional medical advisory service, which for a small fee or annual subscription provides medical advice to sailors and travelers.

If a serious medical emergency occurs far from hospitals but near other boats, a general radio call for medical help may sometimes produce someone able to assist or at least able to relay the call further. On one cruise, we dropped the hook in a remote Exuma anchorage and had started ashore in the dinghy when a woman ran onto the deck of a nearby trawler, screaming that her husband had just fallen down a ladder and was injured. Fortunately, the crew of our dinghy included an orthopedic surgeon and a urologist, who immediately climbed aboard the trawler. They reset and immobilized the victim's dislocated shoulder and we were again on our way in less than twenty minutes. Though this may not qualify as the fastest recorded medical response at sea, it was remarkably cost-effective considering that the proffered and accepted fee was one liter of Canadian whiskey.

Last, when in need of medical advice or assistance, call the Coast Guard. They will refer the request to the U.S. Public Health Service for specific medical advice and will deliver medications and evacuate the patient if needed. This service should only be requested in urgent or serious situations.

In life-threatening medical emergencies, Coast Guard aircraft frequently transport patients from remote outlying medical or first-aid facilities to medical centers on the mainland. This service is usually provided only in the absence of other available air transport and will not be authorized if commercial air ambulance service is readily available. This humanitarian service is provided by the Coast Guard for the citizens of any nation when needed.

On 30 May 1987, the 600-foot Soviet grain ship *Grigority Aleksandrov*, northeast of Attu in the Aleutians, radioed requesting help for a 29-year-old female crew member with appendicitis. A rendezvous was scheduled at Attu Island, though neither the Russian ship nor the crew of the Coast Guard loran station there had access to a boat. Undaunted, Air Station Kodiak made ready a C-130 Hercules, borrowed a Zodiac rigid hull inflatable boat (RHIB) and a boat crew from the cutter *Storis*, and with all on board the plane, dispatched it to Attu. The Soviet ship was dropping anchor off the island as the C-130 landed on the Attu strip. Transporting the RHIB to the water's edge on a loran station vehicle, the boat crew ran the flight surgeon out to the freighter and returned with the patient. Loading the patient, crew, and now deflated boat back aboard, the C-130 proceeded to Anchorage, where an emergency appendectomy was performed. Rescue at sea seems to be an oasis of international understanding and cooperation based on common needs and purposes.

Communications procedures for obtaining medical help are covered in chapter 12 and medical evacuation techniques are outlined in chapter 15.

STORING MEDICAL SUPPLIES

Having determined the scope of your cruising area, the medical training of your crew, and how to call for medical advice if needed, you are now ready to compile a medical chest inventory. If you later decide to cruise further offshore, both the training and supplies can be upgraded. Redundant supplies are costly and wasteful, because many have short shelf lives. Before obtaining and stowing any medical supplies, make sure you have suitable dry containers and a safe but accessible place to stow them. Plastic multicompartmented fishing kits with transparent covers that allow an examination of the contents without opening the lid are excellent containers. Medications are best stowed in one kit, while the bulkier trauma gear is kept in another. Tool kits make excellent containers, but insist on plastic rather than metal, which will rust around water.

Any crew members having their own prescription or patent medicines should keep them with their own belongings. If any are medications that may be crucial in an emergency, such as a seizure, the user should mention the circumstances to the designated medic or the skipper. This is essential for heart patients, diabetics, asthmatics, and persons subject to other acute episodes and allergies. They should carry an extra large supply of medications, because voyages can be delayed or extended.

All prescription and controlled drugs, especially narcotics, must be in properly labeled prescription bottles. Narcotics or controlled substances not in labeled prescription bottles could raise questions if the boat is boarded by the Coast Guard or Drug Enforcement Administration (DEA) agents.

INVENTORY OF MEDICAL SUPPLIES

Most medical and first-aid texts recommended for cruising provide a list of suggested pharmaceuticals and supplies. Because of many variables such as the length and place of the cruise, number and makeup of the crew, and first-aid know-how, the list of medical supplies should be tailored to individual requirements. Consult your own physician or one who is also a sailor. Be conservative in developing the list. If more extended cruising is planned for the future, then the stores can be augmented.

The improper use of medications can cause severe side effects and even death. Know how to use the pharmaceuticals in your inventory. The updated reference *The Ship's Medical Chest and Medical Aid at Sea* contains a section that will probably cover any medications used on a boat. Your pharmacist should be able to give you the manufacturer's data on any prescription you have filled. A readily available information packet on medications can be put together by photocopying or reproducing the data on each medication carried and stowing the information in the medical chest. This is a handy reference to safeguard against improper dosages or mixtures of drugs, and side effects.

SUMMARY

Every boat should have a minimal amount of first-aid supplies. Crews going out for long periods will require more complete medical supplies; someone aboard should be proficient in first aid with some training in treating acute and sudden illnesses, and should be familiar with the boat's medical reference book. The crew of a boat with VHF/FM communications should know how to use the VHF marine operator service. Arrangements to obtain medical advice by cellular or radio-phone patch with a physician or a medical advisory group should be made before sailing. If the boat is outside VHF range, such contact may be made by single side band (SSB) or ham-radio patch. In serious cases, the Coast Guard can be contacted for medical advice and evacuation of the victim if indicated.

To avoid delay and confusion, the skipper should keep on board the telephone numbers of the cruise's medical advisors and his or her own telephone or marine operator credit card.

II

A Problem Grab Bag

CAPSIZING

Small, Open Boats

Although capsizing constituted only 11 percent of all small boat accident cases handled by the Coast Guard in 1989, it resulted in more than a third of all deaths in pleasure boat accidents. The Coast Guard cases are only a small part of the whole picture, because most capsizings occur on inland lakes and waters and are generally dealt with by other boaters or local public safety agencies. In 1990 there were 144,376 capsizings nationally, resulting in 289 deaths. Capsizings were exceeded in number by 296,000 falls overboard or within the boat, leading to another 424 fatalities. Most capsizings involved small boats less than 18 feet long, and the causes were quite different from those involving offshore boats, which were covered in chapter 8, "Heavy Weather."

The greatest single factor in the mishaps of small, open boats is human error—standing in a small boat and improper seating and loading are the most frequent problems. Going out in weather too severe for the boat is a common mistake, which is compounded if the boat is improperly loaded and operated. Under federal regulations (46 USC 4307 A1) all monohull boats less than 20 feet in length whose construction began after 1 November 1972 must display capacity information on an attached plate. This information is sometimes combined with a certificate of compliance with USCG safety standards. Sailboats, canoes, kayaks, and inflatable boats are exempt.

Weight-carrying capacity roughly varies from two people (or 410 pounds) for a 10-foot boat to five persons (or 975 pounds) for a 16-foot boat. The same relationship is shown by a formula in which Personnel Capacity = Length × Width/15, assuming a weight of 150 pounds per person. The load that can safely be carried is dependent on the weather conditions, for high winds and seas may quickly swamp an open boat with low freeboard.

Caution must be observed when anchoring small boats in a choppy sea or strong current where the downward pull of the anchor rode can drag a boat under. The stern of a small open outboard motorboat is vulnerable, especially when it is built with a lowered transom to accommodate the motor. The combination of a low transom and the weight of the motor, tank, and operator aft has resulted in numerous swampings of small boats. Although they are not inherently dangerous, such boats must not be used in conditions beyond their designed limits.

A large search operation was launched off Los Angeles on 20 May 1986, when a fishing vessel spotted a nine-year-old girl clinging to the overturned hull of a 28-foot motorboat that had capsized twelve hours earlier. Two bodies were found nearby, but a search failed to locate the other three occupants of the boat. The child, suffering severe emotional trauma, could not tell what happened. No signs of collision could be found, and the sea was unusually mild during that period. The cause of capsizing was presumed to be a freak wave, but an excessive wake from a passing vessel cannot be ruled out.

At Lake Talquin, Florida, a church picnic was in progress and a deacon was taking children for rides in a 15-foot flat bottom boat with a 6-horsepower motor. Conditions were ideal and the water was glassy calm. After taking four teenagers for a ride, the deacon asked if the smaller children wished to go. Eighteen swarmed aboard and the boat left the dock with only 2 to 6 inches of freeboard. There was no life-saving equipment aboard and not one of the children could swim! Soon the boat began to take water over the gunwales, and as the children scrambled to avoid it, the boat capsized. Although other boats were nearby and raced to the scene, only one boy was saved. The seventeen others, ranging in age from five to fourteen including seven children from one family, drowned in eight feet of water—a tragedy that could have easily been avoided.

In North Florida a stiff breeze on the wide Saint Johns River quickly produced a three-foot chop that proved too much for the small, open outboard motorboat in which a Georgia family was sight-seeing near the lee shore. When the boat swamped and capsized, the nonswimmers had no life jackets; three people drowned with numerous other boats nearby but unaware of the tragedy.

Boats of rigid construction less than 20 feet long built since 31 July 1973 are required to have built-in buoyancy, which will provide flotation for the occupants even after the boat is swamped or flooded. Although this buoyancy provides considerable protection to the occupants against drowning and hypothermia, it does not eliminate a boat's tendency to capsize.

Small sailboats of open construction, or those with disproportionately large cockpits or deep open hatches, are vulnerable to knockdowns from heavy gusts of wind resulting in flooding and capsize. If the crew is properly equipped with PFDs and hatches are closed, a knockdown is not usually serious. Most small boats under 20 feet long will usually float and can be righted. If possible, the occupants should stay with the boat until help arrives, because they will be much easier to spot and the boat aids their flotation (see figure 11.1). They should avoid the temptation to try to swim to shore, which may prove dangerous and sometimes fatal. Most swimmers have only a fifty-fifty chance of swimming fifty yards in 50-degree F water (the Rule of Fifties).

The dangers of trying to swim ashore were again tragically shown on 8 August 1987 when a 15-foot pleasure craft with four people aboard was swamped in Saginaw Bay, Lake Huron, Michigan. A search for the overdue boat by Coast Guard helicopters and boats located two women early on Sunday morning, 9 Au-

Figure 11.1 Helicopter hoists survivors from a trawler that capsized while trying to enter a rough inlet. None are wearing PFDs, though one man has grabbed a Type IV life ring. *Courtesy USCG*

gust. Both survivors were clinging to the swamped boat in the cold lake waters. They reported that the owner of the boat, wearing a PFD, decided to swim for shore after the boat capsized. He was later located by a helicopter floating in his PFD, having died from hypothermia. The second man, also wearing a PFD, also tried to swim for shore later, but when the case was finally closed, he had not yet been located. It seems highly likely that had the men stayed with the swamped boat, all four persons would have been saved.

Larger Boats

Most larger well-designed sailboats and motor yachts used offshore and in unprotected waters are highly resistant to capsizing and are not easily overloaded. If properly handled, only an unusual combination of very high winds and rogue seas can create serious trouble. Even if capsized, most monohull sailboats will quickly recover on their own. In the Fastnet disaster already mentioned, a third of the three hundred boats in the race were either knocked down or rolled over 180 degrees, yet all but five recovered.

Inflatable Rubber Dinghies

Given similar lengths, the inflatable rubber dinghy can carry more weight and has more flotation and stability than its rigid counterpart. Even a partially inflated rubber dinghy will usually provide adequate buoyancy, and one filled with water still provides a floating platform. Capsized, they are easily righted when a line has been provided for the purpose. Inflatable rubber dinghies have thus become increasingly popular as tenders for yachts. The Coast Guard's 19-foot inflatable rescue boat with rigid keel and bottom (RHIB) has operated safely in heavy seas and storms, though its use in surf or breaking seas is restricted, as it is difficult to right after capsizing.

Waterskiing accidents are akin to capsizing and falling, though in the past they have not been included in SAR statistics, perhaps because it is largely an inland sport and accidents are usually handled by friends or other boaters. The 81,460 cases resulting in damage or injuries, nevertheless, evidence a serious problem. These accidents can usually be attributed to high speeds in crowded or confined areas, a lack of proper lookouts (a minimum of two are required in the towboat), and striking fixed objects or other boats.

Falling overboard can be as dangerous as capsizing and chapter 9 covers methods of retrieving such victims while under way. But falling over from a moored or anchored boat can also be dangerous, especially if the person is alone or the water cold. Most boats are extremely difficult to board without help when the swimmer is encumbered with a life jacket or clothing or weakened from hypothermia or injury. Know the best place to climb back aboard your boat, preferably on a ready rigged ladder. In a marina, look around and know the closest and best place to climb on another boat or the dock.

FOG AND REDUCED VISIBILITY

The risk of collision or navigational mishaps is greatly increased by reduced visibility, which can be caused by snow, heavy rain, fog, or other weather mechanisms created by the cooling of the air mass. As it cools, the air becomes less capable of retaining its water content. When the air mass reaches the critical saturation point, the water content separates out as tiny visible particles of water, which are seen as fog, rain, or snow.

Fog can often be predicted in the regular weather forecasts. In many areas, such as our Northeast Coast and much of our Pacific Coast, fog is almost a certainty at some seasons of the year. (See figure 11.2.) A typical prefog condition will involve high humidity, little or no wind over cool water, an observed drop in visibility, or a halo around lights. In offshore areas, fog banks can often be seen at some distance as a solid wall of low lying clouds reaching to the water.

If thick fog is encountered, speed should be immediately reduced to dead slow, the crew should don life jackets, and the following steps taken:

• Get a good fix before the fog closes in and lay out a DR (dead reckoning) track. List sound and light characteristics of buoys along the track and the ETA (estimated time of arrival) at each.

Figure 11.2 Fog rolls in through the Golden Gate. Such fog banks are a frequent sight to sailors on the Pacific and New England coasts. *Courtesy National Oceanic and Atmospheric Administration*

• Break out a reference and check on the whistle and bell signals used by boats in fog. Keep the reference handy. Few people can remember all signals.

• Begin sounding the appropriate fog signal and turn on navigation lights. Activate the radar and radar reflector if available.

• Post a sharp lookout on the bow to look and listen for bells, whistles, other boats, and seagulls, which may indicate that land is near.

• Stop the engine periodically and listen for several minutes for other vessels or the sound of surf if near shore. If near high land, listen for an echo of your horn.

• Move from buoy to buoy, steering a close heading, using all available navigation devices and keeping a current DR plot.

• If a marker or navigation aid does not appear at the ETA, stop. Recheck the navigation and obtain another fix if possible. Listen for any signal from the aid. Remember that both sound and visibility can be deceptive in fog.

• In deciding whether to proceed without precise fixes, mark two DR positions, one based on maximum possible progress or set and the other the minimum. If either indicates a position of danger, take action to avoid that possibility.

• Unless confident of your position and ability to navigate safely, lie to or preferably anchor at the first opportunity well out of the channel and in shallow water where the big boys can't run you down. Sound appropriate signals while at anchor or lying to.

• If near shipping or ferry routes, be aware that large vessels in fog move at speeds that will make their stopping in the reduced distance of visibility impossible. Though they rely on radar, it may not pick up a small boat. If you hear a large vessel, use VHF/FM sound signals, including the discharge of firearms if necessary, and take evasive action if possible.

In May 1986, the 72-foot fishing vessel *Jack Jr*, which was hauling in its nets off Point Reyes, California, transmitted a Mayday saying it was about to be rammed by a large steamer coming out of the fog. The SS *Golden Gate* was nearby and heard the call but had no radar or visual target. It turned hard right as a precaution and began searching for the vessel. Despite dense fog, Coast

Guard and air force searchers immediately responded and on the next afternoon located large quantities of debris from the *Jack Jr,* including an unopened life raft. No trace was ever found of the two crewmen. The skipper of the *Golden Gate* was charged with violation of 18 USC 115, misconduct or neglect by ship's officer causing loss of life (failure of skipper to come to bridge when entering fog and failure to exercise due caution in fog). The skipper was also charged with failure to render appropriate aid on becoming aware of a distress at sea. The charges were thrown out on a technicality on appeal, and the case is still in the hands of the Justice Department. As of 1992, no action against the master has been taken by the Coast Guard.*

RIGGING FAILURE

Rigging failure in a sailboat can be extremely serious unless quickly handled, for a break in the standing rigging may lead to loss of the mast. This problem most often results from a faulty or broken fitting such as a turnbuckle, spreader, or the shroud itself. Poor tuning with an improper bend in the mast can also result in mast failure. Routine inspections of the standing rigging can often detect pending failures before they occur (chapter 2), and this is especially important in racing or offshore boats subjected to heavy wind and sea stresses.

If a shroud or stay gives way or even displays serious defects, immediate action is called for. With a weather shroud gone, an immediate tack may save the rig. If a forestay parts while going to windward, the headsail will probably hold the mast temporarily, but aft pressure on the mast should be reduced by easing the boom vang and mainsheet and turning downwind. If already running before the wind with no strain on it, forestay failure is not as critical. In either case, once the strain is off the forestay, a jury rig must be set up to replace the broken stay.

If a backstay parts going down wind, the mast will get some support from the boom vang, but both the vang and the main sheet must immediately be sheeted in hard to increase the sup-

*Source: Lt. Mike Jandrossak, USCG Headquarters, Washington, D.C.

port and the boat brought around promptly into the wind. If the backstay parts while going to windward, continue to windward until a jury stay can be rigged. (See figure 11.3.)

With the loss of either a fore- or backstay, the load can be partially taken by the inner forestay or running backstay if the boat is so rigged, but this will not protect the portion of the mast above these stays, so support for the upper mast must be promptly rigged.

If a lee shroud parts, stay on the same tack until emergency repairs are made. If a weather shroud parts, tack promptly to relieve the strain before starting repairs. Shrouds often fail because of excessive play in the lee shrouds causing pins to work loose or hardware fail. The next time you are heeling in a stiff breeze, check the play in both windward and lee shrouds. The first should be taut, whereas the lee ones should have a couple of inches of give laterally but no feeling of looseness. Also look up along the mast and check it for bend. A slight bend is normal but should be equal on both tacks. If a weather shroud parts, tack promptly to relieve the strain on the mast.

Following shroud failure, all sails should not be dropped if seas are such as to cause heavy rolling, for the motion of the boat without the steadying effect of sails may generate a whiplash effect that can cause the mast to go by the board. In the days of tall ships, some were reputedly dismasted in the doldrums while rolling excessively in heavy ground swells with no steadying wind.

Damage Control Measures
Following the first steps outlined above, further measures must be taken to save the mast, even if you are close to a port of refuge. The most obvious precaution is to lead down a halyard as a substitute for the parted stay of shroud. After fastening it to the chain plate or other strong attachment point, lead the other end to a winch and take a healthy strain. This will serve as a stopgap until the boat can reach the nearest port.

The topping lift may be used instead of a halyard. It can be led to the stern fitting or chain plates and tightened with a purchase; a readily available one is either the mainsail vang or the Cunningham.

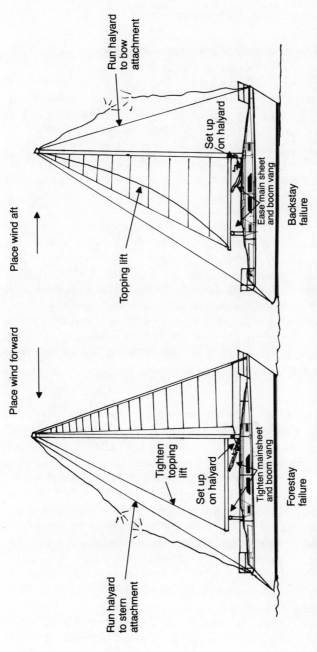

Figure II.3 First aid for forestay and backstay failure. Forestay failure: 1. Place wind aft. 2. Set up hard on jib halyard so that jib temporarily takes part of load. 3. Ease mainsheet and boom vang. 4. Lead a spare halyard (if none, use the main halyard) to a bow strong point and secure it. 5. Set up hard on the halyard with a winch. 6. Take in jib. Backstay failure: 1. Tighten topping lift, mainsheet, and boom vang. 2. Place wind forward. 3. Run a halyard to a stern strong point. 4. Set up hard on the halyard with a winch. 5. Take in mainsail.

If the break in a stay or shroud is near the deck and accessible, the broken ends of the cable can be bent into eyes fastened by cable or wire clips, then joined by a turnbuckle and tightened. If no turnbuckle is available, the upper eye can be connected to a vang or Cunningham and this led to the other eye or a deck fitting and set up tight (see figure 11.4). Combined with the halyard or topping lift rig, this affords added security.

With the jury rig completed, the boat should proceed promptly toward port under power, selecting a heading and tack to ease the strain on the damaged rigging and carrying only enough sail to minimize rolling.

While they are working on the rigging, crew members should favor the side of the break to avoid the danger of the mast falling on them. If the mast goes, the objective should be (except in flat seas) to cut loose and cast off the mast and attached rigging quickly before the wreckage holes the boat or fouls the screw and rudder. The engine must not be used until the rig and all lines are clear of the boat or water. The fastest method is to drive out the retaining clevis pins of the turnbuckle assemblies. Cutting larger-sized shrouds with wire or bolt cutters, a hack saw, or a hammer and chisel is a time-consuming and frustrating job.

Communications after Dismasting

If the mast cannot be jettisoned, it's time to call for help. This may be difficult after the loss of a mast-top VHF antenna, but a small emergency antenna may work out to four to five miles, a portable walkie-talkie to five to ten miles, and a cellular phone about fifteen to twenty. Stern whip antennae are not affected by mast damage. An EPIRB will provide a long-range, reliable, and sometimes delayed means of alerting SAR stations in an emergency regardless of antenna and radio damage. Visual and sound signals may also be effective if near land or other boats or aircraft.

On 19 December 1986, the 76-foot ketch *Scheherazade* reported to the Coast Guard via SSB radio that it had suffered rudder, engine, and sail damage 280 miles southeast of Montauk, New York, cutters *Vigilant* and *Sanibel* were ordered to assist, and three commercial vessels were diverted but were unable to help after arriving because of 22-foot seas and 65-knot winds.

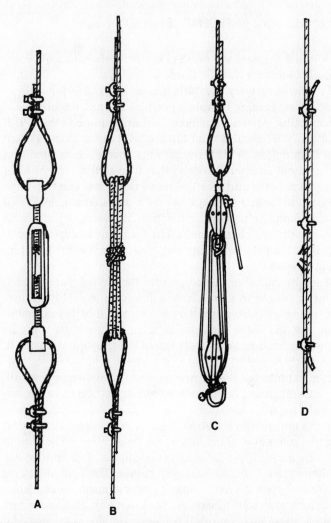

Figure II.4 Stay and shroud repairs. To make a temporary repair on a stay or shroud after taking emergency first-aid measures (fig. 11.3), bend both ends of the wire into eyes and fasten them with wire clamps. Join the two eyes together with (a) a turnbuckle, (b) strong lashings set up while the broken side is to leeward and not under tension, or (c) a strong multiple purchase such as a vang or Cunningham, securing the lower end to a strong point on the boat or to the lower eye. If a cable frays or shows signs of failure but has not broken, reinforce it with a length of cable secured with cable clamps (d).

The *Vigilant* relieved the *Sanibel* on the scene and took *Scheherazade* in tow for New Bedford.

As dawn broke on the 20th, numerous SARSAT (satellite) contacts were coming in from a position 370 miles southeast of New York City. After a commercial airliner confirmed the EPIRB signal, a C-130 Hercules from Elizabeth City located the 47-foot sloop *Commotion*, with three persons aboard, dismasted and adrift without communications other than EPIRB. The *Sanibel* was again diverted and took the vessel under tow and into Cape Cod. Despite the loss of the yacht's radio and antenna, the EPIRB brought prompt help to the *Commotion* and her crew just as SSB radio did for the *Scheherazade*. The decisions to declare a distress rather than attempt temporary repairs were wise in the prevailing weather.

When in coastal or inland areas of the United States, elaborate jury rigs beyond those already described make little sense. Most sailing boats have auxiliary power, and if help and shelter are nearby, the delay incurred in attempting repairs must be weighed against reaching safety before the situation worsens. If, however, there is little chance of matters getting worse, self-reliance in protected waters may save a big commercial tow bill, for the Coast Guard is unlikely to render assistance in the absence of danger.

In the uncommon situation where a boat has neither power, sails, nor communications, there may be no other choice but to try to rig a means to get the boat under command and under way (see figure 11.5). It will at least help morale. The kind of jury rig will depend upon the remaining rigging and materials available. A compact and well-illustrated book by Neil Hollander and Harold Mertes, *Yachtsman's Emergency Handbook* (Hearst Marine Books: New York, 1986), shows how to effect simple marine repairs or temporary fixes and is arranged in alphabetical order for easy reference.

FATIGUE

Most emergencies at sea are caused by human error, often attributable to exhaustion and fatigue. Fatigue is both insidious in onset and cumulative in effect. The condition is aggravated by anxiety,

Figure II.5   The sloop *Joie de Mer*, after losing 15 feet of its mast and drifting for eight more days, is taken in tow 550 miles southwest of Hawaii by a Coast Guard cutter. A jury rig could have helped in this case. *Courtesy USCG*

the physical beating in a tossing small boat, seasickness, hunger, and cold. No one, however tough and experienced, can escape for long the cumulative effects of fatigue unless rest or relief is provided.

The behavioral symptoms of fatigue include poor judgment, failure to carry out essential tasks, irritability, irrational actions, and in the later stages, hallucinations or panic. Even normally simple navigational calculations prove difficult, and bizarre errors are made by usually competent navigators. As the exhaustion deepens, there is a strong tendency to evaluate facts in the light of how one wishes they were rather than how they actually are.

A number of disasters have resulted when a skipper or watch-stander identified a distant light as the one sought, though the actual light characteristics were entirely different from the one they had been seeking. The same phenomenon has caused exhausted skippers to run a dangerous inlet trying to reach shelter, in situations where they never would have attempted it if they had been rested and rational. The final result of fatigue is to give up, which has cost many lives in circumstances where more rested and fit individuals survived.

Other than heaving to or lying ahull in order to obtain rest, there is little that the crew can do about the weather and sea. It is essential to keep as warm as possible and eat when hungry. Hot coffee, tea, soup, or cocoa are good stimulants up to a point. Though brandy or whiskey may give a temporary lift, the longer-term result is even more fatigue. Since its worst effect will be the further impairment of already questionable judgment, alcohol must not be used under these conditions.

The use of amphetamines was common during World War II and the ensuing years, when they were readily issued to flight or combat crews on long missions. This practice was largely discontinued some years ago because of the side effects and because the drug gave users an illusion of well-being and control, which they did not in fact have. The amphetamines masked rather than relieved the effects of fatigue.

Since fatigue dangerously clouds judgment, the skipper in adverse conditions should openly discuss the situation with the crew, invite their comments on his or her decisions, and counsel with them. Though command of a vessel is not normally a democratic process, the thinking of several people may be better than a tired individual's solo decision. Because the captain has the final responsibility for the boat and crew, he or she should consider abstaining from any watchstander rotation in heavy weather. The captain will be subject to numerous calls as well as the burden of responsibility, and these combined with a watch rotation will cause excessive fatigue and an increased risk of poor command decisions.

NAVIGATION ERROR

Assuming that the navigator is competent, alert, and diligent, getting lost is rare. But all of us have at times been unsure of our position, and this can result from several factors:

• *Failure of a navigation device.* With the increasing use of loran and GPS (global positioning system) in small craft, many people place too much faith in them and fail to maintain the traditional dead reckoning (DR) plot. Navigators should never rely on the input from a single source but rather weigh all available evidence—loran, GPS or SATNAV, celestial, soundings, visual or radio bearings, and always a current DR. Dead reckoning can be thrown off by knotmeter or compass errors (such as that caused by a metal object placed near the compass), by unknown currents, or by human errors in calculations. Visibility may preclude celestial shots or visual bearings, the depth of water may prevent soundings, and electronic failures can occur.

• *Discrepancies in position data.* If all inputs agree, the position can be relied on; if there are discrepancies in the input evidence, the position must be viewed with caution until further observations can resolve the differences. *No good navigator places all eggs in one basket, especially in restricted waters.*

• *Unpredictable currents and poor leeway estimates* can contribute to DR error. Even a powerful current such as the Gulf Stream can be greatly slowed by strong opposing winds blowing over long periods, and local wind-driven currents can develop where currents are normally nonexistent. Near inlets and rivers, changing tidal currents must be taken into account.

• *Fatigue.* Fatigue causes errors in calculations and judgment. To an exhausted crew, any evidence showing them nearer shelter may be accepted more readily than evidence to the contrary. An exhausted navigator may fail to double check all data, which he or she would normally do when rested.

If a combination of equipment failures or circumstances has resulted in serious doubt about the boat's position, the action to be taken will depend on the possible threat to the boat's safety. (See figure 11.6.) If well clear of land, it may be safest to wait for the weather to clear to allow observations. If making a landfall, however, the risks are greater and the following steps may be advisable:

1. Heave to and wait until the weather and situation clear.

2. Ask a passing boat or vessel for a position. Check on its accuracy by asking how and when the last fix was obtained.

Figure II.6 The Coast Guard cutter *Cape Corwin* takes over the tow of the 45-foot sloop *Galilee* from the USS *Niagara Falls*, which had sighted the disabled boat 250 miles northwest of Hawaii. After departing Tahiti and suffering a series of navigation mishaps and errors, the sloop missed Hawaii entirely. When chanced upon by the navy ship, the three crew members had been missing for two months. *Courtesy USCG*

3. If the situation becomes threatening, contact the Coast Guard for advice. Some stations can take bearings on your radio transmissions to estimate your position or a station can dispatch a search craft to home in with its own RDF (radio direction finder) and locate you. If you request help, the Coast Guard will take steps to locate you. They will not, as a rule, offer navigational advice if not in company with you because of possible error and legal liability.

DRUG INTERDICTION BOARDINGS

The Coast Guard and U.S. Customs Service have much broader powers to search vessels at sea than do police ashore. This precedent derives from the early days of the nation when its survival depended largely on the revenues from import duties, and the founding fathers vested broad powers in the enforcement units afloat to insure that these duties were collected. Today the Coast Guard is fighting drug smugglers, and the interdiction pressure brought against these ruthless criminals is sometimes felt by pleasure boaters.

Those cruising in areas traversed by drug smugglers will occasionally be stopped and checked by Coast Guard, navy, or customs patrols. Because drugs are smuggled in all types of craft, from dilapidated fishing vessels to sleek luxury yachts crewed by clean-cut young men and women, no vessel can be presumed innocent.

A random sampling of craft interdicted by the Coast Guard may afford an idea of the extent of drug running by what at first appear to be innocent pleasure craft (see table 11.1). Drugs were secreted in compartments.

Boarding parties try to minimize inconvenience or delays to

Table 11.1 Examples of Drug-running Craft Interdicted by U.S. Coast Guard

Name	Type	Registry	Location	Contraband	Amount (lbs)
Reel Dive	Cabin cruiser	U.S.	Yucatan Passage	Marijuana Cocaine	1,500 2,500
Derriere Rouge	Sloop	U.S.	West Florida	Marijuana	60
FL-7175-GX	Cabin cruiser	U.S.	Cape Canaveral	Cocaine	1,210
Islander	Sailing	U.S.	Key West	Marijuana	532
Blue Whale	Sailing	U.S.	Cayman Islands	Cocaine	800

SOURCE: Information provided by Commander, 7th Coast Guard District, Miami, Florida. Based on sampling of cases in 1991.

the boating public, and many inspections are carried out while the boat continues under way (fig. 11.7). The legitimate pleasure craft operator has nothing to fear from a boarding party. If hailed by a Coast Guard or navy vessel, follow its instructions. The boarding party of three to four men and women will come alongside in a boat or rubber dinghy and request permission to come aboard. Comply with the instructions of the boarding officer, once aboard. The usual routine is to check the boat's papers and crew's identities, carry out a walk-through inspection of the boat, give the operator a copy of the inspection report, and depart. The inspectors are nearly all businesslike and polite (if not, report the facts to the Coast Guard on the toll-free boating safety hotline, 1-800-368-5647).

In 1991, 22,315 boardings were made by the Coast Guard, and 13,393 of these involved pleasure craft. Sixty-five calls were re-

Figure II.7 A boarding party from a Coast Guard cutter comes alongside a ketch in one of the cutter's small boats. When directed, the yacht must heave to and prepare to take the boarding party on board. *Courtesy USCG*

ceived by the Coast Guard concerning these boardings. Of these, twenty-nine were complimentary, twenty-one asked for further information, and only fifteen contained complaints.

The inconvenience of a boarding is obviously minimal and a small price to pay in protecting the country from a ruinous flood of illegal drugs. Any policy to exempt pleasure boats from surveillance would immediately open a floodgate of drug imports carried in yachts and pleasure craft operated by drug runners.

Because of the effectiveness of the maritime interdiction effort, bulky and easily detected marijuana shipments have largely been replaced by hard drugs such as cocaine and heroin, which are more easily concealed and more profitable. Drug boats are increasingly being fitted out with cleverly concealed built-in compartments. Although some of these can be located by careful exterior and interior measurements, others can only be located by drilling small holes to allow the insertion of a detection device. If suspicious evidence is found, the boat may then be taken into port for a more thorough screen using trained narcotics dogs, chemical testing for traces of narcotics, hull inspection by divers, and if indicated, cutting into the boat's structure. Despite a few wild sea stories, legitimate pleasure boats have rarely been subjected to such an inspection, and then only when intelligence reports and a nonintrusive search uncovers strong evidence of drug activity.

Recreational boaters should be aware that under the provisions of federal law (19 USC 1590), a *concealed* void compartment is strong evidence of an intent to use the boat for smuggling, and the boat can be seized. Several recent random cases will illustrate the point.

In September 1990 off Islamorada, Florida, a 35-foot pleasure craft was stopped and an empty concealed compartment was located in the bow. A chemical test of the space was positive and the vessel was seized.

The CGC *Maui* boarded a vessel off the southeast coast of Florida suspected of being the drop vessel for a drug plane that had fled. A hidden compartment was found, along with paneling and adhesive materials to seal the compartment after the drugs were stowed. The boat was seized.

Another fast boat was stopped off Hillsborough Inlet, Florida, and a secret compartment with drugs was found where one of the fuel tanks had been removed. This frugal but dumb boat captain had stowed the removed fuel tank in his lazaret. The boat was seized.

A violation of the law against secret compartments will result in the loss of the boat. If narcotics are also found in these compartments, the boat operators will also be arrested.

Another complaint by boaters involves repeated boardings of the same boat while passing through an area of heavy drug interdiction such as the waters of the Southeastern United States. A new computer data system, which can be interrogated before stopping a suspect boat, has greatly reduced the number of repeat boardings with less inconvenience for all parties. A copy of a recent boarding report will also probably prevent a repeat search.

Pleasure boats traveling alone should not chance reporting suspected drug activity to the Coast Guard by radio because of the risk of being overheard by the drug traffickers, but you should do so by landline telephone after docking. Call the U.S. Customs Service's toll-free hotline, 1-800-BE ALERT (232-5378). The call and source will be kept confidential.

12
Emergency Communications

When confronted with a really threatening situation afloat, *immediately* let someone else know your position and predicament. Events often move rapidly. If the situation worsens, and you are unable to transmit again, the other party will probably take action or alert people who can. At sea a cry for help is usually made first by radio, but it can also be done by visual or sound signals if other boats, aircraft, or people are nearby. Such nonradio signals were, until only forty years ago, the principal means of indicating small craft in distress.

In late 1979, while single-handing offshore from Charleston, South Carolina, to Mayport, Florida, I chanced at sunset upon three men in the water in life jackets five miles offshore. Alerted by their shouts, I hauled them aboard. While they were fishing that morning, their boat's transom had given way and rapidly flooded the boat. There was barely time to grab life jackets, and no distress message was sent out. Though the weather was fair, three shrimp trawlers passed close to them during the day without hearing their shouts. No one was even aware that they were in trouble, and my passage through the area of the sinking was mere chance. Thirty minutes later I could easily have missed them in the darkness.

Several months later, while some thirty miles off the south Florida coast, we heard a weak Mayday call, which we answered but heard nothing further. I reported the call to the Coast Guard; no one else had heard it. An hour later we sighted a 40-foot cabin cruiser on the horizon, and through glasses we saw a flag being waved on a long pole. Closing it, we learned that the boat's engine and batteries were dead, and it had been drifting north in the axis of the Gulf Stream for two days. The batteries had been run down attempting to start the engines, and the weak call I had heard earlier had been made with the last gasp of battery power. If you have problems starting the engine, let someone else know of your problem, intentions, and position before using up the last battery power.

The third case, two months later, involved an experienced crew nearing Stuart, Florida, after a five-hundred-mile delivery job from Chesapeake Bay. After a routine watch change at daybreak, an off-watch crew member was awakened by water coming over the sole. A distress call was hurriedly broadcast in the blind, and the crew took to a life raft as the boat sank beneath them. Though the boat was only five miles off the coast when the accident occurred, the distress call was not picked up, nor was their later EPIRB signal; the reasons were never determined. Four days later the survivors were picked up eighty miles offshore by a merchant vessel. They had drifted north several hundred miles from the sinking site, without food or emergency signals.

All three of these emergency cases could have ended in tragedy had it not been for chance sightings, and in each case the crew failed to get through a distress message. The best insurance against this is an overdue report to the Coast Guard from a person holding the boat's *float plan*. Unfortunately only half of all recreational boaters use float plans; many of the others believe that in case of trouble a call on VHF radio will get a quick response. Lack of time, electronic failure, distance, or other traffic, however, may prevent a distress call from getting through.

VHF RADIO

The VHF/FM radio transceiver is by far the most popular and most often used communications gear in small boats. Few experienced or knowledgeable sailors will venture far from land without it. A good VHF can make up for a lot of omissions and nautical sins. With proper installation and a well-charged boat battery, present-day VHF gear is nearly idiot proof, yet there are a few simple human errors that can undo even the best VHF/FM set, such as:

- Turning the receiver volume or squelch down too far
- Setting transmit power to *Low* instead of *High*
- Setting in the wrong channel or international channel group
- Allowing batteries to get low

Other than these simple human errors, the VHF, if properly protected from the elements, seldom fails within the ranges for which it was designed. Exceptions would be electronic black-box failures, a lightning strike, or dismasting. When lightning strikes, a mast-mounted VHF antenna at the highest point of the boat is the most likely target. Many skippers disconnect the VHF coax cable when electrical storms are nearby. If a sailing vessel with a mast-top antenna is dismasted, the VHF becomes inoperative. For this reason, many boats use a whip antenna mounted near the stern, though this gives a reduced range. In the event of any antenna loss, a small, folding emergency antenna can be inserted into the VHF radio jack to afford short-range communications. A portable VHF/FM walkie-talkie also provides a reliable backup and can be invaluable in survival situations. In an emergency, VHF/FM is a proved, primary alerting device.

VHF PROPAGATION

The VHF signal is line of sight, although a slight bending along the earth's curvature may extend the range slightly beyond the horizon. The higher the transmitting and receiving antennas, the longer the line of sight and thus the VHF range. Assuming a sloop with a VHF antenna 36 feet high (Height, H boat), and a Coast Guard–receiving antenna of 300 feet (Height, Hcg) the communication range should be:

$$1.4\sqrt{\text{H boat}} + 1.4\sqrt{\text{Hcg}} = 8.4 + 24.2 = 32.6 \text{ miles}$$

This is a reasonable range of communications to expect in the coastal regions of the United States. The well-guarded Coast Guard VHF net will likely pick up any VHF call within twenty to twenty-five miles of the coast. To facilitate this coverage, each Coast Guard group has additional remote antennas situated at intervals along the coast and tied to its operations center by land lines. This effectively extends the VHF range, and it is common to maintain VHF communications via these remote antennas at ranges of 150 miles from the group commander's operations center, provided the boat is within 25 miles of the coast.

Although it has a relatively short range, VHF can prove useful far offshore if other craft are in its area. On 1 October 1986, the British merchant vessel *London Spirit* received a Mayday from the 41-foot sailing vessel *Aqua Vit* while the British ship was 360 miles south of New Orleans. Though she answered the call, she heard no further transmissions, nor were any position or the nature of distress given. The Coast Guard was notified and Air Station Clearwater launched a C-130 and Mobile launched a Guardian jet. The C-130 soon picked up a weak EPIRB signal and made voice contact with the two survivors on their VHF portable. They were located on a raft nearly four hundred miles south of New Orleans and the merchant vessel *Fantasy L* diverted to pick them up. The Mayday call, made "in the blind" (broadcast without first establishing two-way contact with another ship) and relayed by a nearby ship, led to the dispatch of search aircraft, which in turn flew within range of the EPIRB and portable VHF radio and homed in with radio direction finders to locate the raft. The *Aqua Vit* had flooded and sunk early that morning from unknown causes.

All Coast Guard aircraft carry VHF/FM equipment in addition to the VHF, UHF, and high-frequency SSB (single side band) radios required for their many multiple missions. Coast Guard units also have radio direction-finder equipment to home on a distressed boat's VHF/FM signal. Because of the high altitude flown, aircraft can establish VHF contact at ranges in excess of one hundred miles. On one occasion, scrambling to intercept a distressed aircraft, I picked up his VHF transmission on my direction finder at a range of nearly two hundred miles. By contrast,

Coast Guard small boats with antennas only a few feet high will usually not be heard more than ten to fifteen miles by other small boats.

GUARDING VHF

Although a modern VHF set may have more than one hundred channels, only about a dozen of these are normally required by the coastal sailor. The most important of these is Channel 16—the calling, safety, and distress frequency required by law on every vessel equipped with VHF/FM. Channel 6 for intership safety communications is the other channel required by law. All vessels under way should listen on Channel 16 at all times. Other boats wishing to contact you will attempt initial contact on that channel. After contact, shift promptly to a mutually agreed working channel to handle nonurgent traffic. A station transmitting distress signals or urgent traffic may remain on Channel 16 unless directed by the Coast Guard to shift to Channel 22, the Coast Guard working channel. By allowing the brief use of Channel 16 for initial common calling, the FCC encourages all boats to guard it continuously, thus affording greater coverage and safety to all at sea.

A difficulty in monitoring the frequency is that some VHF installations on sailboats are below deck for weather protection and are hard to hear topside, so the volume must be up when all hands are on deck. The electrical drain in *receiver only* mode is very modest and continuous monitoring won't seriously deplete the batteries.

One should be alert if the short warbling signal from a Class C EPIRB is heard while guarding VHF; this information should be promptly passed to the Coast Guard. Some Coast Guard stations use a two-tone VHF alarm signal to indicate to listeners that a distress or safety message will follow.

If a distress message is heard, copy it down immediately. If a tape recorder is handy, tape the traffic verbatim—it could be the only clue to a vessel's fate. After hearing a Mayday (distress) or Pan (urgent) call, listen for ten more seconds for an answer, but remember that another replying station may be within VHF range of the victim but beyond your range. It will soon be evident from the conversation if the distressed boat is in contact with anyone. If not, call and acknowledge the distress message. Obtain the essential information (name, position, number of persons on board, nature of the trouble, and intentions). Transmit this immediately to the Coast Guard, steer for the victim at best speed, and be ready to act as a relay between the victim and assisting units. If no contact can be made with the Coast Guard, broadcast to any other unit. For your safety and that of everyone at sea, guard Channel 16 while under way. It is seldom noisy, and its short range limits the number of callers heard. Guarding it is made easier by the dual channel-guard capability on newer VHF sets.

DISTRESS CALLING PROCEDURES

Anyone using VHF should know emergency communication procedures. Make a copy of table 12.1 and post by the VHF.

VHF/FM CHANNELS

Frequencies between 156 and 163 MHz have been allocated by international agreement for marine use. Within this band, channels are established and numbered at 25 kHz spacing, and each channel is designated by a number as well as a frequency. The channels most used by pleasure craft are shown in table 12.2.

VHF MARINE OPERATORS

A system of commercial marine telephone VHF operators serves the needs of VHF equipped boats wishing to contact persons ashore through the commercial telephone system. Operated by various commercial communication corporations, the listing and locations of these stations can be found in most coastal cruising guides or on fliers obtainable from the communication companies or marine electronics dealers. The listing in the telephone book is usually "Marine Telephone VHF Operator."

After you have identified the location and working frequency of the nearest marine operator, use the working frequency or

Table 12.1 Distress Calling Procedures

DISTRESS CALLING
- Switch VHF to Channel 16.
- Repeat: *"Mayday—Mayday—Mayday,"* followed by the name of your vessel and your call sign three times.
- Give your position—in latitude / longitude bearing or distance and bearing from commonly known landmark.
- State type of assistance needed—example: vessel sinking . . . medical assistance.
- Description of vessel, color, type, length, and number of persons on board.
- End message with "Over."

DISTRESS, URGENT, SAFETY MESSAGES
- Distress signal—*Mayday* Example: Immediate danger of loss of life or property
- Urgency Signal—*Pan* Example: Safety of a person or a vessel is in jeopardy
- Safety Signal—*Security* Example: Precedes storm warnings or other navigational safety messages

MAKING A SHIP-TO-SHIP CALL
- Switch VHF to Channel 16.
- After making sure the channel is clear, depress the microphone button and give the name of the vessel you are calling, followed by your call sign and the name of your vessel.

- If the vessel called does not reply within 30 seconds, do not call that vessel again for another 2 minutes.
- If the called vessel replies, select a clear working channel to continue communications.
- End transmission with "Over."
- End your completed communications with "Out."

REPORTING ANOTHER VESSEL IN DISTRESS
- Transmit: *"Mayday Relay—Mayday Relay—Mayday Relay."*
- Give your vessel name and call sign three times.
- Give your position, bearing and distance from vessel in distress.
- State nature of distress.
- Give complete, detailed description of the vessel in distress.

ACKNOWLEDGING A MAYDAY CALL
- Repeat the call sign and name of the vessel sending distress signal three times.
- Transmit: "This is (Your call sign and name of vessel)" three times.
- Transmit: "Received Mayday."
- Pause—Listen—if another vessel is closer, let that boat proceed with the communications and rescue operations

(Continued on next page)

(Table 12.1, continued)

while you stand by and monitor. • If you are closest to the vessel in distress, recontact the vessel and give your position, latitude / longitude, and bearing or distance and bearing from a commonly known landmark. • State the speed of your vessel and estimated time of arrival (ETA) to vessel in distress.	**MAKING SHIP-TO-SHORE CALLS** • Select proper ship-to-shore channel and make sure it is not already in use. • Alert the operator by depressing the microphone button for approximately 5 seconds. • Call the operator by location. Example: "Chicago Marine Operator . . . this is (Your vessel name and call sign)." • Give the operator your vessel name, call sign, and the number you wish to call. • End completed communications with "Out."

SOURCE: Derived from FCC rules

Channel 16. If you use the working frequency, first listen to insure that a telephone conversation is not already in progress. If you use Channel 16, promptly shift to the working frequency designated by the marine operator after you make initial contact.

The marine operator will request the name of the boat, the owner, the radio call sign, and the telephone number being called. Calls may be person-to-person or station-to-station; they can be made collect, charged to the caller's home number, or to a credit account if the boat's owner has established one with the marine telephone corporation. The operator dials the number, electronically connects the boat's radio signal to the telephone system by a "patch," and a normal two-way phone conversation follows (remember to press the mike key to talk).

If you make frequent ship-to-shore calls, it is more economical and faster for the boat owner to establish an account with the marine telephone company for a small annual fee. There is no charge by the marine operator for distress or urgency calls.

Persons ashore can make a call to the boat through the marine operator nearest to the boat if the approximate location of the

Table 12.2   VHF/FM Channels for Small Boats

Channel	Purpose
06	Intership safety communications (mandatory)
12	Port operations—traffic advisories—CG shore working channel
13	Ship bridge to ship bridge. Mandatory for ocean vessels, dredges, and some tugs. (This channel is restricted to 1 watt power.) Guarded by some bridge tenders.
14	Port operations, some USCG shore stations
16	**DISTRESS, SAFETY,** and **CALLING** (mandatory)
22	For working USCG ships and shore stations and for USCG marine information broadcasts
25	VHF Marine Operator (public telephone)
26	VHF Marine Operator (public telephone)
27	VHF Marine Operator (public telephone)
28	VHF Marine Operator (public telephone)
68	Noncommercial intership and ship-to-coast
69	Noncommercial intership and ship-to-coast
70	Noncommercial only, ship-to-ship
71	Noncommercial intership and ship-to-coast
72	Noncommercial intership
78	Noncommercial intership and ship-to-coast
WX-1	Weather broadcast
WX-2	Weather broadcast
WX-3	Weather broadcast

boat and a listing of locations and phone numbers of the various marine operators is known. If such calls are anticipated, you should leave a marine operator's listing with the potential callers. The marine operator will call the boat on Channel 16, then shift to a working frequency.

Traffic through the marine operator is unrestricted except for obscene or profane language, which are forbidden under FCC rules, but the user must remember that anyone within thirty miles with a VHF receiver can listen in.

If a boat in distress is unable to reach a Coast Guard unit but can contact the marine operator, he or she can alert the Coast Guard or patch the call through by phone. If a call back from a party is expected, remind the marine operator to give the other party the marine operator's phone number.

CELLULAR TELEPHONES

Cellular phones, now in wide use ashore, offer much promise afloat. In many areas within twenty-five miles of the coast, they provide reliable and convenient direct-dialing ship-ashore service. In the near future, satellites may extend the service several hundred miles offshore, which will provide an invaluable backup to existing radio channels.

Tests were begun along the mid-Atlantic seaboard by Bell Atlantic Telephone Company in 1991 to determine the feasibility of using cellular phones to conduct urgent and distress marine traffic. Using a three-digit number (* C G), similar to the 911 number for public safety calls, a caller in the area between Toms River, New Jersey, and Chincoteague, Virginia, including Chesapeake Bay, can be routed by the company's switching network to the Coast Guard group operations center for the caller's area. The service did not see heavy use in the early test stages, but there were no significant problems or incidents of abuse.

In other areas, boat operators began using cellular phones on their own initiative. In early 1991, fisherman James Clemons's boat began sinking seventeen miles off the coast of Maine. Grabbing his cellular phone, he jumped into a raft, dialed his wife, and asked her to look up the number of the Coast Guard Station. He then added, "I'm on a life raft and the boat is sinking." Said his wife, Ann Clemons, "It was a little bit odd." Those were also the sentiments of Petty Officer Bob Van Gordon, who took the call at the station, remarking later, "We were pretty surprised." Two aircraft and a boat were promptly dispatched, but Clemons was picked up first by nearby fishermen.

Several months later a couple in a high-speed boat smashed into a lighted three-ton navigation buoy at 4:00 A.M. near the Jacksonville, Florida, midtown docks. The twenty-five-year-old operator, Robert Allen III, was killed instantly, but his twenty-year-old female companion used the boat's cellular phone to call 911 for help and was rescued soon afterward.

Even if a three-digit distress number is adopted nationally, however, cellular phones are not an adequate substitute for VHF/FM radio. Coast Guard direction finders cannot take bearings on a cellular signal to help locate the caller, nor can nearby boaters hear the call for help. Coast Guard units attempting to help have no direct contact with a boat equipped only with a cellular phone. VHF/FM remains the primary communications link for pleasure craft, with cellular communications only a secondary resource, but the future holds considerable promise for cellular communications as its use is expanded.

SINGLE SIDE BAND (SSB) RADIO

When a vessel is outside VHF range, the use of single side band (SSB) radio in the frequency bands 2–3 MHz and 4–24 MHz will permit long-range communications around the clock if the proper frequencies are selected. The uses and purpose of these long-range frequencies are very similar to that of the short-range VHF. The distress, safety, and calling frequency is 2181 kHz, whereas blocs of frequencies in the 4, 6, 8, 12, 16, 21, and 22 MHz bands are allocated for intership, Coast Guard, and public coast station (SSB marine operator) calls. The Marine Radio Service has the advantages of available long-range, professional operators if trouble develops, and few restrictions on message contents, third-party traffic, or operating in foreign waters. Direct contact can be made with the Coast Guard or commercial vessels on 2182 kHz or a higher working frequency if you are further out. Unlike amateur (ham) radio, an operator's license is not required, and the SSB station license can be included or endorsed on the VHF station license. A VHF set is a prerequisite before an SSB license can be issued for shipboard use.

SSB is little used by small-boat coastal sailors, who feel that VHF/FM meets their needs. But even on larger offshore boats its use is limited by a number of factors:

1. The initial cost is high, between $2,500 and $4,000.
2. Calls patched through the public coast stations are expensive.

3. Some knowledge of the effects of distance, time of day, period of the year, atmospheric activity, and band selection is necessary for good communications.

4. General misinformation is common about the operational effectiveness and cost of SSB. The past decade has seen vast improvements in equipment and performance while costs have steadily decreased.

AMATEUR RADIO SERVICE (HAM)

Amateur (ham) radio has become very popular with yacht owners in recent years, largely because it affords an informal link with the rest of the world from far and lonely places. It is generally cheaper than SSB marine radio gear, there are no service, or patch, charges, and the bands can be used for social chatter. But there are serious drawbacks to amateur radio in both normal and emergency use.

The primary obstacle to many people is the strict and sometimes difficult licensing requirement. An applicant for a general license must pass a written test on radio theory and FCC regulations and then a Morse code receiving test at a minimum rate of thirteen words per minute. These tests may require months of study. As a result, the various bands, though busy, are not as crowded as are the free access services like citizen's band (CB) radio, and the circuit discipline, courtesy, and helpfulness of most hams are first-rate. Though the price of a good transceiver and antenna tuner approximates that of a marine SSB radio, ham gear can be installed by an owner with the necessary know-how.

Other drawbacks are the absence of designated guard stations on the ham frequencies, such as the coast stations and Coast Guard provide on marine SSB, and there is no designated emergency frequency. There are informal groups of ham operators called "nets" that operate at regular times each day, and some are dedicated to the passage of maritime mobile traffic between boats and shore. Other nets will accept and monitor float plans. It is sometimes difficult with the relatively low transmitter power on boats to break into busy circuits, and band conditions vary so much with the time of day and year that considerable expertise may be required to get through. If time allows, contact can be made, but time is the big uncertainty. Though a ham operator for many years, I have never had the occasion to work a distress or urgent call on the ham bands, perhaps because I only turn the set on when sending a message. But hundreds of hams ashore are using the bands at all times and are often instrumental in obtaining help for those in distress, especially cruisers in distant waters.

Amateur radio has many legal restrictions. Most foreign governments require a temporary license in their territorial waters. The issuance of these permits is dependent on mutual international agreements. For example, the United States and Bahamas have such an agreement, and a temporary permit for the Bahamas can be obtained for a few dollars on application. Third-party traffic, meaning anyone other than the two licensed operators, is forbidden in *international* traffic, and this of course rules out phone patches. Phone patches are made by a device at the receiving station that interconnects radio and telephone signals, allowing a radio operator to converse with another party using a telephone. The transaction of business or commerce on ham frequencies is strictly forbidden in both foreign and domestic traffic, and this includes such mundane things as ordering spare parts. None of these restrictions apply to the Maritime Radio Service, nor do any such restrictions exist in an emergency situation.

Because of the skip characteristics of SSB, a transmission may be received by another ham operator thousands of miles away. How can a ham operator help? It would be better, of course, to use a frequency workable in your local area, but in either case, be prepared to tell the other ham how specifically to help you. Give the ham one of the following Coast Guard telephone numbers and ask the operator to patch you through (if your position is not known, call either number):

1. If distressed vessel is in the Atlantic or Gulf of Mexico:
   Commander Atlantic Area   (212) 668-7055
   New York, N.Y.
2. If distressed vessel is in the Pacific:
   Commander Pacific Area   (415) 437-3700
   San Francisco, Cal.

If the operator has no patch equipment, or time is running out, give the ham the Coast Guard phone number and ask that he or she pass on or relay your distress message. The Coast Guard will accept collect distress messages, but there are heavy penalties for malicious false alarms and fraud.

The use of ham radio to obtain medical advice is also obvious if the receiving operator has patch equipment. In a large anchorage, someone nearly always has ham gear aboard and will be eager to cooperate. Boats with SSB can be recognized by a backstay with an insulator near each end, or by a long whip antenna.

MARINE SSB OR HAM RADIO?

If a reliable network for the conduct of business or urgent personal matters is needed and affordable in areas outside of VHF range, marine SSB is the obvious choice. If chatting, telling sea stories, and recreation are your aims, and the various restrictions not too binding, ham radio may be the answer, but a license requires preparation and study.

For emergency and safety use, marine SSB has a clear edge over ham radio, because of the twenty-four-hour professional watchstanders at the powerful shore and marine stations and the established procedures for alerting SAR centers. If ham gear is all you have, however, there is a good chance you can get through, but start early. If you have a real distress, forget the general Coast Guard call. Use the Mayday distress call. If the danger is lesser but serious, use the urgent call Pan. Use a frequency regularly used by one of the marine nets, or break in on any net where you are receiving a clear signal. If you hear them, they will probably hear you.

COMMERCIAL BROADCAST STATIONS

If you are operating in areas outside shore VHF/FM range, weather information can be obtained by listening to reports on the AM and FM commercial broadcast bands. Though FM range is similar to VHF/FM, the AM stations can be received at much greater distances, depending on the power used. The time of these weather forecasts and station frequencies should be obtained before leaving or from other boaters. This source of weather information is often used in the Bahama out islands.

HANDY COMMUNICATIONS NUMBERS LIST

Keep on board in a small notebook or the radio log essential communications data such as:

1. Phone numbers for your doctor, hospital or clinic; holder of your float plan; family and business associates; and friends who may have to be contacted.

2. Phone numbers of the two primary Coast Guard Atlantic and Pacific area rescue coordination centers (RCCs) and the number of the nearest Coast Guard station or group in your local area.

3. Broadcast schedule for Coast Guard and commercial broadcast station weather reports.

4. Locations, frequencies, and telephone numbers of marine VHF telephone operators in your operating area.

5. SSB frequency guards of public coast stations and Coast Guard communication stations (for boats with marine SSB). Because these are subject to change, a list of frequencies should be obtained when your SSB is installed and checked again before extended cruises.

6. Frequency and time schedule of ham marine nets (for ham operators).

EPIRBS

The use of electronic locator aids dates from the bulky "Gibson Girl" and hand-cranked transmitter of World War II. Using long antennas carried aloft by a kite or balloon, their alternate transmissions on 500 kHc and 8364 kHc could be heard for hundreds of miles, and the endurance of the signal was limited only by the crew's stamina. In 1953, a 500-kHc SOS signal was picked up by an overseas Coast Guard radio station, and we scrambled in a PBM-5G Mariner to locate it. Climbing through five hundred feet, I tuned the aircraft's automatic direction finder (ADF) to the freqency, and a loud clear SOS came banging through the earphones. Switching to *auto* mode, the ADF needle swung toward the signal source, and a little over an hour later we sighted a 35-foot sloop. After dropping a walkie-talkie to them, we learned that they were college students en route to Bermuda for the Easter holidays, though now 150 miles off course. They were given a position and course to steer, and told to report in on arrival, which they did two days later. They insisted that they were not lost, merely unsure of their position.

Manually cranked homing devices were soon replaced on aircraft by emergency locator transmitters (ELTs), which are automatically actuated in the event of a crash to send out a distress beacon signal on 121.5 and 243 MHz, the civil and military VHF/UHF emergency frequencies. These frequencies are routinely guarded by other pilots in flight. Though the automatic actuation by heavy G-forces is essential in a crash, the large number of aircraft false alarms may be saying something about the landing techniques of some pilots.

It was only a matter of time until a maritime equivalent of the ELT, known as an EPIRB (Emergency Position Indicating Radio Beacon), emerged. The class-A EPIRB, automatically deploying like its aerial cousin, operates on the same frequencies and in a like manner. The class-B EPIRB differs only because it is manually deployed and must first be actuated by a switch. The class-C EPIRB, designed for coastal use, is also manually deployed but alternates transmissions between VHF/FM Channel 16 (1.5 seconds) and Channel 15 (14.5 seconds). The intermittent two-tone short wail on Channel 16 alerts the listener, after which Channel 15 can be used as a homing beacon signal by SAR craft. Battery endurance is two to four days, depending on temperature and battery condition. The FCC will endorse the VHF/FM station license for use of an EPIRB, though few EPIRB owners bother with this technicality.

Class-A EPIRBs are more expensive and the automatic deployment feature is not needed by small-boat sailors. The question of whether to use a class-B or class-C beacon has received much attention. Theoretically, the class C, which uses Channels 15 and 16, should be best in the coastal areas because of the widespread use of VHF/FM by small craft and the Coast Guard's radio guard on the channel. In actual practice, however, the surface-to-surface range of a class-C beacon is far less than the surface-to-air range of a class B. This short range, and the fact that many small-boat operators are careless about guarding Channel 16 and do not even know the EPIRB signal characteristics, greatly reduces the chance that a class-C signal will be heard or recognized.

The major advantage of the class-B device is that its signal can be heard by either aircraft or a SAR satellite (SARSAT) and relayed to SAR centers. Few class-C models are in use, and with the updating of the class B and the advent of the newer 406 MHz model EPIRB, it seems unlikely that they will be in the future. We recommend that a class B, updated to present standards, be used until the 406 MHz EPIRB becomes more affordable.

Until the coming of the satellites, most reports of emergency beacon signals came from aircraft. Pilots of my generation guarded the VHF and UHF distress frequencies at all times, just as most good seamen still guard Channel 16 on VHF/FM.

At noon of 27 October 1986, the FAA traffic control center in Oakland, California, notified the Joint RCC in Honolulu that several trans-Pacific aircraft had reported picking up an ELT signal about one thousand miles west of Oahu. An emergency broadcast was made to all ships and planes in that area, and before 2 P.M., an Air Force C-141 confirmed the earlier reports. A Coast Guard turboprop C-130 was dispatched from Oahu and on arrival at the scene three hours later sighted a large tanker engulfed in flames and three miles away, a motor lifeboat with a life raft in tow. Relays of long-range aircraft were kept over the scene until the arrival of the Japanese fishing vessel *Shoshi Maru* and the Singapore vessel *Dresden*. It was then learned that the burning vessel was the 811-foot tanker *O.M.I. Yukon*, which had suffered a series of engine-room explosions followed by fire that engulfed its superstructure and control spaces. No SOS could be sent. Four men were killed in the explosion and thirty-three abandoned ship in midocean. They owed their rescue to the small ELT, a number of alert overseas pilots passing near the scene, and a prompt response by the SAR forces and other mariners.

An ELT might have been just as important to the twenty-eight crew members of the M/V *Tuxpan*, a 474-foot container ship en route from Europe to Mexico with five hundred containers stacked seven deep. On 24 February 1987, the vessel reported heavy weather 720 miles WSW of the Azores and four days later was reported overdue. Coast Guard and navy aircraft searched over nineteen thousand square miles without results. Six days later a floating container from the *Tuxpan*, which had been stowed well below the main deck level, was sighted 150 miles south of the original search area and another intensive search was conducted. No other trace of the *Tuxpan* or her crew was ever found. The ship was supposed to have an ELT. For reasons unknown, it was not carried on her final voyage, and twenty-eight men perished possibly because of the lack of a small device costing several hundred dollars.

Where in a recreational boat should an EPIRB be carried? Although a few sailors pack it in the life raft container, it is not easily accessible there for periodic testing and upkeep. In a distress situation, breaking out an EPIRB would mean unpacking the raft. A better stowage is in a convenient location below deck, protected from the weather but handy in an emergency.

An unusual double save in November 1985 was credited to EPIRB. The Coast Guard at San Juan, Puerto Rico, picked up an EPIRB distress signal sent out by the crew of the 60-foot ketch *Sun Quest*, who had taken to their life raft in the heavy seas kicked up by Hurricane Kate. Jets were launched from Florida and Puerto Rico, which sighted an orange flare and a life raft three hundred miles northeast of Puerto Rico. Further search revealed not only the life raft from the *Sun Quest* but the previously unreported and dismasted sailing vessel *Taxi Dancer* and its crew. A nearby tug and barge were diverted to the scene and recovered all the men from the two boats.

SARSAT/COSPAC

During the mid-1970s NASA, with added funding from the air force and Coast Guard, began development of a system for monitoring distress beacons by satellite. The design was to be compatible with both the existing ELTs and EPIRBs, as well as the proposed new 406.025 MHz EPIRB. The SARSAT (search and rescue satellite) package was built to attach to the NOAA TIROS (television and infrared observation satellite) weather satellites. To service these and process the information, a ground network and processing system were also developed.

During this same period, the Russians developed their own COSPAC (Space System for Search of Vessels in Distress), which was the first to become operational. Both the U.S. and Russian SAR satellites operate in a similar manner, differing primarily in the processing and distribution of the data generated. They are now combined in one system (SARSAT/COSPAC). The French developed the ARGOS satellite gear first used to monitor long-distance ocean sailing events and were among a number of nations that contributed resources to the highly successful international effort. Racing vessels in the major ocean races are required to carry ARGOS transponders, which relay daily position and other information when interrogated by the satellites. The effectiveness of the system was proved yet again in two nearly identical tragedies at the end of 1986. On 13 November, the ARGOS satellite detected the big trimaran *Royale*, which had been leading the Route du Rhum Race in heavy weather, moving on erratic courses in the mid-Atlantic. Another vessel later sighted it capsized but Luic Caradeo, the sole crew and world-famous racer, was missing. A little over a month later, *Skoiern IV*, racing in the BOC, was detected by ARGOS wandering off the southeast corner of Australia. When the boat was located with sails still up, the sole crew member, Jacques de Roux, was missing.

Both the Russian and U.S. satellites use the changes in doppler effect as the satellite passes over a beacon in order to compute the survivor's position. The process is complex, and the time required is affected by the relative positions of the satellite, the beacon, the ground station, and the number of satellites and their tracks. At least two satellite passes are required to confirm a position, and the average time between transits is two hours. It is vital to the working of the system that *if you turn on an EPIRB, do not turn it off unless the emergency has terminated.*

Many racing sailors are familiar with the rescue in 1983 of Walter Greene, a trimaran designer, builder, and sailor, and his crew from the capsized *Gonzo* the day after activating his EPIRB following a capsize on a transatlantic voyage. Two years later, a fifty-year-old man was rescued after he had clung for thirteen hours to his life raft and EPIRB in the chilly and rough North Pacific.

More recent cases dramatically demonstrate the potential of the satellite detection system. A single-engine Cessna en route from Monterey, California, to Hawaii failed to make a scheduled position report. Only moments after the alert was passed to Honolulu RCC, an orbiting satellite picked up an ELT signal on the flight path three hundred miles northeast of Hawaii. A Coast Guard C-130 was scrambled from Oahu and located the partially submerged Cessna within fifteen minutes after arrival on the scene—only five miles from the position reported by the satellite. Helicopters from Hickam Air Force Base picked up the pilot three miles from the wreck and only two miles from the datum.

On 15 September 1986, the 42-foot motor vessel *Rhea C* with five persons on board was reported overdue on a six-day hunting trip from Homer, Alaska, to Port Chatham on the Kenai Peninsula. A composite SARSAT solution was received in the vicinity of Gore Point and an H-3 helicopter was scrambled from Kodiak. The helo found all five survivors on the beach only 1.5 miles from the SARSAT indicated position. The boat had sunk five days before after hitting a rock. The occupants abandoned ship in a life raft, rowed ashore, and were making their way along the beach using the EPIRB.

As of April 1988, more than one thousand lives had been saved by satellite reception of EPIRB and ELT signals. More than five hundred involved air crashes, and most of the others were marine cases.

The processing time of the class-B EPIRB signals, at least two and as much as twenty-four hours, will be drastically reduced by the 406 MHz EPIRB. The stowage of data and the computations will be done within the satellite computer and a position accurate within one to three miles transmitted to the nearest ground station. The new equipment will provide global coverage, which is not possible with the present 121.5/243 MHz EPIRB. Perhaps equally important is the ability of the new system to send a coded signal giving a boat's number and nationality, which will allow access to a data bank for information on the craft. This information is important in both SAR and in stopping the rash of false alarms, which threaten the effectiveness of the entire concept of search and rescue. Though the cost of the 406 MHz is about four times that of a class-B EPIRB, it affords rapid and accurate fixes worldwide. The 406 MHz is now mandatory equipment for commercial vessels, and mass production and competition should eventually make it affordable for recreational boaters. Some makers are offering updating programs for older class-B EPIRBs so that they can be used for years to come.

In November 1986, thirteen nations cooperated in the first worldwide test of the then new American-Soviet SARSAT/COSPAC system. Twenty-four emergency beacon transmitters on five continents were activated and monitored by three Soviet and two U.S. satellites.

The value of the new 406 MHz global system was proved dramatically during the testing phases. Two Belgian racing-car drivers were participating in the thirty-week car race from Cape Town to Cape Horn: via Africa, the Middle East, India, China, by boat to Canada, and thence, to the tip of South America. In a remote part of Africa, one of the cars flipped, severely injuring the driver. The other driver switched on an experimental 406 MHz transmitter. The signal was picked up by SARSAT and "dumped off" at the next ground station. The United States notified the French government, whose ambassador arranged for a doctor and medical evacuation to a hospital in Belgium. The driver recovered and later rejoined the race.

COST BENEFITS OF THE EPIRB

Two recent cases conclusively demonstrate the economic benefits of the EPIRB. On 9 May 1991, the Miami Rescue Coordination Center (RCC) received an alert via SARSAT from a vessel identified as the *Patricia Ann*, a 36-foot fishing vessel. The 406 MHz signal not only gave its identification and an accurate position 130 miles northwest of Tampa, Florida, but also the phone numbers of two shore contacts. Phone calls to them verified that the vessel was fishing near this position, and twenty-six minutes after the first SARSAT signal, a helicopter and a jet were airborne and immediately acquired the 121.5 MHz homing signal of the EPIRB. A little over an hour after launch, the aircraft sighted two men clinging to a hatch cover in six- to eight-foot seas and another in a life ring with the EPIRB. All three were picked up by the helicopter less than two hours after the sinking. The boat had been capsized by a large wave over the transom and sunk immediately with no time to grab PFDs or send a Mayday. The 406 MHz EPIRB had detached and actuated automatically. Total cost of the two-hour rescue effort was $6,500.

Less than two weeks later, the Miami RCC received a call from a concerned family that an 18-foot outboard with three adults and one child was overdue from a day fishing trip off Florida's west coast. The boat's destination was *thought* to be eighteen miles off Marcos Island, and weather was worsening. On the fourth day of an intensive search, a Coast Guard C-130 located the drifting boat and deployed two pararescue men to determine the condition of the survivors. The boat was over one hundred miles from its reported fishing position, but the survivors were in good condition. The boat had sailed with a past history of engine trouble, an adverse weather forecast, lack of reliable communications and signaling gear, and no EPIRB. Total cost to U.S. taxpayers for the massive four-day search and rescue was $554,000.

With the introduction of the new system, the use of EPIRBs will undoubtedly increase greatly. Wide usage promises to have as great an effect on marine and air safety as the coming of affordable and reliable voice radio did following World War II. In a large percentage of SARSAT cases to date, no other distress signal was transmitted, nor were authorities aware of a distress until receipt of the EPIRB/SARSAT signal.

EPIRB/ELT FALSE ALERTS

Though new technology offers tremendous potential for saving lives, its effectiveness and sensitivity in detecting weak signals ironically threatens to nullify some of its promise. In California, the state with the greatest total number of boats and aircraft, the EPIRB/ELT false alarm rate in 1986 was 98 percent! In September of that year, all nineteen rescue missions stemming from satellite detections were caused by beacons accidentally sending out distress signals. Although a few may be the result of negligence or malice, most are caused by human factors, material failure, or rough handling. The Coast Guard and other federal agencies have started a campaign to correct this problem, and a theme that will be repeatedly emphasized is, "Test your EPIRB in accord with instructions, but insure that it is off before getting under way or *after handling it.*"

TESTING THE EPIRB

Manufacturer's handbooks will recommend the proper operational tests for the EPIRB, usually consisting of briefly switching it on to a *test* position until a pulsing red light on the equipment indicates that it is working. A more reliable test, which is used by Coast Guard marine inspectors to test class-A or -B EPIRBs on commercial vessels, can be used by any boat owner:

1. Test only during the International Distress Frequency Test Period—from 00 to 05 minutes of any hour.
2. Turn on an FM stereo radio and tune it precisely to 99.5 MHz.
3. Operate the EPIRB's switch. If it is working, you will hear an oscillating tone on the radio.
4. Shut off the test switch as soon as you hear the tone. The test must not last more than ten seconds or three audio sweeps.
5. If you get no signal on the radio, first shut off the EPIRB. Then carefully check the FM radio to see that it is on 99.5 MHz. Repeat the test *once*. If you still hear no tone, have the EPIRB serviced by a qualified technician.

Warning: When conducting any test or handling an EPIRB, make sure it is turned off before putting it away.

MALICIOUS FALSE ALARMS AND HOAXES

Although they are few in number, deliberately false voice distress calls are a very serious matter. In a 1986 case in New England waters, a distress call reported a boat sinking with ten persons aboard and position uncertain. A large-scale search effort was launched. Later, a report claiming to be from the CGC *Spencer* was received.

The report later proved to be false and malicious. By the time the original distress call was determined to be a hoax, the search costs had risen to $77,000. Working on a number of calls and tips, Coast Guard intelligence agents and police arrested two men. Charges against them carried maximum penalties of $525,000 and eleven years in prison. In a similar case in New Jersey, the man convicted was given five years in prison and a fine of $10,000.

In both cases, malicious intent was the key element of the charges. This is a completely different matter from a legitimate distress call made in good faith, which turns out not to be serious. If a sailor believes that a situation is life threatening or beyond his or her capabilities to handle, the person can call for help without fear of later criticism.

VISUAL AND SOUND COMMUNICATIONS

Long before the days of electronics, seamen used visual and audio signals to attract help in time of trouble, and such signals still prove effective. The accepted forms of distress signals are incorporated in both International and Inland Rules of the Road. These are shown in Annex IV of the Rules (see also chapter 14). They are also covered in the handy and well-illustrated pamphlet "Visual Distress Signals for Recreational Boaters," available at no cost from the nearest Coast Guard unit (see Appendix F). Every boat should carry a copy.

SUMMARY

- Do not go alone offshore or in unprotected waters without VHF/FM radio, an EPIRB, and visual distress signals. File a float plan as a backup.
- Guard VHF Channel 16 at all times when under way at sea.

• Assist any vessel in distress and relay information if required.

• If your crew or vessel is in extreme danger, broadcast a Mayday message. If the danger is urgent rather than extreme, use the Pan call rather than Mayday. Messages prefaced with either Mayday or Pan are broadcast "in the blind," that is, without waiting for any other station to answer. If two-way contact is desired for advisory or safety reasons, call the Coast Guard on Channel 16. When they answer, request a shift to Channel 22 to work.

• If unable to reach a Coast Guard unit with less urgent traffic, try the marine operator or another boat for relay. For medical advice, call a physician or medical advisory service through the marine operator. If unable to do so, or a medevac is required, contact the Coast Guard.

• Beyond VHF range, use marine or amateur SSB if available, or relay through other vessels. If unable to communicate and a distress situation exists or threatens, actuate the EPIRB and do not turn it off until the emergency is over. Display appropriate visual distress signals, but do not use the expendable pyrotechnic signals until another craft is in sight, or until you are where watchers on shore can see the signal.

13
Abandoning Ship

Abandoning ship is, or should be, one of the most unlikely events at sea. Even if this improbable event occurs, there is usually advance warning and time to prepare. Only a fire, explosion, or a catastrophic collision is likely to force a hurried evacuation with little time for preparation. Heavy weather or a resultant capsizing may finally force abandonment of vessel, but it is unlikely to come as a surprise, nor is it advisable to leave a capsized or swamped boat until her demise seems sure. Stay with the vessel as long as possible, but assign a person with a sharp knife to tend the tether line and be ready to cast off the raft if the boat starts down. By staying on or close by the disabled boat, the survivors will be easier to spot and may have time to get more supplies from the vessel. The boat's predicament may also appear brighter as the weather moderates.

Not all abandon-ship evolutions involve a life raft or dinghy. Yachtsmen have been taken off by merchantmen, helicopters, or other boats, and others have jumped off grounded boats and waded ashore. A few have simply stepped from a burning or sinking boat onto a dock.

BOAT-TO-SHIP TRANSFERS

At any time, there are hundreds of commercial and naval ships at sea, but the chances of encountering one will depend on your nearness to their transit lanes. The Coast Guard tracks thousands of these ships with its AMVER system and on receiving a distress report, can within minutes have a computer printout (surface picture, or SURPIC) of all participating vessels within a specified area. The most suitable one is then called by radio, or an auto-alarm broadcast is made on 500 kHc, the International C-W Distress Frequency, to alert all ship radio operators. The distress information is broadcast, and a query is made about available help. As the various nearby ships answer, one or more are requested to assist and in nearly every case quickly do. If no distress communications have been sent or received, however, the survivors will have to chance being seen by a passing vessel or aircraft. When such a craft is sighted, the crew of the stricken boat must use all means—visual, radio, and audible—to alert the approaching plane or ship, because survivors are often difficult to see. Nearly all merchant ship captains will cooperate fully in saving people from a small craft, and a few may offer to try to save the boat if they have the capability, though they have no obligation to do so. If the boat is saved, the owner or the insurance company are obligated to pay a salvage claim from the ship.

Although merchant ships are a major source of help, transferring to a large ship with high freeboard can be a perilous operation for the crew of a small boat when alongside with high seas running (see figure 13.1). A sailboat with its high masts is more vulnerable than a motorboat, and loss of the mast while alongside is most likely. The mast striking against the side of the ship can be hazardous to those being hauled on board, so they should be taken from the stricken boat as far aft or forward as possible.

Jacob ladders and cargo nets are extremely difficult to climb, especially for storm-beaten and exhausted people, who may not realize the extent of their weakness until physical exertion is required. They should be assisted with bowlines tended by the ship's crew. A strain should be taken on the line when the boat rises to the top of a swell, and the victim assisted on board. The greatest danger is being caught or falling between a small boat and the side of the ship. Such a mishap is often fatal. I once saw a dozen survivors from the British freighter *Newton Ash* crushed between the side of the Coast Guard cutter *Ingham* and a large metal lifeboat that had capsized moments earlier as it came

Figure 13.1 The crew of the sloop *Yard Mystery* is taken aboard a large container ship after being located by a Coast Guard C-130 in heavy seas. In such a transfer, damage to the small boat is almost certain. *Courtesy USCG*

alongside. Though a cargo net was already rigged and swimmers went over the side to help, only three men survived.

In a more recent case in 1987, nineteen crew members from the 345-foot Philippine cargo vessel *Balsa 24* abandoned ship into life rafts five hundred miles northeast of Bermuda. The winter seas were 45 feet high and winds were 60 knots. A Coast Guard C-130, a navy P-3 from Bermuda, and a Canadian forces Aurora aircraft responded to the distress call. The navy plane dropped another life raft and soon all crew members had abandoned into either the life raft or the ship's lifeboat. The Russian *Adler*, the Panamanian *Frisia*, and an Israeli vessel all diverted to help. Air cover was flown over the survivors throughout the night by Coast Guard C-130s from Elizabeth City, North Carolina, and Clearwater, Florida. The USS *Scamp*, an attack submarine, and the *Frisia* arrived at first light. The submarine, though ill suited by its hull shape for picking up people, recovered one person before the raft capsized in the 40-foot seas. Four other occupants who were thrown into the water were never recovered. The *Frisia* came alongside the lifeboat but found only one person, who subsequently drowned during an attempt to take him aboard. The other occupants of the boat had died or drowned during the night. Though most survivors are rescued after being located, the fate of the *Balsa 24*'s crew is a solemn warning that there are no guarantees (even with a multinational effort by hundreds of able rescuers). It should also serve as a warning of the danger in the early abandonment of a storm-wracked vessel.

Because of these dangers, many captains of large rescue ships will launch their ship's lifeboat (obviously impossible because of the weather in the *Balsa 24* incident) to remove the crew of a disabled vessel or will ask the crew to take to their own inflatable life raft to provide a safer transfer platform. In a few cases lines have been passed to the survivors with instructions to make them fast and jump in the sea. Though the rescue ship can usually drag such victims aboard in a minute or so, it is a dangerous procedure in cold, rough seas, and people have drowned in the short time they were exposed.

With smaller, more maneuverable rescue vessels such as destroyers or Coast Guard cutters, the vessel will come alongside to weather in moderate seas, and employ specially trained swimmers to help survivors, or lie off in heavy seas and launch a boat to effect the transfer. The 19-foot fixed-keel inflatable Avon boat (RHIB) used by the Coast Guard can operate in most open sea conditions, and is much easier to launch and recover than the heavier ship's boats, though less capable in very heavy seas (see figure 13.2). If the commanding officer of the cutter deems the conditions too hazardous for surface transfer, the CO may summon a helicopter to evacuate the survivors. Whatever method is used, the survivors should follow orders from the professional rescuers whenever possible. The decision whether to abandon the boat or not, however, is a final responsibility of the skipper of the distressed craft.

In deciding whether to abandon the boat for another craft, the skipper should realize that the boat probably will be lost after the crew is removed. Most merchant ships do not have the capability or desire to risk lifting a small yacht aboard, nor are they well suited to tow, even if the small craft could withstand the imposed stresses. A Coast Guard rescue cutter will usually attempt to save the disabled boat, but the safety of personnel will always have first priority.

Figure 13.2 A rigid hull inflatable boat (RHIB). Fast, seaworthy, and easily handled, it can be used in either shoal water or offshore. *Courtesy USCG*

The case of the *Born Free II*, however, proved that ingenuity and strong motivation can overcome even the most difficult problems. The 41-foot sailboat, en route from Dana Point, California, to Hawaii with three persons on board had suffered a broken rudder near the midway point and had actuated her EPIRB, resulting in Coast Guard C-130s being launched from Hawaii and San Francisco. The disabled boat was quickly located by homing in on the EPIRB signal and the Dutch freighter *Kapelle*, plotted eighty-five miles north of the yacht by *Amver*, was diverted to assist. When the *Kapelle* was unable to fix the rudder, the USS *Fredrick*, an amphibious ship, was ordered to assist. Even the skilled technicians on the *Fredrick* could not fix the rudder. Towing the *Born Free II* would have been a slow and risky procedure, and in any event, the *Fredrick's* crew was heading for home port, which they had not seen for many months. Swinging out one of her deck booms, the *Fredrick* hoisted the *Born Free II* to her deck and resumed course for her home port, San Diego, where she deposited the yacht and her crew several days later. Liberty was granted on schedule.

BOAT-TO-HELICOPTER TRANSFERS

Boat-to-helicopter transfers are routine with SAR pilots, though they are more difficult and dangerous at night, in heavy seas, and for sailboats with tall masts. With the new generation of fast, long-range helicopters, small-boat sailors in distress will see even more helicopter rescues. Detailed hoisting procedures are described in chapter 15 (see figure 13.3).

BOAT-TO-BOAT TRANSFERS

The majority of rescues in the coastal and inland areas are made by small Coast Guard utility boats or civilian and fishing craft rather than the more dramatic rescues by helicopter or large ships. The workhorse of the Coast Guard's coastal and inland SAR effort is the fast and rugged 41-foot utility boat (UTB), which last year conducted over half of the rescues made by Coast Guard boats under 45 feet in length. The various small boats and yachts operated by the civilian Coast Guard Auxiliary carried out another 7,420 missions. Transferring people from a disabled vessel to one of these small rescue boats is far easier than transferring survivors to a large ship.

Personnel from the rescue boat will often be placed on board a disabled vessel to help in the transfer and to try to save the craft. Often just the presence of these experienced men will so bolster the morale of a storm-beaten crew that they will elect to stay with the boat. Because of their comparable size and power, these small rescue boats are more suitable for towing small boats than large ships are.

TRANSFERRING TO A LIFE RAFT OR DINGHY

If abandonment becomes necessary before help arrives, the crew in distress must act calmly and avoid panic. If the boat has been

Figure 13.3 A helicopter moves in to remove the crew of the yacht *Skivvy Waver* 160 miles off New Jersey. With one engine out because of fuel contamination, the yacht began taking on water. When two crew members were unable to climb the ladder to the rescue cutter, a rescue team was put aboard to help. When conditions worsened, two helicopters were called in to remove everyone before the boat sank. *Courtesy USCG*

properly equipped and the crew well briefed, the dangers are not insurmountable, even in difficult conditions.

Unlike a transfer to a waiting vessel or helicopter, abandoning a ship with no outside help requires that the crew take adequate equipment to guarantee their survival and location. So that nothing is overlooked, each crew member should have been thoroughly briefed beforehand on his or her duties and the equipment to be provided by him or her. The process involves two stages: (1) Prepare to abandon ship, in which equipment is collected and the life raft made ready for launching, and (2) Abandon ship, in which the raft is inflated and equipment loaded, followed by the crew. The type of raft, the equipment contained in it, the equipment to be loaded, and the launching procedures should have been decided long before the vessel leaves the dock.

Since World War II, when they were first widely used by aviators, the quick-inflatable rubber life raft has become highly popular with yachtsmen (see figure 13.4). It is easily stowed in a compact valise or canister, is light and simple to deploy, and inflates with the jerk of a lanyard. Once inflated and loaded, it is comparatively stable. The two main types are open single-tube rafts designed for use in coastal areas for short periods, and the more expensive double-banked circular rafts with canopies, insulated floors, and water ballast bags suitable for use over long periods of time in heavy sea conditions. The small-boat owner should avoid the temptation to save money by purchasing a cheap light rubber raft such as the ones used by children in swimming pools.

Figure 13.4 Survivors of the ill-fated 75-foot yacht *Marana* in dinghies and a life raft dropped by Coast Guard aircraft after the boat sank 17 miles off Miami, Florida. *Courtesy USCG*

Though they are sometimes advertised as *life rafts* and sold at a tenth of the cost of a proper inflatable raft, such cheap substitutes should not be taken offshore.

One school of thought holds that inflatable life rafts are not required for coastal cruising. Drowning and hypothermia are just as rapid in eighty feet of water two miles off shore as they are in a thousand fathoms five hundred miles out. Rescue may be more rapid in coastal waters, however, if a distress call was transmitted and received.

A quick-inflatable raft is not mandatory in coastal waters if an inflated rubber dinghy is carried on deck or towed astern. Time adrift is likely to be short and the stability of an open dinghy is unlikely to be critical. But carrying such a dinghy uninflated and stowed is a dubious answer, for in a sudden emergency one may not have enough time to inflate it with the hand pump.

Some yachts carry small rigid dinghies, which properly handled make good tenders in protected harbors. Most, however, can be too easily capsized or swamped and are simply too unstable for survival in open water. Those built in this country after mid-1973 have built-in flotation, should float in rough water, and afford some protection against hypothermia. They are infinitely better than being immersed in a PFD but not as suitable as an inflatable dinghy or life raft. If for any reason one of the above means of flotation cannot be carried, it is unwise to cruise offshore except in company with another boat.

AERIAL DELIVERY OF LIFE RAFTS AND EQUIPMENT

Coast Guard aircraft often drop life rafts and equipment to survivors in the water. The raft may be dropped inflated or left in the valise to be inflated by the survivors. When people are in the water, the raft will normally be dropped to inflate upwind of the survivors and drift down on them. If a drop is made to a boat still capable of maneuvering, the raft may be dropped uninflated close downwind. In either case, a long trail line is streamed from the raft to aid in retrieval.

After locating thirty-seven survivors of a ditched passenger plane 450 miles east of Jacksonville, Florida, we dropped six rafts upwind of the survivors and six more downwind, all set to inflate as they dropped. Eight of these were quickly retrieved by the survivors, who then rode in comparative comfort until picked up by a navy destroyer two hours later. Helicopters also carry droppable rafts, but there is little reason to use them because the survivors can be hoisted directly into the helicopter.

ABANDON-SHIP SUPPLIES

Most life rafts come packed with certain minimum supplies. Other required equipment for abandoning ship should be stowed in a secure but readily accessible location in the boat. Crew members should each be given specific responsiblity to see that the equipment is provided when needed. The equipment list is relatively simple for boats cruising in coastal areas where rescue can be expected in a reasonably short time if suitable communications gear is carried and a float plan filed. The essential requirements are:

- *Flotation*—Life raft or dinghy and PFDs
- *Protection*—Wear warm and snug-fitting clothes, including shoes, gloves, and hat, which will protect against exposure and will slow heat loss even when wet. If time permits, bring a small sail or blanket for protection against wetness, cold, or sun.
- *Detection Devices*—EPIRB, portable radio, day and night visual signals, whistles, a freon hand horn with spare can, and several flashlights with spare batteries.
- *Water*—A five-gallon plastic jug filled to 80 percent capacity so that it floats, with a lanyard attached to secure it to the raft. Water can become a major problem within three to four days, especially in hot weather. Seawater can be used to keep the skin cool but must not be used for drinking under any circumstances. Do not worry about food supplies in a coastal survival situation; in any area, deprivation of food should not become critical for most people for days or weeks.

MISCELLANEOUS

All crew members should carry folding or sheathed knives, being careful not to leave them loose and open in the raft where they can inflict damage. Insure that a hand air pump is in the life raft for reinflation if required.

Most of this equipment can be stowed in a duffle bag. Equipment that is used daily should be kept nearby to add to the equipment if the boat must be abandoned. Flashlights, batteries, portable radios, and other equipment can be stowed in waterproof zipper packages such as those used to stow foods.

INSPECTIONS AND STOWAGE OF LIFE RAFTS

Whichever type of inflatable life raft is used, it should be inspected periodically as recommended by the manufacturer, repaired and resupplied if necessary, and repacked by a qualified life raft specialist. Although such inspections are expensive, they are necessary for both safety and peace of mind. Take the opportunity when the life raft is inspected to watch it inflate and familiarize yourself with the types of equipment and stowage in the raft.

LAUNCHING THE LIFE RAFT

Secure the painter of the life raft firmly to a strong point such as a stanchion or cleat. Release the hold-down straps, stand clear of the painter, and launch the canister or valise on the lee side. Do *not* inflate the life raft on deck, especially in a high wind. Give a sharp tug on the painter to inflate the raft in the water. It will pop out of the container and take about a minute to inflate. After boarding, complete the inflation by hand pump if required (see figure 13.5).

Put one crew member into the raft to receive and stow the equipment. If seas are heavy, attach a backup retaining line with a quick-release knot. Tie the equipment to the raft after it is put on board. If the raft capsizes with unsecured gear, much of it will be lost.

1 Secure painter line to strong point	2 Stand clear of line and launch canister or valise
3 A sharp tug on painter will inflate the life raft	4 Remove shoes and any sharp objects from person; jump onto the life raft.
5 Cut or untie the painter from vessel when ready to cast off	6 Arrange occupants in a comfortable manner and secure survival equipment

Figure 13.5 Launching the life raft. *Courtesy Avon Corporation*

When survival gear is aboard the raft and secured, do not load the rest of the crew until the boat appears ready to sink. All hands should drink their fill of fresh water before leaving the boat. When the decision is made to leave, all persons must climb or jump into the raft, having removed shoes (take them with you) and sharp objects. If the raft is open, jump for the center of the raft so as to land on the buttocks and back. The give of the raft and water will cushion the impact, help prevent leg and ankle injuries, and protect the raft bottom by spreading the impact area. If the raft is covered, jump into the opening or dive face first on to the canopy structure and hang on until you can get into the opening.

If possible, avoid going into the water before boarding the raft. In cold weather, a swimmer can be quickly disabled. In any weather, it is difficult for even a strong swimmer, clothed and wearing a PFD, to climb from the water into a raft. Once in the raft, move quickly aside to clear a landing spot and assist the next person.

When loaded, check and inventory the raft's equipment and supplies. If any important items have been forgotten, weigh the risk in sending someone back to get them.

PREMATURE ABANDONMENT—A WARNING

Leaving a vessel still afloat to enter a life raft in heavy weather is often an ill-advised decision that over the years has resulted in many needless deaths (see figure 13.6). This seems to have been the case in the famous mystery of the *Mary Celeste*, found wandering under sail with no crew off the Azores in 1872. Fifty years later the sailing vessel *Carol A. Deering* ran onto Diamond Shoals off Cape Hatteras on a winter night in sight of the beach. When boarded soon after by a Coast Guard crew, food was on the table, charts were laid out, but no one was aboard and there were no signs of preparation for abandonment. No clues to the fate of the crew were ever found. In 1943, the crew of the SS *Coulmore* precipitately abandoned ship after being torpedoed. We located the ship the following morning, riding well in the water, and it was subsequently towed to Britain for repairs. It was still engaged in trade a quarter of a century later, but not a trace of the crew was ever found.

During the wooden sailing ship days, so many ships were abandoned but remained afloat that the United States in 1907 commissioned a special "derelict destroyer," and ordered the

Figure 13.6 The owner of a cabin cruiser hangs on to the bow of his boat, kept afloat by trapped air while awaiting pickup by a Coast Guard boat. This is usually wiser than trying to swim to a distant shore. *Courtesy USCG*

Revenue Cutter Service to cruise the shipping lanes and sink these floating navigation hazards. In the years since, dozens of other vessels, large and small, have been abandoned in heavy weather, only to be found later in sound condition and towed in to sail again. In the 1979 Fastnet disaster many lives were tragically lost as sailing craft were abandoned too hastily in severe weather. Most of the abandoned boats were subsequently towed safely into port.

Not only panic but fatigue and despair contribute to premature abandonment. An attitude of "Let's get it over with and get out of here" often prevails with weary and beaten crews, and even a life raft in rough seas seems preferable to staying with the boat. On the other hand, abandonment triggered by the arrival of a rescue vessel is a different story.

ADRIFT IN THE RAFT

Even before casting off, deploy the EPIRB and activate it. If a portable radio is on board, give a short twenty- to thirty-second Mayday call every half hour and listen for a reply for another twenty seconds. Set up a lookout to watch for aircraft and ships. Have visual aids readily accessible for quick use when needed.

After casting off, deploy the sea drogue as required. If your Mayday call or position was received by anyone, try to stay as close to the position as possible. If on a lee shore, the decision whether or not to slow the raft's drift will depend on the weather. With good weather and an onshore wind, pick up the drogue and close the coast. If surf conditions are bad, use the drogue to help hold you off the coast. Do the opposite with an offshore wind. If the direction of drift is not a factor, a drogue does help steady the raft in heavy seas. Some survivors have reported that a partially deflated raft seems to ride better in heavy seas, but this will cause wear on both the raft and crew and is inadvisable.

Survivors should huddle together for warmth, keep the sea water pumped or bailed out, and maintain a lookout. Do not use expendable pyrotechnics unless a vessel, aircraft, or inhabited shore is in sight. When it is, fire a signal, followed by another ten seconds later. The first is to attract attention, the second is to help confirm the sighting.

If seas are rough, ask a strong swimmer to attach a lanyard to his or her PFD and take station near the raft entrance. If the raft capsizes, the swimmer acts as a human sea anchor until the crew can reboard.

If the raft drifts toward shore and the surf is running, stream the sea anchor and cut off the canopy before entering the surf line. This will avoid trapping someone under the canopy if the raft capsizes.

Even the best rafts have a lively motion that is apt to cause discomfort and seasickness. The person in command of the raft must display a positive attitude, try to keep morale up, and establish a watch schedule. Do not, however, offer assurance of rescue in a *specific time period*. If not realized, the letdown is devastating.

THE DILEMMA WITHOUT FLOTATION

Those who proceed very far from land with no flotation equipment other than PFDs are literally betting their life that nothing will happen. True, some boats are too small to carry rafts or dinghies of any kind, but if their owners insist on going far from land, they should travel in company with another boat. I was once thrown into the water on a bitter cold January day when a boat capsized while we were duck hunting. We were five miles from any civilization, and we undoubtedly would have quickly succumbed had another boat not passed nearby. But even without a life raft, dinghy, or another boat in company, the situation is not hopeless. Survival equipment can be air dropped within a short time. The lack of flotation is also a powerful incentive not to prematurely abandon a disabled boat. Even one awash is better than being in the water with only a PFD.

Some survivors, for whatever reasons, may have no choice but to go overboard into the water. The degree of danger will be dependent on the water temperature and sea conditions. In warm water and moderate seas, people in PFDs have lived for days. In two cases involving bailouts from aircraft in Florida waters, the air crews were picked up nearly two days later in good condition. None were molested by sharks, though one pilot reported that he was circled by first two and then three sharks for long periods. The chief complaints by one crew were stings from jellyfish, and the other complained of small fish nibbling at the pilot's life jacket. This nuisance ended when one of the sharks ate some of the offending small fish.

People sometimes survive in northern climates. Shortly after sunrise on 14 September 1986, the 32-foot ocean racer *Super Heat* was swamped by a heavy sea off Ocean City, New Jersey. The five-member crew had time only to broadcast a Mayday before taking to the water in life jackets. An all-day search by a cutter and helicopter did not locate any survivors. Shortly after midnight, the motor vessel *Melvin H. Baker* heard a shout from a person in the water and picked up three men after lowering a boat. A Coast Guard helicopter was scrambled, located the other two men before dawn, and hoisted them from the 70-degree water. Despite over eighteen hours in the chilly water, all were treated for exposure and soon released from the hospital.

When properly equipped with a PFD, a person immersed in the water faces three principal dangers—sharks and other marine life, hypothermia, and discouragement or surrender—not necessarily in that order.

SHARKS

Of the millions of sharks inhabiting the oceans, only four types account for most human casualties. They are the white, tiger, hammerhead, and blue. Two other types, mako and gray nurse (sand) sharks, are occasionally involved. Despite a history extending for over a million years, surprisingly little is known about shark behavior.

Sharks live in oceans, seas, and river mouths and are found in great numbers where garbage or sewage is dumped. Most attacks occur in water temperatures above 65 degrees F, probably because swimmers are found only in warmer water. They seem to feed most actively at night and are attracted by light. After dark they tend to move toward the surface and into shore waters. Most attacks on humans have occurred in shoulder-deep water or less, but this is also where most swimmers are. A shark's natural food consists of small marine animals and fish, but it is also a scavenger and seeks easy prey such as dead bodies or wounded fish. It locates prey by smell, sight, and other mechanisms not fully understood. Sharks often swim in circles around a survivor to investigate and often leave with no further action. No proved chemical shark repellent has been found.

The following defensive measures are recommended when in shark-infested waters:

- Get injured or bleeding survivors out of the water and into a raft if possible.
- Do not remove clothes or shoes. They will help protect you against the shark's sandpaper-like skin, as well as against hypothermia.
- Survivors should stay in a group, facing outward. If a shark approaches, push it away with any object available. Always face the shark.
- Do not dangle hands or feet over the side of a raft or dinghy.

Considering the number of sharks and people swimming in the ocean at the same time, shark attacks on humans are comparatively rare. Many survivors have had no problems with sharks but have reported painful encounters with jellyfish and Portuguese men-of-war. Others have been bitten by bluefish and other smaller fish. In March 1987, a seventy-one-year-old retired navy officer was bitten badly by a wahoo, a mackerel-like fish, that had surfaced near his boat off the Pacific coast of Mexico. Because of a heavy loss of blood and the severity of the wound, he was evacuated by a Coast Guard Falcon jet from Isla Socorro one thousand miles to San Diego.

The case of the *Southern Isle*, which broke apart in heavy seas in the wake of a hurricane five hundred miles east of Jacksonville, Florida, had a more tragic ending. Though the water temperature was not cold, a number of crew members who were sleeping when the ship broke apart had to jump into the water with no clothing. When we reached the site several hours later, all those seen without clothes were already dead, and sharks were among their bodies. Others in clothing and orange life jackets appeared to be unmolested. Although most attacks do involve swimmers who are scantily clad, there is not enough evidence to generalize about the effect of clothing on shark attacks.

HYPOTHERMIA

Loss of body heat, called hypothermia, is a condition that can be just as deadly as drowning. Hypothermia occurs when a person is exposed to cold long enough to cause a marked drop in core body temperature (the temperature of the inner organs). The degree of hypothermia depends on the temperature of the water, whether protective clothing is worn, and the length of time of exposure.

Hypothermia may not be an immediate problem for persons who restrict their boating activities to the seasons when the water temperature is 75 degrees F or higher. Over a prolonged period, however, any water temperature below 98.6 degrees F can induce symptoms. If you go boating on the upland lakes or streams where the water stays cold all year, if you use your boat for hunting or fishing during the winter months, or if you just like to go boating in cold weather, hypothermia is an immediate danger. More hunters die from this and drowning than from gunshot wounds, because of the instability of most small boats used for hunting. Immersion or exposure can quickly become critical, and you should be aware of hypothermia, its symptoms, its prevention, and its treatment.

Hypothermia is most dangerous from a failure to recognize the symptoms and react promptly. The first indications are usually intense shivering, hyperventilation, or both. These denote a body temperature drop of about 2 to 5 degrees. If the body temperature continues to drop, shivering and respiration will diminish and the person will pass into a state of clouded consciousness. At that point the body's core temperature will be about 5 to 10 degrees below normal. Continued exposure will result in loss of consciousness, heart arrhythmia, and death. (See figure 13.7.)

In cold or rough seas, death from exhaustion, drowning, or hypothermia can come quickly. But there are numerous cases where people survived for hours in cold water because of the insulating effect of clothing and the support of a PFD. A fisherman dressed for December weather ten miles south of Pensacola, Flor-

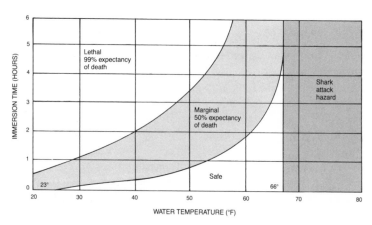

Figure 13.7 Water chill without antiexposure suit. *U.S. Coast Guard*, National Search and Rescue Manual, *1986*.

ida, was hoisted by a Coast Guard helicopter after seven hours in the water on a December day. In another case on 6 December 1986, fortunately dressed for New England winter weather, Bob Tuz swam ashore on Hicket Island, Maine, after a 30-foot fishing boat capsized in five-foot seas. Though the night was bitter cold with water temperature of 44 degrees F, Tuz survived the swim and the cold night on the island. After his rescue the next morning, his only symptom on arrival at the hospital was a slight fever.

Experience in hundreds of cases and follow-ups in controlled tests have proved conclusively that the following measures will greatly prolong life if a person is forced to go into the water:

- Don a survival or wet suit before entering the water. Though the dry type of rubber survival suit is rarely carried by recreational boaters, many do have wet suits used for snorkel or scuba diving. These can provide prolonged flotation and protection against hypothermia, even under severe conditions. If there is no wet suit, wear snug-fitting clothing, including shoes, gloves, cap, and a PFD. The clothing and accessories will provide an insulating effect akin to that of a wet suit, reduce the wind-chill effect, and once in the water add little to the swimmer's weight.

- Do not attempt to swim. Instead, assume a fetal position with arms across the chest and legs tucked up to the body, relying on the PFD for flotation. Any movement, even that caused by rough water, expends the body's heat reserve and hastens the onset of hypothermia.

- If several people are in the water, cling together as close as possible for mutual support and warmth. Most important, if there is a swamped boat, hatch cover, or any floating object, climb on it as high as possible to keep the vital organs of the torso out of the water. The loss of body heat is far greater in the water than in the wind. (See figure 13.8.)

A dramatic example involved the torpedoing and sinking of the U.S. troop transport *Henry Mallory* on a rough, cold February night in 1943 about four hundred miles south of Iceland. Hundreds of soldiers and sailors were forced into the water when the ship went down. When the sinking was finally discovered sev-

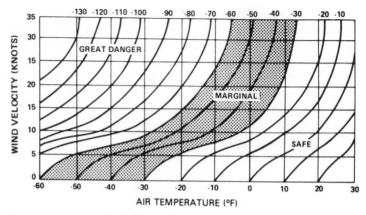

Figure 13.8 Wind chill graph—equivalent temperature curves. *U.S. Coast Guard*, National Search and Rescue Manual, *1986.*

eral hours later, and the CGC *Ingham*, CGC *Bibb*, and other escorts dispatched by the British escort commander arrived, all of the men in the water in life jackets were dead. In a lifeboat lowered from the *Ingham*, we checked dozens of men floating in life jackets, most dead within an hour of going in the water and already stiff with rigor mortis. Yet, three men sitting in a swamped lifeboat, five on a partially submerged float, and one marine on a hatch cover were picked up in relatively good condition twelve hours after the sinking. The common factor among the several hundred who survived was that they were in boats or on floating objects, and their vital core organs were not immersed, though they were wet, cold, and miserable. (See figure 13.9.) None who were immersed with only life jackets survived more than an hour or so in the 50-degree water. The difference has been repeatedly confirmed by tests and actual survival experience. As recently as 14 April 1987 the U.S. vessel *Reef Runner* located three Cubans on three innertubes tied together, fifteen miles off Alligator Reef Light in the Straits of Florida. They had been adrift several days but remained mostly out of the water and were in satisfactory condition when turned over to immigration officials on arrival in port.

Figure 13.9   Three merchant seamen are picked up by a Coast Guard cutter from the cold North Atlantic after many hours adrift. Though suffering acute discomfort, they were protected from deep hypothermia by remaining out of the water. *Courtesy USCG*

TREATMENT OF HYPOTHERMIA

Not only is hypothermia the leading cause of death among shipwrecked survivors, but it is almost always found to some degree in such persons. The victims are very pale; have general muscular rigidity; shiver, often uncontrollably; and exhibit varying levels of consciousness and shock.

Such persons should be assumed to have subnormal body-core temperatures, wrapped in warm blankets and clothing, and warmed as rapidly as possible. A medical treatment manual should be consulted. Lying close to others under cover to share body heat may help. The greatest risk during the warming process is ventricular fibrillation followed by cardiac arrest. If this occurs, strike a sharp blow to the victim's chest and initiate CPR. Nothing but warmed sweetened drinks should be given by mouth for some hours, and both alcohol and smoking must be avoided, all a radical departure from traditional treatments.

Severe cases of hypothermia (with core body temperatures below 90 degrees F) will have lost the ability to rewarm themselves without outside assistance and are at great risk. Accurate core temperatures can seldom be obtained under field conditions, so look for clinical signs such as confusion, poor coordination, apathy or lack of cooperation, and absence of shivering. If these are present, the patient should be air-evacuated as soon as possible. This is rarely required if the patient is alert, shivering, and can stand up.

THE WILL TO LIVE

An intangible yet decisive survival factor is a determination to live. Some people endure incredible hardships and survive; others die quickly without obvious cause. Physiological factors play a part, but the bigger role may involve the human spirit. Three recent episodes illustrate the point.

On 5 July 1986, the USS *Indomitable*, a navy auxiliary vessel, rescued six people from life rafts 240 miles north of Oahu. Their vessel had sunk two weeks earlier 500 miles northeast of Hawaii, leaving eight crewmen adrift. One soon died and was buried at sea. The first mate left his raft and set off for Hawaii alone in a 17-foot skiff to seek help, equipped only with oars and a sextant. Two navy and two Coast Guard aircraft searched 160,000 square miles looking for the missing man after the other survivors were located. After seventeen days (three days after the others were rescued), the missing first mate landed on the privately owned island of Niihau. He was found by the owner of the island, who flew him to Kauai.

Less than three months later, the 25-foot *Shell Game* radioed that it was sinking off the California coast. A three-day search by numerous SAR units made no sightings because of 35-knot winds and eight-foot seas. On the evening of the third day, the sailing vessel *Windsong* located one man on Santa Cruz Island. He had swum ten miles in heavy seas and had been in the chilly water for seventeen hours in a wet suit and PFD. He was flown to a hospital by Coast Guard helicopter and found to be in good condition. The other crewman had died the day before.

Ingenuity as well as courage plays a part in survival. Two men, adrift for ten days in a small 16-foot boat in the remote and lonely waters of the Gulf of California, between Baja California and the Mexican state of Sonora, fought off death from dehydration by rigging a still to convert salt water to fresh. The boiler, a used gallon gas can partially filled with sea water, was set atop two quart oil cans in which a mixture of oil and gas was burned. The salt-free distillate was caught in a plastic jug sitting in a seawater-cooled fishing tackle box. Three times the device caught fire in the small boat and was extinguished. On the last day of a three-day air search, the two survivors were found by a Coast Guard search aircraft and picked up by a helicopter. They had drifted over two hundred miles and were little the worse for the experience. (See figure 13.10.)

SUMMARY

- Do not abandon ship until it becomes clearly necessary. Even a beaten and waterlogged boat may be better than a life raft and certainly better than being in the water.
- Thoroughly brief the crew on abandon-ship duties and conduct in periodic walk-through drills.
- Carry a quick-inflatable life raft stowed in an accessible location. Insure that it is of adequate capacity for the crew and have it inspected regularly.
- If a life raft is not carried, carry a dinghy partially inflated on deck (it can be topped off after launching), or a rigid dinghy with built-in flotation. For short trips in protected waters, a dinghy may be towed.
- Carry out abandon-ship procedures in two stages— preparation and evacuation.

Figure 13.10 The only survivor of a yacht that broke up off the Bahamas stands on the wreck of the cabin top to keep out of the water. His companion had died the night before.

- If transferring directly to another ship, boat, or helicopter, carry only essential valuables. If loading into a life raft or dinghy with no other help present, provide adequate survival gear to assist in survival and rescue.
- If abandoning ship, wear a wet suit or snug-fitting clothes and a PFD.
- After loading the raft, stay by the boat until it sinks.
- Keep a sharp lookout, activate the EPIRB and portable radio, and be prepared to use detection aids if another craft is sighted. With flares, use two signals ten seconds apart. If the other craft is approaching, do not use signals prematurely.
- If in the water, avoid exertion. Keep the torso as clear of the water as possible.
- Do not give up. *Most people who are forced to abandon ship are rescued.*

14
Search and Location

SAR has two major phases—search (location) and then rescue. Most Americans cruise on interior waters or within a few miles of U.S. coasts and are often equipped with radio and some means of navigation. If an accurate distress position is promptly reported, little effort is required to locate the victim, and a rescue can be quickly made. The other cases can be time-consuming, costly, and occasionally are found too late. These difficult searches occur when:

- The boat has no radio
- A boat transmits a distress message but is unsure of its position and loses radio contact before it can be located
- A boat is unable, because of equipment failure or lack of time, to get through any distress message. The only clue then may be a report of an overdue boat.

When no one is even aware of the distress, especially in areas with strong winds and currents, water too deep to anchor, and a resultant high drift rate, there is potential for big trouble. Delay in alerting searchers will force an expansion of the search area to allow for drift. Even more doubts are introduced if there is no information on the cruising plans of the missing boat.

FLOAT PLANS

Anyone going onto exposed waters should leave a float plan (see Appendix A) with a reliable person. Tell the person whom to notify and when, if the boat is overdue. Failing to take this simple precaution wagers your life that a $300 radio set will work, that you will be able to use it in time, that someone else is not blocking the frequency, and that someone within range is listening. With neither a float plan nor radio, the odds can be grim should an accident or breakdown occur.

Once a float plan is filed, changes in routing should be radioed, phoned, or on long cruises, mailed back to the plan holder, as must be major changes in estimated time of arrival (ETA). Finally, there is the absolute responsibility to close out the float plan on arrival. The Coast Guard will assist you in contacting your float plan holder when necessary. The use of a float plan insures that an overdue boat will be reported, even if it is a considerable time after an accident occurs.

Despite the obvious rationale of a float plan, perhaps half of boaters still sail without one. One single-handing sailor left Florida for New York via the coastal route without a float plan. It was not for some weeks that anyone became concerned. When harbor checks failed to turn up the boat, the possible search area, taking into account drift and other unknowns, encompassed a large part of the western Atlantic. The boat was finally sighted by a merchant vessel drifting hundreds of miles off the Canadian Maritimes. (See figure 14.1.) Hundreds of other boaters, however, owe their prompt location and rescue to the fact that a float-plan holder or worried relative phoned in an overdue report.

ALERTING

Anyone seeing or learning of a distress incident, or anyone who is concerned that a boat is overdue, should promptly contact the nearest Coast Guard unit, or if none is nearby, the nearest public safety agency (police, sheriff, or fire department). The information will then be passed to the appropriate rescue center for action. If doubt exists, look at the emergency numbers listed in the

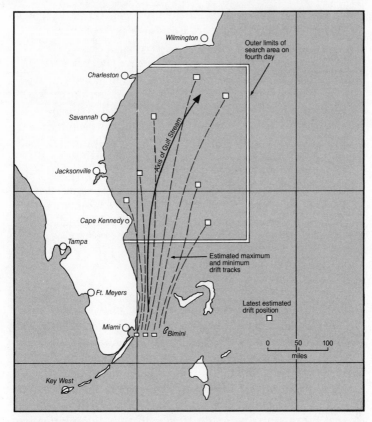

Figure 14.1 Expansion of the search area with time. A boat missing on a trip from Miami to Bimini was probably within an area of less than 500 square miles on the first night. Because of a long delay in alerting the Coast Guard, on the fourth day the area for search had expanded to over 90,000 square miles, requiring sixty times the number of aircraft search hours. The drift projections differ widely because of strong winds and currents, variations in their effects (drifting boat or life raft?), and uncertainty when and where along the route the boat's casualty occurred. Most of these variables could have been eliminated by a distress call or prompt action by the float-plan holder.

front of most telephone directories. A number is usually shown for "marine and air emergency" if an SAR facility is in the local area.

On becoming aware of a verified or strongly suspected distress incident, SAR units will be dispatched immediately and additional information gathered while they are en route. Additional help will then be dispatched if needed. With overdue craft, where no distress call or EPIRB signal has been received, the process is more deliberate, for many reportedly overdue boats are found safely tied up.

Generally a surface craft is considered overdue when it fails to arrive at its destination within a reasonable time after its ETA. When an overdue boat is reported, the rescue coordination center (RCC) will conduct a communications search before dispatching search craft.

COMMUNICATIONS SEARCHES

Communications searches involve basic detective work using radio and telephone to track down leads, as well as actual physical checks of docks and anchorages where the missing craft could be. Relatives and associates who may have information are contacted. Radio calls to the missing vessel are broadcast by Coast Guard units and the marine radio operators in the area, and a general radio broadcast is made to all ships at sea to maintain a lookout for the missing craft. After evaluating the information from all sources, the SAR mission coordinator (SMC) classifies the case in one of three phases: *uncertainty, alert,* or *distress.*

SEARCH PLANNING

If the overdue or missing craft is not located within a reasonable time by communication searches, an active search will be launched. (See figure 14.2.) Because of the large cost and effort involved in a maritime search operation, it must be carefully planned, especially if large numbers of search units are involved. The search planner must:

Figure 14.2 Rescue Coordination Center (RCC). A dozen of these centers stand continuous watch over the various U.S. maritime search-and-rescue areas extending from the mid-Atlantic to the Pacific Far East. *Courtesy USCG*

• Determine the probable position of the emergency or survivors, considering the drift since the initial occurrence.
• Determine the size of the area to be searched.
• Select the search patterns to use.

The search patterns will be one or a variation of the following (figure 14.3):

Sector search (a): used when position of distress is known within close limits.
Parallel track search (b): for search of large areas when there is little information on the missing boat's position.
Track line search (c): used when the proposed track of the distressed boat is known but not its position along the route.

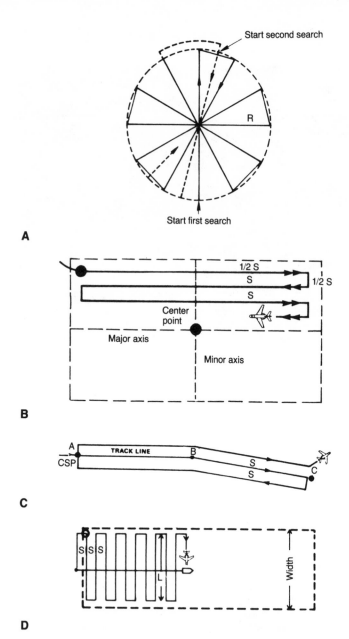

Figure 14.3 Search patterns. A. Sector search, for use when datum known within close limits. B. Parallel track search, for coverage of large areas. C. Track line search. D. Ship-plane search. *U.S. Coast Guard*, National Search and Rescue Manual, *1986*.

Coordinated ship-plane search (d): used when a ship and air-craft are working in company. An excellent pattern for Coast Guard cutters carrying a helicopter and with refuel-ing capability.

REPEATED SEARCHES

Even with search legs close together, it is very common in poor weather to fly over a small target without sighting it, or a momen-tary distraction within the search aircraft may cause a lookout to miss a nearby target. To compensate for this, repeated searches of the area, often five or more, are made. Survivors should not de-spair if passing search units do not sight them when passing nearby. The searchers will pass close by on the next leg and any number of times on repeat searches. Every attempt should be made to attract attention when any search unit is sighted, but re-straint must be exercised in expending limited pyrotechnics when the search craft is at the outer limits of visibility.

DETECTION AIDS

Visually sighting a small object in heavy seas is extremely diffi-cult because a person, life raft, or small boat may be concealed amid hundreds of whitecaps and wind streaks. Ahead-scanning radar is not very effective in detecting small fiberglass or wood boats in heavy seas because of the poor reflective surfaces and sea return clutter. As the search progresses, fatigue adversely affects the ability of an aircrew to see small objects. Survivors must use aids such as flares, smoke, mirrors, bright color fabrics, lights, and dye marker to attract attention.

On a search for survivors in a life raft several hundred miles off the coast of Florida, my copilot sighted the raft close under us at dawn after an all-night search. I wrapped the plane up into a steep turn and dropped a smoke float to mark the spot. As we circled, however, no raft could be seen. After ten minutes, both of us were questioning if we had seen a life raft or a patch of Gulf weed similar in color. Fortunately, we once again sighted the raft only four hundred yards from the burning smoke float. That he had seen it at all in the dim light was miraculous, for the occu-pants of the raft had no visual aids.

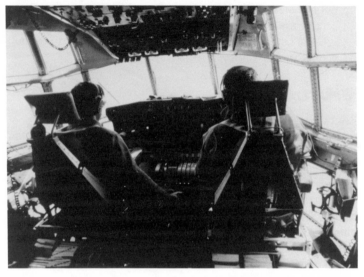

Figure 14.4   Most visual sightings by aircraft are made by the forward flight deck personnel, such as these on a C-130 Hercules search aircraft. *Courtesy USCG*

Even with detection aids, there is no guarantee that a survivor will be seen. A forty-year-old commercial pilot sighted an oncoming freighter the day after his 26-foot trimaran *L'Escargot* capsized off the coast of Costa Rica after hitting a submerged object. He confidently fired a flare, then four more, until one remained. The freighter continued on its way after passing only a mile away. Though the capsized pilot had deployed an EPIRB, it was apparently outside the coverage area of the SARSAT satellite, and there was no transient air traffic to hear it. Later another ship passed five miles away, but the now-skeptical survivor chose not to use his last flare. On the fifth day, he sighted a ship, the *Venus Diamond*, heading directly for him and only three miles away. He began signalling with a mirror, but as the ship neared, it showed no signs of slowing. Aiming the flare gun directly at the bridge, he tried to fire, but he had forgotten to cock the gun. After quickly cocking it, he fired the last flare almost vertically at the bridge and was immediately thrown into the water by the ship's bow wave. This last flare was seen by the officer of the watch as he stepped from the chart room, the ship was brought about, and a quick pickup effected. All the while, a ten-foot-long hammerhead shark was circling the site.

Distress signals are relatively expensive and may never be used, but if one is ever needed, it may literally be worth its weight in gold. Unfortunately, the effectiveness of the signal usually correlates with cost. A high-altitude parachute flare, which will burn for twenty to thirty seconds, will be much costlier than a hand-held version with only half the detection range and burning time.

Night visual aids and lights are especially useful in heavy seas. Though the whitecaps and spray may effectively hide a small boat in daylight, a night search may have a better chance of success. White caps and seas have little adverse effect on the aerial sighting of pyrotechnics and lights. One of the most cost-effective investments is a three- to four-battery waterproof halogen flashlight and a good supply of spare batteries. An SOS on either a flashlight or horn will be recognized by nearly everyone on the water as a distress signal.

At close range, a whistle is also good for as long as the user can blow and is not blocked by intervening swells. No one who has seen a flashlight blink in the night at a range of five miles or heard the whistle signals from survivors in the water near a rescue ship will ever forget their effectiveness. Likewise, the flashing of a signal mirror on a bright day will attract the attention of even a weary search crew at a range of several miles. Its effectiveness, however, depends upon the cloud cover and angle between the survivors, the sun, and the search craft. Waving an orange or white shirt side-to-side on a long pole is also effective; few people will interpret it as a mere greeting, as too often happens with arm waving. Nonpyrotechnic signals have the great advantage of being reusable over long periods.

Pyrotechnics as a rule should not be used until a rescue craft is sighted. Their effectiveness will then depend on the alertness of the passing vessel. During December 1986, the CGC *Cape George* was returning to Guam after seaching eleven days in heavy seas for two missing boats. Midway through a rough mid-watch with 35 knots of wind and twelve-foot seas ahead of Typhoon Kim, a tired but alert lookout sighted a dim white light off the bow. Investigation showed it to be a flashlight waved by one of the three men in a missing 14-foot boat. All were quickly taken on board and removed from the path of the approaching typhoon.

The ultimate detection aid is a radio signal from an EPIRB or portable radio. The signal can be picked up by a satellite or search craft while still many miles away, and searchers can home quickly to the scene using a radio direction finder (RDF) until visual contact is made.

Sound	Sight
Mayday by fixed or portable radio	SOS by flashlight
EPIRB radio	parachute flares
cellular phone	red pistol flares
continuous horn signals or SOS by horn	hand-held smoke or flares
gun fired at one-minute intervals	open flames
mouth whistle	strobe lights, on jacket or floating
yelling	signal mirror
	dye marker
	waving bright color on pole
	national ensign inverted
	black square and ball on orange flag
	signal flags November and Charlie
	square object and ball

There is a catch-22 in planning searches for visual aids. In order to use a light or a flare, the survivors must first sight the search craft. It is therefore necessary that they maintain a continual sharp lookout, not always an easy task in a cramped heaving life raft. There is also the chance that the visual aids have been exhausted or lost, in which case a night search is futile unless the position is known within fairly narrow limits that will permit a close search with high-tech detectors. These include

Air-Eye, a multisensor system installed on some of the new HU-25 Falcon jets. Air-Eye uses a side-looking airborne radar (SLAR), an infrared/ultraviolet line scanner, an aerial reconnaissance camera, and active gated laser television, as well as a display and control console. All of the information can be videotaped and processed in the air. The powerful SLAR system can detect small boats and life rafts at ranges up to twenty-two miles and cargo vessels out to sixty-eight miles. Once detected, the vessel can be examined by the night sensors even in darkness. Helicopters are also being equipped with forward-looking infrared sensors (FLIR), which detect targets at sea using the temperature differences between the target and the surrounding water. In the night detection array are also the Litton M909 night-vision goggles for aircrews, which allows the detection of small objects at ranges of half a mile using only starlight or moonlight, and the powerful Night Sun airborne searchlights for helicopters. In June 1985, a helicopter from CG Air Station Borinquen used its Night Sun lights to guide rescue boats through a treacherous reef to rescue nine shipwrecked pleasure boaters off the coast of Puerto Rico.

SIGHTINGS

On sighting the survivors, a search craft will first mark the spot with pyrotechnics and perhaps an electronic datum marker buoy, notify the on-scene commander, and prepare to make the rescue or assist as directed. Unless confronted with severe weather or a large number of survivors, the rescue should follow quickly. If the sighting was made by a helicopter or surface unit, they may complete the rescue without further delay. If the search unit is a fixed-wing aircraft, it will call in the nearest surface unit or helicopter or divert other nearby vessels.

INTERNATIONAL AIRCRAFT–TO–SURFACE CRAFT SIGNALS

The following maneuvers performed in sequence by an aircraft indicates that it wishes to direct a surface craft toward people or craft in distress:

- Circling the surface craft at least once.
- Crossing the course of the surface craft *close ahead* at low altitude and (1) rocking wings, (2) opening and closing throttle, or (3) changing propeller pitch.
- Then heading in the direction in which the surface vessel is to follow.

When a plane goes through such a sequence, a pleasure boat skipper should follow the aircraft and guard radio emergency Channel 16 and 2182 kHz if equipped with SSB.

When assistance is no longer required, the aircraft will cross *the wake* of the surface craft, flying close astern at low altitude and (1) rocking wings, (2) opening and closing throttle, or (3) changing propeller pitch.

SUMMARY

The average small-boat sailor will have little need to delve deeply into maritime search techniques other than to understand his or her role in not becoming a prolonged search target. The most important points are the following:

- Have a workable radio and use it promptly if needed.
- Know your position at all times and transmit it with your distress message. Maintain communications as long as possible so that rescuers can home on the radio signal.
- *Always leave a float plan*, even if it is only a verbal one. If you do not get out a distress or EPIRB signal, the float plan may be your only hope of alerting help in time.
- Notify your float-plan holder if your plans change.
- On extended trips, make scheduled position reports to someone if possible. Use ham radio, a marine operator, or (if touching land) a telephone. If badly delayed, advise any Coast Guard station of your situation and request it be relayed to the float-plan holder. Regularly scheduled position reports will reduce the uncertainties if you later encounter trouble. On extended voyages, use postcards if necessary to update your travel plans and location.

• Activate your EPIRB if in serious trouble and not in two-way radio contact. *Leave it on* until located or the emergency passes.

• Keep a sharp lookout for search craft and have detection aids ready. Your rapid location is as dependent on you as on the search crews.

• On arrival, *close out* your float plan.

15

Specialized Rescue Procedures

Many basic rescues can be accomplished or aided by nearly any vessel or boat, or by aircraft and helicopters not specifically equipped for SAR. Some situations, however, require special equipment and training that is only possessed by the primary SAR forces, the other military services that assist them in SAR, or commercial salvors. The most highly specialized rescue techniques involve helicopter rescues, airdrop of equipment, underwater SAR, and towing and salvage.

HELICOPTER MEDICAL EVACUATION (MEDEVAC)

Other than antibiotics, no development in the past fifty years has proved more beneficial to sick and injured sailors than the helicopter. The first SAR mission by a helicopter was the delivery in 1944 by the Coast Guard of medical supplies to the victims of an explosion on a navy destroyer. Since that time, thousands of medevacs have been conducted in peace and war, peaking in the universal use of helicopters for the rapid evacuation of wounded during the Vietnam War.

A modern SAR helicopter can proceed out to 250 miles offshore and return in less than four hours. Except in heavy weather or darkness, only normal flight risks are involved. Unfortunately many medical emergencies cannot wait on weather or daylight, and over the years a number of Coast Guard helicopters and crews have been lost on such missions.

For this reason, a medevac is undertaken only after complete information on the case is obtained, the medical need confirmed by a staff medical officer, and the flight feasibility approved by the operational commander. In an urgent case, this approval process will move quickly. Even so, the Coast Guard is sometimes fooled.

While I was commanding the Coast Guard air station at Salem, Massachusetts, we received a radio call for a medevac from a yacht reported ninety miles offshore. A crew member had appendicitis, which had been diagnosed by a doctor on board. Despite heavy fog in the area, a helicopter was dispatched with a fixed-wing aircraft as escort and cover. When the yacht was finally located, it was over fifty miles further out to sea than it had reported. Already short of fuel, the helicopter pilot was unable to see the yacht because of fog, and had to break off, landing at an island with 20 minutes of fuel remaining. Another helicopter was sent out and brought in the patient. The following morning, the patient walked out of the hospital in good health. He did not have appendicitis. It turned out that the patient was also the doctor and had diagnosed his own illness; the patient-doctor was also the navigator who had a fifty-mile error in his position.

PREPARATIONS

As soon as a medevac is approved, the boat with the patient will be advised of the expected arrival time of the helicopter and given instructions on how to prepare. A typical instruction message will read as follows:

A Coast Guard helicopter is en route to your position. Request that you make the following preparations for hoisting. Lower all masts and booms that can be lowered. Provide a clear area for hoisting, preferably on the stern. Keep all unnecessary personnel out of the way. When the helicopter arrives in your area, change course to place the wind on your bow and slow to a comfortable speed to minimize boat motion. This may be modified on request from the helicopter pilot.

The helicopter will provide all of the required equipment. The rescue device (basket, litter, or sling) should be guided to the selected location on deck by the ship's crew by means of the steadying line. On each approach, allow the rescue device to touch your vessel or the water to discharge any static electricity. If the rescue device has to be moved to the person being evacuated, unhook it from the hoist cable. Do not move the rescue device from the hoisting area with the hoist cable still attached. If the cable is unhooked, *do not*, I repeat, *do not* attach the cable to any part of your vessel.

For safety, the helicopter may move to one side while the patient is being prepared for hoisting. Ensure that the person being hoisted is wearing a life jacket if his or her condition permits. The patient should be made as comfortable as possible, and if conscious, should be informed of the instructions about the rescue device. Upon signal from your vessel, the aircraft will move back over the vessel and lower the hook. Allow the hook to touch your vessel to discharge static electricity. Then refasten the hook to the rescue device.

When the vessel is ready to hoist, a "thumbs up" signal should be given to the aircraft. Ensure that personnel tend the steadying line to prevent the rescue device from swinging excessively. During the hoist, strong gale- and even hurricane-force winds may be caused by the helicopter's downwash. These winds may make it difficult to steer your vessel. Ensure that all loose gear, sails, and covers on the vessel are securely tied down and hatches are closed. Attempt to contact Coast Guard rescue helicopter (number) on (frequency) at (time).

It is especially important that all gear topside be well secured, especially sails, awnings, and rigging, for any loose object could be swept up by the very high winds generated by the helicopter blades and ingested into the turbine or rotor blades. The helicopter should also be informed if the patient's condition will permit the use of a hoist basket (fig. 15.1) or will require being hoisted in a horizontal position in a Stokes litter (fig. 15.2). Be sure that all instructions are clear before hoisting begins, because the noise of the helicopter will make radio conversation during hoisting difficult or impossible. Either advise the pilot by radio about medications already given the patient or enclose a written note with the patient.

Figure 15.1   A survivor of a capsized boat is hoisted by a helicopter off the Florida coast. The victim is seated in a standard Erickson rescue basket used by the Coast Guard for most helicopter rescue hoists. *Courtesy USCG*

Occasionally a paramedic will be lowered to the boat to examine the patient and assist in the hoist, and in a few cases para-rescue men have been parachuted from fixed-wing aircraft. In such cases, the boat will be fully instructed beforehand by the pilot.

It is imperative that all preparations be completed before the hoist, that no unnecessary delays be caused, and that under NO circumstances should a light be directed at the helicopter at night. The pilot often has to hover with the helo's rotor blades turning only a few feet from a swaying mast, and any contact between them could result in instant death for both the flight crew and the boat crew below. Though thousands of such hoists have been safely made, there is little room for error or carelessness.

Figure 15.2   An HH-3 helicopter hoists an injured crew member, strapped in a Stokes litter, from a cabin cruiser. The ample deck space and low antennas make this hoist much easier than one from a sailboat with high masts and rigging. *Courtesy USCG*

HOISTING SURVIVORS

Though similar to a medevac hoist, the rescue of survivors from a sinking boat or the water usually has to be done without a prior briefing. The rescue will normally be made with the basket, though a horseshoe sling may be used with experienced military or physically able people. If so, the center of the sling must be at the back and under the shoulder blades of the person being hoisted. If the sling position is reversed, the survivor can slip out. If a victim in the water is unable to get into a sling or basket alone, a rescue swimmer from the helicopter crew may be lowered into the water to assist, or an amphibious helicopter such as the HH-3 Pelican can land beside the victim (fig. 15.3).

Figure 15.3   A helicopter crew member crouches on the rescue platform and prepares to haul in the survivor of a boating accident after the helicopter landed alongside. *Courtesy USCG*

On the night of 28 October 1991, at the height of Hurricane Grace, a Coast Guard HH-60 helicopter from the air station at Elizabeth City, North Carolina, fought its way through the hurricane to reach the foundering 95-foot schooner *Anne Kristina* at a position 350 miles off Cape Hatteras. Because of the extreme range, Lieutenant Paul Lange landed his helicopter on the carrier USS *America*, which was sixty miles off the coast in thirty-foot seas, refueled, and was again airborne within ten minutes. The schooner was sighted near midnight by using night-vision goggles, and evacuation of the nine crew members began. The rescue swimmer, twenty-nine-year-old Duane R. Jones, was lowered into the howling storm and forty-foot seas. In one of the great rescue feats of maritime history, the nine crew members were all hoisted and the helicopter headed back to home base, 350 miles away, refueling again from the USS *America* enroute. It landed at Elizabeth City after a 7.7 hour flight. The following day, a fresh crew using the same helicopter and similar techniques, rescued four more people from the sailing vessel *Snowy Egret*.

AERIAL DELIVERY

Both helicopters and fixed-wing aircraft can be used to deliver SAR gear and survival supplies to people or boats in distress. This includes life rafts, survival gear, detection aids, portable radios, pumps, mechanical parts, and medications. Because of the rapid scramble time and high speed of the latest generation of rescue aircraft, it is probable that a fixed-wing aircraft can reach most positions within 150 miles of the U.S. mainland within an hour of the alarm and within 500 miles in two hours. A helicopter can reach its maximum offshore distance of 250 miles within 2½ hours. The long-range C-130 Hercules can reach mid-Atlantic or mid-Pacific in four to six hours. There are few places in the northern hemisphere where help cannot reach a cruising sailor within hours.

If survivors are in the water or on a sinking boat, a fixed-wing aircraft can drop flotation and survival gear either by free fall or parachute. A fixed-wing aircraft cannot deliver supplies with the accuracy of the slower helicopter, and weary survivors cannot always retrieve the gear. The helicopter may often dispense with delivering gear and hoist the survivors directly into the helicopter if the situation is critical.

The rescue of four men from the small fishing vessel *Chabro* in May 1986 was a classic example of a triple-effort rescue. A distress call, relayed by another boat, reported the boat sinking 160 miles southwest of Cordova, Alaska. A C-130 was diverted from a logistics flight, found the survivors floating in survival suits, and dropped them a life raft. The fishing vessel *Kodiak* soon arrived on scene and recovered all five people, one with no signs of life. An HH-3 then arrived and hoisted the comatose victim and delivered him to medical help at Seward, but he was pronounced DOA (dead on arrival).

Both helicopters and fixed-wing aircraft are used to deliver pumps for dewatering swamped boats, but the helicopter with its hoist can do so far more accurately than a fixed-wing aircraft using a parachute drop.

If personnel must be placed aboard a boat to assist the victims, lowering them from a helicopter is obviously far safer than parachuting, even using crack pararescuers. The latter may have to be used, however, on long-range missions outside helicopter range.

SURFACE RESCUE CRAFT

Since neither high speed nor extensive searching are essential in most recreational boat rescues, it is not surprising that over 80 percent of such surface aid is rendered by small Coast Guard utility boats such as the 41-footer, with the remainder performed by larger patrol boats and high- and medium-endurance cutters. All the large and most medium cutters have helicopter platforms and refueling facilities and carry helicopters on board on many missions. Such a combination affords the best of all worlds: speed, search capability, endurance, and adequate on-scene personnel.

Whatever the distress incident, Coast Guard surface units are capable of pumping and dewatering, firefighting, towing, first aid, limited repairs, and other general assistance on board. Few cases arise that cannot be dealt with by one or a combination of SAR units. Yet failures still occur, primarily as a result of delayed alerting, uncertainty about position, a rapidly progressing medical casualty, or extreme weather stresses.

UNDERWATER RESCUE

Pleasure boaters are seldom involved in underwater mishaps. The SAR system, however, has available a variety of resources to assist scuba divers, an occasional miniature submersible, or persons trapped in a capsized boat. These include the underwater capabilities of the Coast Guard's Atlantic, Pacific, and Gulf strike teams; the navy SEAL teams; and the navy's submarine rescue division.

SALVAGE OPERATIONS

Coast Guard units engage in salvage other than towing only when no commercial salvage facilities are on scene and immediate action such as ungrounding, pumping, and damage control is necessary to prevent further damage or loss. When no commercial salvage companies are available within a reasonable time or distance, the Coast Guard may refloat a grounded boat even though it is not in danger of further damage or loss, provided:

- Coast Guard units are capable of doing the job.
- The owner requests the assistance and agrees to the specific effort to be made.
- Coast Guard units and personnel are not placed in jeopardy.

Because most salvage jobs are covered by insurance reimbursements, the issue is less emotionally charged than is towing, which is covered by fairly rigid liability restrictions.

LIABILITY IN MUTUAL ASSISTANCE BETWEEN PLEASURE BOATERS

There is a good possibility that any small-boat operator at some time will either require a tow or be in a position to assist another boat with one. In either case, a tow should not be undertaken lightly or without full preparations. Although under both federal law and the Rules of the Road a good samaritan is protected from liability, the protection exists only as long as the rescuer exercises reasonable care. The good samaritan principle also does not apply to a person charging a fee for services, so if volunteering aid to a disabled boat, make it clear that no fee will be charged. The acceptance of any payment not only increases the liability risk but can void a pleasure boater's insurance coverage while so doing. A waiver of liability from the disabled boat is of little use in distress cases. The courts have ruled that a person in distress is not in a position to bargain, and any such agreement would be under duress. Unless confident of your ability to properly carry out the tow, it is best to stand by while the disabled boat calls for a more capable towing vessel or the Coast Guard.

If you are the person in need, it is highly likely that another boater will come along and willingly and capably assist you. In some isolated instances, however, a person or business assisting you may attempt to take advantage of your troubles, and you should take defensive actions to protect yourself under the salvage laws, which are quite different from those used ashore. These are quite complex and a large portion of salvage claims end up in court or arbitration. Fortunately, few of them involve small pleasure craft.

Although any vessel at sea is required by custom and law to render aid to save *life*, there is no legal obligation to save *property*. The incentive to do so is provided by the use of salvage awards. To have a valid claim, the salvor must prove that the disabled vessel was in peril; that the salvor volunteered to help; that the salvor's own life and vessel were risked in so doing; and finally, that the effort was successful.

To minimize such a claim, the disabled vessel should display no emergency flags or signals and should use as little of the salvor's gear as possible. The disabled boat's towline or anchor rode should be used if feasible. The crew should leave either one crew member on board or leave a written notice that the crew will return and that the abandonment is temporary. The mere acceptance of aid or a tow does not in itself entitle a salvor to an award or ownership claim.

The simplest protection is to agree on a towing fee or a non-charge before the operation begins. Such an agreement, even an oral one in the presence of witnesses, will bar any further claims for salvage fees beyond the agreed terms.

TOWING PROCEDURES

Should a tow be decided upon, the two boat crews should fully discuss the procedures to be used:

• The disabled boat should secure all sails and loose objects on deck, and prepare an anchor for quick release if the towline snaps.

• The crews should agree on hand signals or a VHF/FM channel to pass instructions.

• The salvor should make a slow, cautious approach from leeward and pass or take a towingline or hawser as the boat passes the disabled boat's bow. Do not get too close in a seaway. If conditions appear marginal, pay out a long towline buoyed with PFDs or cushions and make a circling pass around the stern of the disabled boat so that the line can be retrieved from the cockpit with a boat hook. Have plenty of slack line on deck to pay out and afford time for the other boat to make the line fast (see figure 15.4).

• The towing boat should use a bridle fastened to strong points well forward on either side such as winches or heavy backed cleats. Do not fasten the line to the stern or pass it through a stern chock, as it restricts the swinging of the stern. This is known to seamen as a "bound rudder." (See figure 15.5.)

The longer the towline the more resistant it is to sudden forces and shock. Twisted nylon lines have good stretch and shock-cushioning characteristics but also have a dangerous lash if they snap under strain. The use of a length of chain or a small anchor midpoint of the hawser will produce a greater catenary and more cushioning effect, but such rigs should be left to experienced tow crews. Double-braid nylon is safe and strong and the preferred choice for towing because there is less backlash if the line parts. But it is susceptible to chafing and must be well protected by chafing gear at points of friction.

• The disabled vessel should make the towline fast to a strong point such as the forward bits, or cleats, or to the mast at its junction with the deck, provided it is one that extends to the keel. Whatever strong point is selected, the line should then be

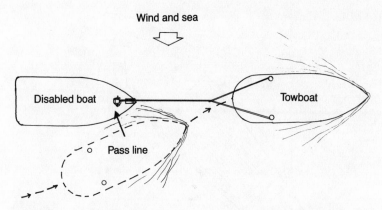

Figure 15.4 Passing a towline to a disabled boat. Adequate line must be on deck to pay out and allow time to make it fast on both boats.

extended aft to a large winch, all the slack taken out, and tension set on the line as a backup for the strong point attachment (fig. 15.6). Powerboats may elect to run a bridle around the deckhouse. If strong points further aft are used, whether a single point or double ones with a bridle, the towline must be led through a stem chock and well secured to prevent its jumping out. If it does, the tow force is exerted further aft on the towed boat, which can quickly slew or broach.

• A sharp knife or axe must be close by on both vessels if it becomes necessary to sever the towline.

• When ready for tow, a safety oberver must be stationed aft on the towing vessel to watch and communicate with the tow. The observer should advise the skipper of the towing vessel if slack develops in the towline, which can foul in the screw. On the towed vessel, someone must be at the helm to keep the disabled vessel lined up and in the wake of the towing vessel.

• A strain must be taken slowly on the towline and speed increased with caution. The most common mistake in towing is to proceed too fast, which can cause severe stresses on the disabled boat and in some cases even a breakup. This is especially true when a large or powerful vessel attempts to tow a smaller one.

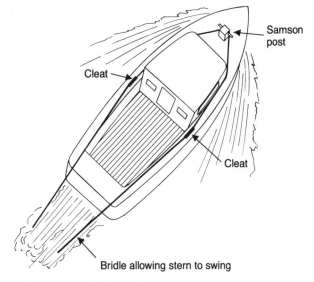

Bridle allowing stern to swing

Figure 15.5 Towing harness. The bridle is secured forward at the samson post, around the deckhouse or at other strong points, then led to the midship cleats. With the bridle secured to cleats well forward of the rudder, the stern will be able to swing more freely and the boat can be more easily maneuvered. Lines must not be fastened to cleats alone, especially not to those without strong backing plates. Avoid leading a towline through a stern chock, which will result in a "bound rudder" and lack of control while towing heavy loads.

The hull speed of a displacement hull (above which a great increase in power is required and a very large wake created by the hull) is shown by the equation:

$$\text{Hull speed (knots)} = 1.35 \sqrt{\text{Waterline length (ft.)}}$$

A 50-foot boat would have a hull speed of 9.5 knots, and if the boat is towing a 15-foot boat with a hull speed of only 5.2 knots, the smaller boat could be damaged unless caution is used. The towing speed should not be greater than 85 percent of the hull speed of the disabled boat in good weather, and this speed

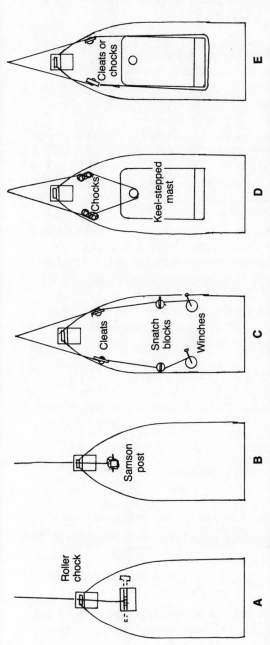

Figure 15.6 Securing the towline. A. Secure towline to a strong spar, such as an emergency tiller, placed inside forward hatch. B. Secure to a strong samson post. C. Secure to forward deck cleats, but only *when backed up by strong points further aft*. Here the lines are led aft through snatch blocks to winches, where a good strain is taken. D. Towline is led around mast, then out through chocks. This must *not be used with masts that are stepped on the deck or cabin top rather than the keel*. Towline must be well secured by preventer ties to prevent it jumping clear of chocks and applying towing force too far aft. E. Towline led around deckhouse and out through chocks. Preventer lines should be used to prevent line jumping out of chocks.

Either a straight towline or a bridle may be used, and the towline may be led through chocks, roller chocks, or cleats, depending on the boat's hardware.

should be reduced even further in rough seas. People in both boats must keep clear of the towline under strain. Failure of the line or a fitting can result in severe injury or death if the line snaps back or recoils.

• The length of towline must be adjusted by the towing vessel so that both boats are in step; that is, both are on the crest of a swell at the same time (fig. 15.7). Failure to do this will result in alternate slack and jerking on the towline and severe strain on both vessels and the towing gear.

• When in sheltered water approaching a dock, it is usually best to shift from a tandem tow to an alongside position for best maneuverability. Use plenty of fenders and do not allow crews to use hands and feet to fend off, because serious injuries could result if the boats are thrown together (see figure 15.8).

In protected waters, a boat may be moved over short distances by the use of the boat's outboard motor dinghy for tandem tow-

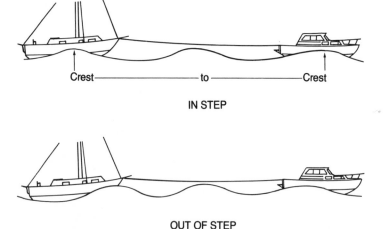

Crest ——————————— to ——————————— Crest

IN STEP

OUT OF STEP

Figure 15.7 Towing in step. The towline length should be equal to one wave length, or multiples of that wave length, so that both boats are "in step" and meet seas simultaneously.

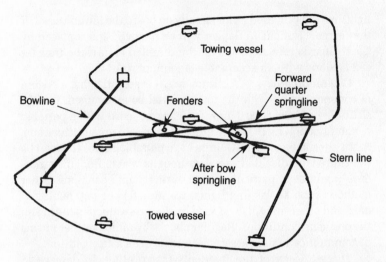

Figure 15.8 Lines rigged for side tow. Towing alongside is often best when in a crowded area or approaching a dock. Both helms must be manned. An outboard powered dinghy may be used as a towboat, but steering in such a case will depend largely on the big boat's rudder.

ing. The dinghy provides the propulsion, but a helmsman on the larger and more controllable boat must do the steering. Before starting, simple sound signals should be agreed on using the hand horn. Ahead, stop, and back signals should be adequate. This dinghy assist may also be used in docking.

Again, towing should only be requested when really necessary. As long as a boat has steering control and either wind or power, towing can seldom be justified.

COAST GUARD SAFETY MEASURES WHEN TOWING VESSELS LESS THAN 65 FEET

The Wearing of Personal Flotation Devices.   Vessels under 65 feet will normally not be taken in tow until all persons on the towed vessel are wearing approved PFDs. In cases where insufficient PFDs are available, Coast Guard PFDs will be furnished. If any portion of the tow will take place during darkness, PFD lights will be provided if not already on board the towed vessel. If they agree, civilians in danger will be removed and replaced by Coast Guard crew members on the disabled craft if the transfer can be done with an acceptable amount of risk.

Communications.   While towing, it is essential that a system of communication with the towed vessel be maintained. Ideally, stationing a Coast Guard crew member on board with a portable communication rig insures a quick response to urgent situations. As an alternative, most CG units have portable radios that can be transferred to a disabled vessel without its own radio. This procedure would be of particular value during night operations. Other methods such as flashing lights, warning flag or rag, hand signals, and others may also be used by the coxswain, depending on the on-scene conditions. Regular checks by radio or other means of communication are essential in insuring a safe evolution.

Tides.   Many of the incidents that resulted in damage to grounded small craft could have been avoided by waiting for a rising tide before attempting to refloat, and by inspecting the hull to determine if it is watertight. Small craft left high and dry by receding tides may not be damaged if suitable preventer lines and fenders are rigged to maintain position and prevent heeling damage and flooding on the incoming tide. Sometimes it is better to wait for high tide even with a rescue craft on scene.

BOARDING AND REPORTS

After rendering assistance, a party from the Coast Guard SAR unit or its base will normally board the disabled boat to obtain information required for the assistance report. At the same time, a routine inspection is made of the boat's safety equipment and papers to insure compliance with the law. Any violations can result in a warning, though in cases where gross negligence or regulatory violations are involved, a citation may be issued.

16
Final Briefing

Having examined the more common mishaps to small boats and yachts, we note from a Coast Guard analysis in 1986 of 8,000 accidents that most seem to be caused by human error:

Operation of vessel (human error)	37 percent
Fault of other vessels (human error)	23 percent
Environment and weather	16 percent
Equipment failure	9 percent

Surprisingly, material failure ranks near the bottom as a cause of *serious accidents*, and even some of these breakdowns are partially attributable to human neglect or mistakes. Reasonable preventative maintenance can minimize such failures.

Bad weather conditions can contribute to material failure, especially if encountered unprepared or not sufficiently downpowered. It also causes fatigue with its unpleasant effects on the performance of people. The pleasure boater can watch the weather and usually avoid severe and prolonged storms—a simple and effective course of action in the coastal area. The stretches of coast with few shelters, or those having numerous thunderstorms or freak or unexpected local conditions are exceptions that require special alertness. Despite the common fear of bad weather among many boaters, it is a relatively minor factor in serious boating accidents.

Most marine accidents attributable to human error are the result of a lack of alertness. In recent years, over half of all serious boating accidents resulted from collision with other boats or objects, almost always because of a lack of attention or unfamiliarity with navigation rules. Alcohol and fatigue contribute to the lack of attention. Another quarter of all serious boating accidents are caused by other boats, a sobering thought for old salts who feel competent to avoid trouble or look out for themselves in any conditions. Knowledge and experience are no guarantee against a drunk boater losing control of a hot-rod boat doing 40 knots, a close encounter with a recreational trawler whose new owner doesn't know the Rules of the Road, or the wake of a big boat passing a small dinghy at high speed.

Over two-thirds of less serious boating *mishaps* do not even involve accidents but mechanical breakdowns that leave the boat immobilized or adrift. Most can be handled without outside help, provided the boat has a tool kit and a minimum of essential spares.

Though self-help and time solve most problems, neither may be advisable in situations where lives or property are actually in danger, or where conditions may worsen. Within twenty-five miles of the U.S. mainland, instant VHF-radio contact can usually be made with the Coast Guard, while SSB radio covers most of the ocean. Advice as well as help can be requested. If you are unsure of the seriousness of the emergency and what action to take, describe the situation to the Coast Guard.

Many recreational boaters have come to believe that the Coast Guard should not be alerted or asked for help unless or until lives and vessels are in extreme danger. But very often, a call at an early stage can be quickly handled with minimum effort, whereas a delay may eventually require an enormous search-and-rescue effort. A relatively simple problem can be quickly worsened by oncoming weather, strong currents, or progressive material failure. Some distress cases, such as fire, will have to be handled by the crew if distance does not permit outside help arriving in time.

Figure 16.1 A Coast Guard boat speeds to the help of a sailboat in trouble. The decision whether to call for help in heavy weather must be made by the skipper of the threatened boat. *Courtesy USCG*

Not clearly in either category is what to do in heavy weather when danger is perceived. Do not overreact. Unless faced with such obvious things as structural failure, a crippling knockdown, or being set onto a dangerous lee shore, this is a subjective judgment that must be made by the skipper, keeping in mind the inevitable results of fatigue on human performance (see figure 16.1).

Do what seems best to you for your crew, your boat, and yourself. Criticism will not come from the professional rescuers, who too often have seen a delayed call for help result in help arriving too late.

Your responsibility is not confined to those on your vessel. One of the oldest human traditions concerns the moral and legal duty of any sailor to help other sailors in distress. The obligation is also a privilege, for few rewards surpass the deep satisfaction in helping others in peril at sea, where we are all truly each others' keepers.

Fair Winds and Good Cruising

Appendix A

Float Plan

Reproduce a copy of the following page. Then fill out the top section describing the boat and equipment. Use this partly completed form to reproduce a large number for future use. The voyage information in the bottom section can be filled out before each departure. Then leave a completed form with a reliable person who will carry out your alerting instructions if you do not arrive on time. Do not attempt to leave the plan with the Coast Guard. Notify them only if you are running behind time and need help in notifying your float plan holder.

BOAT DESCRIPTION: Type _____; Color _____;

Registration no. _____; Length _____;

Make _____; Name _____;

Home port _____; Engine (type) _____;

No. engines _____; Radio (type) _____.

SURVIVAL EQUIPMENT: PFDs _____; Flares _____;

Mirror _____; Smoke signals _____; EPIRB (type) _____;

Flashlights _____; Life raft _____; Dinghy _____;

Water _____; Food _____; Other _____

_____.

VOYAGE INFORMATION: Leave _____
(departure point)

at _____ going to _____ via _____
(date/time)   (destination)

_____
(route)

Expect to arrive by _____.
(date/time)

ALERTING INSTRUCTIONS: If not arrived by _____,
(date/time)

call Coast Guard at _____ or _____
(phone no.)   (local authority)

at _____.
(phone no.)

CREW LIST:

Name   Phone no.

_____

_____

_____

_____

_____

_____

CAR INFO:

Where parked _____; Color/make/model _____

_____; License _____; Trailer license _____.

Appendix B

Emergency Bill

(Four-member crew)

FIRE

No. 1   In charge at fire scene. Broadcast distress message if fire cannot be controlled.

No. 2   Provide extinguishers at fire. Take over at fire scene if directed by no. 1.

No. 3   Provide extinguishers at fire. If under way, take over wheel.

No. 4   Provide buckets of water or other gear as ordered.

PREPARE TO ABANDON SHIP

(All hands don life jackets and protective clothing.)

No. 1   In charge. Send distress message.

No. 2   Provide EPIRB and water jug. Prepare to go into raft when launched and receive equipment.

No. 3   Provide abandon ship kit, knives, flashlights, and portable radio. Stand by to launch raft when ordered.

No. 4   Assist no. 3.

ABANDON SHIP

No. 1 In charge. Direct launching of raft. Last one in.
No. 2 Into raft first when inflated. Receive and stow provisions in raft.
No. 3 Pass gear to raft. Board when ordered.
No. 4 Assist no. 3.

MAN OVERBOARD

Helmsman: Sound alarm. Throw over seat cushions and markers, followed by MOB pole, horseshoe, and strobe. Stop boat as close by as possible and keep an eye on the victim!

First person on deck: Keep an eye on the victim. This is your sole responsibility!

Second person on deck: Break out equipment—heaving lines, rig vang for hauling, lead down halyard, drop lifelines, and so on.

NOTES: a. This bill is for a four-person crew. If fewer are aboard, one will have to assume the duties of two billets. Bear in mind that the most essential duties are assigned to no. 1 (always the skipper), while the less important duties go to no. 3 and no. 4, whose duties can be easily assumed by no. 1 or no. 2 if required.
b. As there is no way to know who may be the person overboard, duties must be assumed on an ad hoc basis after the MOB emergency occurs, that is, they cannot be assigned by numbers.

Appendix C
Operating Checklists

The use of checklists to carry out complex tasks has long been an accepted practice in operations as varied as flying an aircraft, operating a power-generating plant, or performing bypass surgery. They are also used by professional seamen, even though they perform the same tasks hundreds of times and are completely familiar with the equipment. Checklists are even more essential for operators who use equipment infrequently, which is the case with many yacht and small-boat owners.

The length of an operating checklist is directly related to the size and complexity of the boat. A small boat with a low-powered trolling motor may have a checklist containing only five to ten items, emphasizing safety, such as stowage of PFDs and smoking precautions. The sample shown here is for a 45-foot offshore sloop with a sizable electronics and equipment suite. The checklist should be hand-tailored to fit the owner's requirements and the rig and equipment of the boat. It should always be used if serious omissions or oversights are to be prevented.

A stowage list is also developed by many skippers. This will prove invaluable in locating gear if the owner or skipper is not always available and will save many questions.

PREBOARDING

1. Compute fuel quantity for cruise plus 50 percent reserve. Sample fuel from Raycor filter for dirt or water. Refuel if required.

2. Check quantity of *lube oil* with dip stick; check reserve oil.

3. Check transmission oil with dip stick; check reserve supply.

4. Check batteries: electrolyte up, gravity normal, voltage normal, connections OK.

5. Check engine coolant: full.

6. Check on manual and auto bilge pumps; check warning horn and light; pump bilges; leave pumps on *Auto* and warning system *On*.

7. Check radios. Set frequencies; check EPIRB and secure.

8. Check navigation, instrument, and binnacle lights; check horn and spare Freon can; check flashlights.

9. Check safety and survival gear.

10. Load icebox with ice or turn on refrigerator.

11. Top off water tanks.

12. Load perishable food and supplies.

13. Secure loose gear.

14. Check spare parts, oil, and filters.

BEFORE STARTING

15. File float plan.

16. Brief crew and assign PFDs.

17. Fenders: as required.

18. In boats with gasoline or propane fuel, run blowers for five minutes.

19. Check fume detectors for fumes; smell engine compartment and bilges.

20. Battery selector: as required.

21. DC switch panel: as required.

22. VHF: *On* and guarding Channel 16.

23. Loran or GPS: as desired.
24. Autopilot: as desired.
25. Stove: burners *Off*; fuel valve *On*.
26. Engine fuel valves *On*.

START ENGINE

27. Oil pressure: Up.
28. Exhaust water discharge: normal.
29. Alternator output: charging.
30. Shore power: disconnect and stow cable.
31. Under way: stow lines and fenders; check engine compartment and bilges.

SECURING AFTER ARRIVAL

1. Engine: *Off*
2. Ignition: *Off*
3. Fenders and lines: as required.
4. Radios: *Off*.
5. Autopilot: *Off*.
6. Navigation, instrument, and binnacle lights: *Off*.
7. DC switches: as desired; battery selector switch: as desired.
8. Connect shore powerline; AC switches: as desired.
9. Stove: burners *Off*; fuel valve *Off*
10. Ports and hatches: as desired.
11. Refrigerator/ice box: as desired.
12. Pump out bilges; leave selector switch on *Auto*.
13. IMPORTANT! *CLOSE OUT FLOAT PLAN WITH THE SHORE CONTACT NOW!*

SUNSET

1. Running and bow lights: *On*.
2. Anchor light: *On* at anchor; *Off* under way.

3. Compass and instrument lights: On.
4. Check man overboard rig.
5. Rig jack line as required; break out safety harnesses.
6. Place safety gear and portable lights in cockpit.
7. Horn: by helmsman.
8. Trim sails for night; stow below any left on deck.
9. Battery selector: as desired.
10. Check loose gear topside and below for security. Check rigging (from deck).

SUNRISE

Same as sunset, but reverse actions as required by daybreak.

HEAVY WEATHER

1. Take motion sickness medication if required.
2. Latch or secure drawers and doors to cabinets.
3. Secure loose gear topside and below. Secure stowage areas against rollover.
4. Run engine to charge batteries.
5. Pump heads dry and secure all nonessential through-hull valves.
6. Rig jack lines and grab lines.
7. Break out life jackets and harnesses to all hands; watch-standers don rig now.
8. Double-secure anchors.
9. Check life raft for security.
10. Check reefing rig; break out storm sails; check rigging for loose parts.
11. Fill thermoses and break out snacks.
12. Secure doors and hatches; remove ventilators and cap dorades.
13. Down-power or reef sails well in advance of the storm's approach.
14. Get best possible fix and lay out a DR track ahead.
15. Check bilges hourly and pump as required.

16. If lightning is severe or expected to be severe, disconnect electronics gear where possible.

17. All crew not on watch should rest.

REFUELING

1. Before fueling, stop all machinery. Shut off all electrical power and fires.

2. Close ports and hatches to prevent fumes below decks.

3. Disembark all crew not engaged in fueling.

4. *Smoking lamp out.* This includes people at dockside.

5. Calculate amount of fuel needed. Sample fuel from Raycor for cleanliness and water.

6. Supervise the fueling yourself or assign the job to a trusted member of the crew. Do not leave it up to dockhands. Open the fuel fill fitting yourself and then check to insure that the proper hose is being used. Boats have fill fittings for fuel, water, and sewage discharge, and fuel has been mistakenly pumped into all of them, as well as fishing rod holders mounted on the gunwale. Keep fuel nozzle in contact with the fill opening to prevent static sparks.

7. Avoid overfilling and spills.

8. Fill outboard tanks on the dock.

9. After completion of fueling, close pipe caps.

10. Hose down boat to wash away spilled fuel.

11. Open all ports and openings; turn on blower and vent boat for five minutes.

12. Check tank and engine compartments by smell. If odor of gasoline is present, *do not start engine.* Check fuel tanks and fume detectors and continue venting boat until no further indications of fuel vapors are noted.

SECURING BOAT FOR LONG ABSENCES

1. Remove all perishable foods from boat.

2. Turn off refrigerator/icebox, and pump dry. Leave door open to air.

3. Clean heads and pump dry.

4. Place cushions, pillows, and damp items where they can dry.

5. Empty trash.

6. In cold weather, check adequacy of engine coolant.

7. Cut off all fuel valves to main engine, stove, and heater.

8. Drain all sinks.

9. Pump bilges dry, checking for any leak around prop shaft and rudder.

10. Place electric bilge pump in *Auto* mode; check float switch for easy operation; leave horn in *On* position so that other boats will be alerted by long continuous pumping.

11. Turn off all DC and AC panel switches except bilge pump selector.

12. Secure all ports and hatches.

13. Close all through-hull seacocks and gate valves except bilge discharge.

14. Turn battery selector switch to *Both* if the bilge pump operates through the selector switch; otherwise turn it *Off*.

15. Arrange for a friend or neighbor, preferably someone familiar with your boat, to check the mooring lines, waterline level, and bilge sump at periodic intervals.

(a) Give the person the key or combo to your boat; also give information on how to reach you in an emergency.

(b) Arrange with an acquaintance on the dock to call the friend if anything goes wrong between checks.

16. Double all lines after checking them for chafe and put on chafing gear. Check the decks for loose or forgotten objects. Check the fenders for adequacy and security. Tie off any halyards that may bang in the night.

HURRICANE PLANNING

Developing a Plan

• Determine if you will trailer or haul your boat, secure it in the marina or move to a previously identified hurricane hole. Keep in mind the hazards hurricanes present: wind, tidal surge ranging from five to twenty-five feet above normal, and flooding, with tidal surge the most destructive.

● Identify and gather equipment and supplies, such as chafing gear, spring lines, anchors, old tires (fenders), and so on.

● Allow sufficient time in your hurricane boat plan for stripping your boat of all movable objects (canvas, sails, dinghies, radios, cushions) and lashing down everything you cannot remove (tiller, wheels, booms).

● Check your lease or storage rental agreement with the marina or storage area and your insurance policies to know your responsibilities and liabilities, as well as those of the marina.

● Practice your hurricane boat plan to see how long it will take to implement.

● At least one other qualified person should know your plan and practice it in case you are out of town in the event of a hurricane.

Options

1. Remove the boat from the water
   A. Trailering
   ● Remove the boat from the water.
   ● Avoid exposure to wind and park away from trees.
   ● Lash boat to trailer and secure boat with heavy lines to fixed objects, preferably from four directions.
   ● Remove half the air from tires and place blocks behind and in front of tires to prevent rolling.
   ● Seal door openings and tape windows that may break.
   ● Remove sails, riggings, and other loose articles and lash down items that cannot be removed (tiller, wheels, and so on).
   ● Remove drain plugs, where appropriate.
   B. Hauling
   ● Be sure the marina can haul your boat and safely store and secure it quickly. Remove loose articles, lashing down items that cannot be removed; seal door openings and tape windows that may break.
   ● Check into a prearranged contract for hauling and have

an alternate plan in the event the marina cannot meet the sudden demand that would be generated by an approaching hurricane.

- Remove drain plugs, where appropriate.

2. Remain at the dock

- Double all lines and protect them from chafing. Use long leads to allow for tidal surge.

- Boats around your boat should be tied down as securely as yours.

- Make sure that boats under roof will not strike the roof as high tides rise.

- Make sure cleats and winches are well secured to boat.

- Cross spring lines fore and aft.

- Adjust lines and make sure water levels are adequate if unusually low tides occur.

- Install fenders to protect boat from rubbing against pier, pilings, and other boats.

- Cut off all electrical devices except bilge pumps for the duration of the storm.

- Cut off all hull valves except bilge pump discharge and cockpit drains.

- Remove all loose items (canvas, sails, dinghies, radios, cushions) and lash down everything you cannot remove (tiller, wheels, booms).

- Seal door openings and tape windows that may break.

- You do not have the right to tie up to the property of others (docks, bulkheads, and so on).

- *Do not stay aboard!*

3. Anchor in a hurricane hole or protected anchorage
These anchorages should be scouted personally well in advance. The further inland you anchor, the safer the boat will be.

- Select a hurricane hole that offers a good bottom and protection from winds and storm surge.

- Before leaving the dock, remove sails, riggings, and other loose articles; lash down those items that cannot be removed (tiller, wheels); seal door openings; tape windows that may break; and seal ventilators and dorades.

- Avoid channels and tidal currents.

- Leave early for your site because others will also be heading out and because of stronger winds and currents.
- Bridges will be locked in the down position when winds reach 40 MPH.
- Do not raft up (tie up with another boat).
- Practice runs should be made to determine accessibility, depth of water, and location of bridges, and to locate obstructions and objects on which to secure lines or from which to drop anchors.
- Make sure cleats and winches are well secured to the boat.
- You do not have the right to tie up to the property of others (docks, bulkheads, and so on).
- Cut off all electrical devices except bilge pumps for the duration of the storm. Close all hull valves except bilge discharge and cockpit drains.
- *Do not stay aboard!*

After the Storm

- Wait to check on your boat until it is safe to travel.
- Check for damage to the marina before returning your boat from a hurricane hole.
- Beware of dangling wires, fuel leaks, weakened docks, bulkheads, seawalls, bridges, pilings floating underwater, and so on.
- A thorough check for seaworthiness and damage should be made, and findings conveyed to your insurance agent and to owners of property damaged by your boat.
- Know what your liabilities are and what your insurance company's responsibilities are.
- Remove water and marine life from the boat.
- If the boat is blocking a navigable waterway, you must remove it immediately.

Table C.I   Hurricane Countdown

Time from Landfall	Hit/Miss Ratio*	What to Expect
72 hours	9:1	Probabilities of hurricane conditions first issued approximately 72 hours before landfall. Now is the time to review your hurricane boat plan. Plot storm's position on hurricane tracking chart. For continuous weather information, tune to an NOAA weather radio frequency.
48 hours	7:1	Continue to monitor storm's progress. If your boat is to remain at the dock, now is the time to take the following minimum precautions. Double all mooring lines including spring lines. Put on chafing gear at all wear points.
36 hours	5:1	Hurricane watch announcement usually issued at this time, indicating a possible threat to coastal areas. You should be nearing completion of your hurricane boat plan. Remember that drawbridges cannot operate in winds greater than 40 MPH.
12 hours	2:1 or 3:1	Hurricane warnings in effect. Occasional squalls accompanied by gusty winds and heavy rains first appear (this depends on size, movement, and quadrant affecting area). All hurricane boat plans should be completed.
6 hours	—	The most devastating winds of a hurricane are usually confined to within 60 miles or less of the storm's eye.
0 hours	—	If the eye crosses your area, you will likely experience a calm before hurricane-force winds return from the opposite direction. Stay away from your boat.

*The ratios reflect the probabilities of hurricane landfall at a specific point at a given time.

Appendix D
Insurance Rating Factors

Insurance premiums and costs are related to the risks perceived by each company's underwriters and actuarial experts. Though insurance is a highly competitive business, very few companies consider exactly the same set of risks, though all view certain ones in common. Therefore, in buying boat insurance, it is best to shop around to determine the best deal for you and your boat. Be sure that you are not comparing apples and oranges and in so doing, giving up essential coverage items or services, such as high seas coverage and towing protection, to save small amounts of money. A number of factors will affect the premium costs, and some idea of a company's risk emphasis can be gained from the questions asked on the policy application.

TYPE OF BOAT

Naturally, the cost of insuring a boat rises with the value of the boat. Motorboats will command higher premiums than sailboats of a similar size, which are slower, usually have more experienced crews, and suffer fewer losses. In a motorboat, the higher the horsepower-to-length ratio, the higher will be the speed and thus the premium. For example, one major company charges twice as much to insure a 20-foot boat with a 200-horsepower engine as it does for the same boat with only 150 horsepower.

Diesel-powered boats have better ratings than gasoline because of their greater safety. Older boats have a higher premium charge, not only because of their greater risk of breakdown and material failure, but also because of the higher repair costs as a percentage of their true value. Many companies will not insure boats older than five to ten years without a complete marine survey. Wooden boats may also be difficult to insure because of their relatively high repair costs.

OPERATOR EXPERIENCE

Because the incidence of human error in boating accidents is high, the proficiency of the operator directly affects the premium costs. Most companies give credit for the completion of formal courses given by the U.S. Coast Guard Auxiliary or the U.S. Power Squadron and for membership in those organizations. Other companies give credit for experience documented by a Coast Guard license, master mariner or mate papers, or other formal marine education; be sure to list all such qualifications and experience on insurance applications. Credit is also given for accident-free experience, and conversely, a company may refuse to insure an operator with one or more accident claims, or even with a poor motor-vehicle accident record. Such persons may have to seek more expensive special policies.

SAFETY EQUIPMENT

Credit is given for special safety equipment over and above the minimum required by law. Examples are built-in automatic fire extinguishers, smoke and fume detectors, and bilge and burglar alarms. Some companies require special added equipment for offshore boats, such as SSB radio.

OPERATING AREA

Protected and inland waters carry the lowest risks and premiums, followed by the Great Lakes, coastal waters, high seas, and foreign cruising, in that order. Because of the rate differences, it may be wise to not carry high seas coverage if you cruise there only occasionally. For such trips, amended short-term coverage can be requested at a reasonable cost for a particular trip. Boats that are laid up for a number of months every year because of weather are given preferential rates over those that are used year round and thus exposed for longer periods. Florida, for example, has higher rates because of its year-round boating. The safety of the layup berth is also considered. Live-aboard boats are also assigned debits due to the greater risk exposure compared to ones that are seldom used.

DEDUCTIBLES

Nearly all boat policies carry a deductible: either a fixed sum, or 1 to 2 percent of insured value, which the owner must pay for repair work. This deductible does not apply to total-loss cases. A larger deductible will allow a lower premium.

REFUSAL TO INSURE

Many companies may refuse to insure a boat because of the operator's loss experience, the age of the boat and construction, the lack of a recent survey or proof of good condition, or the use to which the boat is put. High-powered boats are often subjected to a "machinery exclusion clause," which voids protection in case of damage to the rudder, propeller, shaft, or engine unless such damage results from fire, sinking, collision, or insurable cause not attributable to high power and speed. Higher deductibles may be assigned to such boats and liability coverage limited. A company may also decline to issue further insurance in areas where it has written a large number of policies and does not want too many eggs in one basket.

OTHER USES OF BOATS

Most yacht insurance policies are issued for pleasure use only. If the boat is used for commercial purposes, charter, or hire, a different premium is assessed. This is also true for boats engaged in such sports as racing or waterskiing, and coverage may be denied to motorboats during official races or speed trials unless added premiums are paid. Modifications may also be made in the coverage or deductibles during such use. Sails used during racing events are not usually covered, though related rigging may be. If a boat suffers damages while being used for a purpose not covered in the policy, the insurer may refuse to pay.

NAMED-PERIL AND ALL-RISKS PROVISIONS

Named-peril policies specifically describe the perils against which the boat is insured and does not cover others. This type of policy is used only for the larger and more expensive yachts. Most yacht policies, and all motorboat and small-boat policies, are all-risk types, which offer blanket coverage unless the cause of loss is specifically excluded. A few companies may not cover accidents occurring while docked or berthed. Most policies do not cover breakdowns that result solely from wear and tear and are not caused by the elements or by "the adventures and perils of the sea."

AGREED VALUE AND CASH VALUE

Most yacht policies are of the agreed-value type, where the owner and insurer agree beforehand on the value to be paid in case of total loss. Policies written on small boats and outboard boats are based on actual cash value less depreciation.

PERSONAL EFFECTS

All boat equipment and navigational gear are covered under the boat's hull insurance. Personal items can be covered for an additional small premium or under a separate homeowner's policy.

LIABILITY (PROTECTION AND INDEMNITY)

Sizable increases in liability coverage can be obtained for relatively little increase in premium. If the typical maximum liability coverage of $300,000 is considered inadequate, one of the most cost-effective ways of adding coverage is through an umbrella provision in either a homeowner's policy or a special provision in the marine policy.

SALVAGE RESPONSIBILITIES

Nearly all policies pay expenses for a salvor to raise a sunken yacht or tow a stranded vessel. In the event of an accident, the policy also pays all reasonable expenses you incur to protect the boat and limit the loss. You are expected to take timely action and then notify the insurer. Your time and effort are not reimbursed.

SHOPPING FOR MARINE INSURANCE

Take all the information on your boat to two or three insurance brokers, preferably ones specializing in marine and accident insurance. Ask around the waterfront or marina for recommendations. Service may be as important as price. Above all, make sure that the policy that may seem cheaper does not omit features offered by other companies that may be essential to you. Read the fine print, discuss it with the brokers, and compile a comparison sheet. It will take a little time but can mean hundreds of dollars in savings and perhaps tens of thousands in protection.

Appendix E

Required and Recommended Safety Equipment

Every boat registered or operated in the United States is subject to numerous federal, state, and local laws. On the navigable waters of the United States, these are primarily federal statutes enacted by Congress and the regulations that stem from these statutes and are issued by federal agencies such as the U.S. Coast Guard and the Army Corps of Engineers. The states and local jurisdictions also enact boating laws and regulations, but on the navigable waters they must not conflict with federal laws.

Most of these laws and regulations were enacted to protect the boating public. This includes the protection of our own crew and passengers, as well as those of other boats against our own reckless or negligent actions. Other laws attempt to protect the consumer from substandard manufactured products. COLREGS (Rules of the Road) contain agreed procedures to enable boaters to predict what another boat should do in a close situation and how to avoid collision with it. Afloat as ashore, the criminal laws shield all against the acts of a few wrongdoers. Finally, civil liability laws provide possible redress to victims who suffer injury or damage as a result of others' conduct or negligence.

Perhaps the most important rules affecting pleasure boat owners are those regarding the kind and quality of safety equipment required on board before getting under way (see table E.1).

COAST GUARD–APPROVED EQUIPMENT

Some of the required equipment must be Coast Guard approved, a stamp of approval given by the Coast Guard to a product that meets its specifications and regulations on materials, construction, and performance. This applies to both boat construction and safety devices such as PFDs, carburetor flame arresters, visual distress signals, and fire extinguishers. Other safety items such as horns, ventilation systems, and navigation lights are required but do not have Coast Guard product approval. The buyer should be aware that Coast Guard approval does not guarantee a product's adequacy under all conditions. An item bearing Coast Guard approval may be marketed by several companies under their brand names, and the choice of a particular brand is up to the buyer.

EQUIPMENT RECOMMENDED BUT NOT REQUIRED BY LAW

All of the equipment mentioned in table E.1 is required by federal law on most small boats. Some states require additional equipment. These are only *minimum* requirements and most experienced sailors will carry more. Additional safety equipment should include at least the following:

- additional means of propulsion, such as a paddle, oars, or trolling motor.
- manual bilge pump and a bucket for bailing
- basic first-aid kit
- anchor and line
- simple tool bag
- small spare fuel tank for outboard motor boats

Any boat going out of sight of land or that could be carried out by currents if disabled should have a radio. VHF/FM, either fixed or portable, is best. A citizen's band (CB) radio is a poor second choice and affords little savings over VHF/FM. If no radio is carried, a boat should travel in company with another boat when in exposed waters.

Table E.I Minimum Required Equipment for Recreational Boats

EQUIPMENT	CLASS A (less than 16 ft) (less than 4.9m)	CLASS 1 (16 to less than 26 ft) (4.9 to less than 7.9m)	CLASS 2 (26 to less than 40 ft) (7.9 to less than 12.2m)	CLASS 3 (40 to not more than 65 ft) (12.2 to not more than 19.8m)
BACKFIRE FLAME CONTROL	An effective means of controlling the backfire flame of all gasoline engines installed after 25 April 1940, except outboard motors. Backfire flame arresters must be Coast Guard approved.			
VENTILATION (Boats built before 1 August 1980)	At least two ventilator ducts fitted with cowls or their equivalent for the purpose of properly and efficiently ventilating the bilges of every closed engine and fuel-tank compartment of boats constructed or decked over after 25 April 1940, using gasoline as fuel or other fuels having a flash-point of 110° or less.			
VENTILATION (Boats built on 1 August 1980, or later)	At least two ventilator ducts for the purpose of efficiently ventilating every closed compartment that contains a gasoline engine and every closed compartment containing a gasoline tank, except those having permanently installed tanks that vent outside the boat and contain no unprotected electrical devices. Also, engine compartments containing a gasoline engine having a cranking motor must contain power-operated exhaust blowers that can be controlled from the instrument panel.			
PERSONAL FLOTATION DEVICES (PFDs) [Must say Coast Guard Approved and be in serviceable condition]	One approved Type I, II, III, or IV PFD for each person on board or being towed on water skis.		One approved Type I, II, or III device for each person on board or being towed on water skis; in addition, one throwable Type IV device.	

Note: A Type V hybrid PFD may be substituted for a Type I, II, or III device, but it must be actually worn whenever the vessel is under way and the person is not in the cabin or other enclosed area.

BELL, WHISTLE	Every vessel less than 12 meters (39.4 ft) in length must carry an efficient sound-producing device.	Every vessel 12 meters (39.4 ft) but less than 20 meters (65.6 ft) in length must carry a whistle and a bell. The whistle must be audible for ½ nautical mile. The mouth of the bell must be at least 200 mm (7.87 in) in diameter.
VISUAL DISTRESS SIGNALS (Required on coastal waters only)	Must carry approved visual distress signals for nighttime use. *Note: All boats carrying six or fewer passengers for hire must meet these requirements also.*	Must carry visual distress signals approved for both daytime and nighttime use.
FIRE EXTINGUISHER (Must say Coast Guard Approved and be in serviceable condition)	At least one B-I type approved hand portable fire extinguisher. (Not required on outboard motorboats less than 26 feet in length and not carrying passengers for hire if the construction of such motorboats will not permit the entrapment of explosive or flammable gases or vapors and if fuel tanks are not permanently installed.) *Note: When fixed fire-extinguishing system is installed in machinery space(s), it will replace one B-I type portable fire extinguisher.*	At least two B-I type approved portable fire extinguishers, OR at least one B-II type approved portable fire extinguisher.	At least three B-I type approved portable fire extinguishers, OR at least one B-I type plus one B-II type approved portable fire extinguisher.

SOURCE: "Federal Requirements for Recreational Boats" (cmdr., USCG Instr. M16760.1)

NOTE: Passenger-carrying and other commercial vessels have slightly different requirements. For information, call U.S. Coast Guard.

INSPECTING FOR ADEQUACY OF EQUIPMENT

If doubt exists as to the types and adequacy of mandatory safety equipment, a free examination will be made by a Coast Guard Auxiliary inspector at the request of the boat owner. This courtesy safety inspection is voluntary and no citations will be made, nor will anyone other than the owner be notified of the results. If discrepancies are found, the owner will be advised on corrective measures and a reexam scheduled if the owner desires. Once this strict set of requirements is met, the boat will be issued a special decal good for one year. Regular Coast Guard boarding parties do not conduct routine safety inspections of boats carrying this decal.

Following any case involving assistance by the Coast Guard, members of the rescue crew will board the assisted craft to fill out an assistance report. In the process, they will inspect the boat for compliance with safety-equipment regulations and laws. If a discrepancy is found, a warning (or in flagrant violations, a citation) may be issued. An annual Coast Guard Auxiliary courtesy inspection can prevent such embarrassment.

In view of the widespread potential for legal liability, an owner must insure that his or her boat and equipment are well maintained, that passengers are briefed, and that the boat is operated in a safe and reasonable manner. Despite all this, tort litigation can still result if an accident occurs. Even if the claim lacks any merit or is of the nuisance variety, this may not dissuade a claimant and attorneys from embarking on an action that can be long and costly for both parties.

SUMMARY

- Insure that your boat has aboard all required safety devices prescribed by the FBSA/71 and USCG regulations. The state in which the boat is operated may have other requirements as well, but they must not conflict with federal laws.
- Other safety equipment, though not mandatory, should be carried by the prudent sailor.

• In buying equipment, check that it complies with USCG standards and carries a CG-approval marking. Insure that pyrotechnics are not near or beyond the expiration date. Use your own judgment in choosing the best among the approved gear.

• To insure that equipment is adequate and in compliance with the law, request a Coast Guard Auxiliary courtesy inspection. When completed satisfactorily, place the inspection seal on the boat.

• If you have questions about boating safety, possible safety defects in a boat, or information on a safety recall, or want free pamphlets, call the toll-free Coast Guard number (1-800-368-5647).

• If a Coast Guard vessel orders you to stand by for boarding, comply with its orders unless you are given permission to depart from them by the circumstances of weather, ship control, or other reason. If unable to comply, inform the boarding vessel of the reason and request further instructions.

RECOMMENDED READING

Federal Requirements for Recreational Boats. COMDTINST M16760.2/85. Free from USCG.

Appendix F

Recommended Reading

Experience afloat will be more meaningful if preceded by reading and study. The material may range from books and magazine articles on broad boating topics to specialized subjects as diverse as anchoring, yacht woodwork, cooking, or weather. The level of study is up to the reader, depending on his or her grasp of technical matters.

Start in your local library, looking at listings under "Boats," "Sailing," and "Yachts." In most larger libraries, dozens of fine books will be available. Otherwise, your local book or marine stores will have them, including recent editions and publications.

Books dealing with equipment, especially electronics, are outdated rapidly by technical advances. Seamanship and navigation, on the other hand, evolve slowly and are unlikely to change over a short term. Treatises on engine maintenance and repair are general in nature and, for a particular engine, should be used in conjunction with the handbook issued by the manufacturer. In addition, books on maintenance of a particular brand or model of engine are available at marine bookstores; these may be more understandable to the beginner than the manufacturer's handbook. Beware of voluminous books that you may never finish reading. It is better to digest a short book than to give up halfway through a definitive and detailed one. Size, however, is only one criterion; some large volumes contain chapters on a variety of subjects, each complete in itself, which can be digested at will. However, every boat owner should read one of the following books covering the broad aspects of boating: *Chapman's Piloting, Seamanship and Small Boat Handling* (E.S. Maloney. New York: Hearst) or *The Annapolis Book of Seamanship* (J. Rousmaniere. New York: Simon and Schuster).

Chapman's has been used by sailors and yachtsmen for more than 65 years, and to many is the bible of small boat operation. Rousmaniere's book is a latecomer to the scene, but it is well written and similar in scope. It presents the material in a form perhaps better understandable for beginners and emphasizes sail more than *Chapman's*. One of these two books should be aboard as a reference, even for experienced sailors.

For those interested in a deeper understanding of the various aspects of boating, the following are readable and informative; some are definitive in scope. The books listed in each category are not necessarily the best, but they are representative. In listing them, I considered price and ease of reading.

Navigation
Maloney, Elbert S. *Dutton's Navigation and Piloting*, 14th ed. Annapolis: Naval Institute Press, 1985.

This is the authority on navigation and the standard for professionals and serious yachtsmen alike. Both *Dutton's* and the latest edition of *Chapman's* were prepared by the same author.

Rules of the Road
U.S. Coast Guard. *Navigation Rules, International—Inland*. Washington, D.C.: Government Printing Office, 1983. (COMDTINST M16672.2)

This is the official document on the subject. Although most general boating books carry some discussion of the rules, this book is the source. The Inland Rules must by law be carried on all boats longer than 12 meters.

Medical Aid
Cohen, Michael E. *Dr. Cohen's Healthy Sailor Book*. Camden, Me.: International Marine Publishing Co., 1983.

The book *Ship's Medicine Chest and Medical Aid* has been published by the U.S. Public Health Service for many years for the use of merchant vessels not carrying doctors. This latest edition contains information that is required or should be used by a nonphysician. Dr. Cohen's book, one of a number written by physicians, is recommended for its emphasis on physiology in the marine environment, preventative health care, and good health habits at sea, very necessary for sailors far from professional help.

U.S. Public Health Service. *Ship's Medicine Chest and Medical Aid at Sea*. Washington, D.C.: Government Printing Office, 1984.

Heavy Weather
Coles, K. Adlard. *Heavy Weather Sailing*. 3rd rev. ed. Clinton Corners, N.Y.: John DeGraff, Inc., 1981.
Kotsch, William J. *Weather for the Mariner*. 3d ed. Annapolis: Naval Institute Press, 1983.
Kotsch, William J., and Richard Henderson. *Heavy Weather Guide*. 2d ed. Annapolis: Naval Institute Press, 1984.

Design, Construction, and Maintenance
Brotherton, Miner. *The 12-Volt Bible for Boats*. Camden, Me.: Seven Seas, 1985.
Calder, Nigel. *Marine Diesel Engines: Maintenance, Troubleshooting, and Repair*. 2d ed. Camden, Me.: International Marine Publishing Co., 1987.
Cruising Club of America. *Offshore Yachts*. Edited by John Rousmaniere. New York: W. W. Norton, 1987.
Florence, Ronald. *The Optimum Sailboat*. New York: Harper and Row, 1986.

Emergency Repairs
Hollander, Neil, and Harold Mertes. *The Yachtsman's Emergency Handbook*. New York: Hearst Marine Books, 1986.

A small handy encyclopedia on making emergency repairs and dealing with mishaps yourself.

Sailing
Henderson, Richard. *Sail and Power.* 4th ed. Annapolis: Naval
    Institute Press, 1991.

Navigation Publications and Area Guides
The navigation publications you should carry will depend on the
size and navigational capabilities of your boat and where you
will sail. The list includes a number of annual publications by
the National Ocean Service (NOS) such as *Tide Tables, Tide Current Tables,* and a nautical almanac. The *List of Lights* published
by the Coast Guard should be periodically checked for reported
changes. Some publications cover specific geographical areas
and a number of volumes may be needed to cover a long coastal
cruise. For boaters who sail mostly in a local area, tidal information can usually be obtained from a local paper, or you can reproduce the four or five pages from the tide and current tables
pertaining to the local area.

Replacing many of these publications annually can be expensive. Fortunately, those sailing on the East Coast in the area between New Brunswick and Texas can obtain nearly all of this
information and more from one annual publication, *Reed's Nautical Almanac and Coast Pilot,* American East Coast Edition
(Surrey, England: Thomas Reed Publishers, annual). A new one
can be obtained yearly from most marine dealers for $25.00, and
this includes a free midyear information update. For those not
interested in celestial navigation, *Eldridge Tide and Piloting
Guide* for the East Coast provides the tidal and piloting material
for less than $7.00.

A cruising guide for the area in which you are operating is
invaluable for the detailed local knowledge it contains. There is a
wide selection of these guides for the various cruising areas.
They contain information on navigation, anchorages, marinas,
fuel, and other services, as well as sights of interest along the
way.

Government Publications
A number of very useful free publications and pamphlets can be
obtained from your nearest Coast Guard station, or by calling the

Coast Guard's toll-free boating safety hotline: 1-800-368-5647. These publications include:

"Federal Requirements for Recreational Boats"
"First Aid for Boating"
"Courtesy Marine Examination"
"Visual Distress Signals"
"Emergency Repairs Afloat"
"Marine Aids to Navigation"

Manufacturer's Manuals and Handbooks

Most equipment will have instruction manuals supplied. These should be kept on board for use in the event of an operating problem and for reference in routine maintenance.

Magazines

A large number of good magazines covering boating and current boating news are available. Many specialize in such diverse subjects as motorboats, sail craft, cruising, racing, and other topics. A subscription to at least one of these will afford good reading, as well as provide an update on boating events and news.

Index

About the Author

Captain Waters attended North Carolina State University on a football scholarship. In 1942 he graduated from the U.S. Coast Guard Academy and then served on the cutter *Ingham* for two years. During the four major convoy battles he was involved in, *Ingham* sank the first U-boat by an American man of war on the North Atlantic. In subsequent assignments Captain Waters commanded USS *Savage* (DE-386) in the Seventh Fleet, led a destroyer escort task unit, and commanded the cutter *Aurora*.

After the war he entered aviation and served as a search and rescue pilot, flying seaplanes, amphibians, four engine land planes, and helicopters. He commanded air stations at Miami and Salem before assignment as Chief of the Search and Rescue Division at U.S. Coast Guard Headquarters.

In 1955 his *Aircraft Emergency Procedures Overwater* (a U.S. inter-service publication) was published, and in 1956 he developed and was the principal contributor to the original *National Search and Rescue Manual* and its first subsequent revision. Now in its third edition, this is the recognized international reference for SAR. In 1966 he conceived of and obtained funding for the National Search and Rescue School, and in 1967 he was selected to head up a Department of Transportation task force on Emergency Medical Care for highway victims. He was known in the services as Mr. Search and Rescue.

Captain Waters retired from the Coast Guard in 1968 to become Director of Public Safety in Jacksonville, Florida, until 1979. He was a consultant to public safety organizations, emergency medical systems, commercial airlines, and hospital helicopter services and lectured at numerous universities and medical schools. He was appointed by President Ford to the Interagency Committee on Medical Services, and the University of Florida School of Medicine appointed him a Clinical Professor.

His many previous publications include the books *Bloody Winter* and *Rescue at Sea*, both published by the Naval Institute Press. In 1977 he went back to sea as a full-time hobby, sailing his 46-foot sloop *Meteor* between Cape Hatteras and the lower Bahamas. Captain Waters passed away in August 1992, as this book was in production.

The **Naval Institute Press** is the book-publishing arm of the U.S. Naval Institute, a private, nonprofit society for sea service professionals and others who share an interest in naval and maritime affairs. Established in 1873 at the U.S. Naval Academy in Annapolis, Maryland, where its offices remain today, the Naval Institute has more than 100,000 members worldwide.

Members of the Naval Institute receive the influential monthly magazine *Proceedings* and discounts on fine nautical prints, ship and aircraft photos, and subscriptions to the quarterly *Naval History* magazine. They also have access to the transcripts of the Institute's Oral History Program and get discounted admission to any of the Institute-sponsored seminars offered around the country.

The Naval Institute's book-publishing program, begun in 1898 with basic guides to naval practices, has broadened its scope in recent years to include books of more general interest. Now the Naval Institute Press publishes more than sixty titles each year, ranging from how-to books on boating and navigation to battle histories, biographies, ship and aircraft guides, and novels. Institute members receive discounts on the Press's nearly 400 books in print.

Full-time students are eligible for special half-price membership rates. Life memberships are also available.

For a free catalog describing Naval Institute Press books currently available, and for further information about U.S. Naval Institute membership, please write to:

Membership & Communications Department
U.S. Naval Institute
118 Maryland Avenue
Annapolis, Maryland 21402-5035

Or call, toll-free, (800) 233-USNI.